Studies in Religion

"An important and deeply interesting contribution to our understanding of metaphor as a way of knowing and as a way of organizing and giving meaning to experience. Frank Burch Brown makes it clear that metaphor, being much more than mere rhetorical embellishment, makes important assertions combining thought and feeling."
—James Olney, Louisiana State University

"A lucid and informed study that carries the exploration of the relations between the properties of literary language and the conditions of religious assertion to a new level."
—Giles Gunn, University of North Carolina

In *Transfiguration*, a theory of poetic metaphor is proposed that attempts to account for literature's complex role in the discovery and creation of significant patterns within both language and life. Building on a critique of the work of such philosophers as Whitehead, Wheelwright, and Ricoeur, Frank Burch Brown shows that while poetic and conceptual modes of discovery are different, they are nevertheless mutually interdependent. "The thoughts we reasonably conceive influence the aesthetic metaphors we imagine, with the converse being equally true," Burch Brown writes. "Even if such relations seem illicit, they can no longer be ignored."

In particular, the author offers a new view of the way in which theological and metaphysical concepts grow out of, and are transfigured by, metaphoric expression. The language of poetry reshapes thought and feeling, and it is thus especially able to engender the transformations in experience and understanding that are critical to religious belief. At the same time, Burch Brown suggests how poetic metaphor can itself be transformed and given new significance by theological reflection and religious practice.

Transfiguration

At the heart of *Transfiguration* is a detailed and original study of the structure and dynamics of T. S. Eliot's *Four Quartets*. The author shows how this work as a whole is both a metaphoric representation and a metaphoric argument, constituting a "raid on the inarticulate" that challenges as well as heightens one's prior sense of self and world, of actuality and possibility.

Frank Burch Brown is assistant professor of religion and humanities at Virginia Polytechnic Institute and State University.

FRANK BURCH BROWN

Transfiguration

Poetic Metaphor and the Languages

of Religious Belief

The University of North Carolina Press

Chapel Hill and London

The publication of this work was made possible in part through a grant from the National Endowment for the Humanities, a federal agency whose mission is to award grants to support education, scholarship, media programming, libraries, and museums, in order to bring the results of cultural activities to a broad, general public.

Manufactured in the United States of America

Library of Congress Cataloging in Publication Data

Brown, Frank Burch, 1948–
   Transfiguration: poetic metaphor and the languages of
religious belief.

   (Studies in religion)
   Bibliography: p.
   Includes index.
   1. Religion and poetry. 2. Metaphor. 3. Eliot,
T. S. (Thomas Stearns), 1888–1965. Four quartets.
I. Title. II. Series: Studies in religion (Chapel
Hill, N.C.)
PN1077.B69 1983   801'.951   82-24714
ISBN 0-8078-1560-8

TO CAROL—

Whose art and belief
Are part of my life
And, I hope, of these words.

Contents

Preface

Given the nature of the argument I have pursued in this book, I have found it necessary to venture across the boundaries of a number of academic disciplines. Such an attempt is not without its hazards. The reader's fields of interest and expertise are unlikely to coincide exactly with mine. At the same time, my own capacity to do justice to all the areas of scholarship touched on here is undeniably strained to its limit. In an effort to minimize the potential for misunderstanding on the part of the reader and misrepresentation on the part of the author, I have tried in the following chapters to indicate as plainly as I can the crucial points of the overall argument in such a way as to circumvent some of the technical terminology a scholar specializing in any given area might expect to encounter.

In this regard, however, I have met with only partial success. Technical terms remain, and I have had to presume a readership with wide interests and unusual patience. Even though each chapter is intended to be intelligible to the nonspecialist, I have nonetheless felt that each must offer something of substance to the specialist as well. The three chapters analyzing Eliot's *Four Quartets*, for instance, assume that the reader already has a degree of familiarity with modern poetry and with this cycle of poems in particular. In any case, most readers will want to consult the complete text of the *Quartets*, which is less than thirty pages long. Similarly, my exposition in the chapters focusing on Wheelwright and Whitehead will be followed most easily by students of literary theory and philosophy. Finally, I assume that the reader has at least a marginal curiosity about religious issues and religious thought.

It would be difficult to overestimate the value of the help given me over the years by Nathan A. Scott, Jr., David Tracy, and Anthony C. Yu. So I welcome the chance to thank them, knowing that I am only beginning to realize how much their assistance has meant. Likewise, I am especially indebted to Schubert M. Ogden and Paul Ricoeur. In very different ways, both have stimulated my reflections and challenged my unexamined presuppositions every time I have talked with them or read their writing with the care it deserves. Whatever criticisms I here express with regard to some of their ideas should be understood in this light. More recently, Giles B. Gunn has given considerable aid and encouragement that could not have been better timed or more appreciated. This project would never have been completed at all without the personal support provided by my parents and by friends like Larry Bouchard, Michael Kinnamon, Lynn Poland, and Peg Stearn. One such friend and colleague, Elizabeth Struthers Malbon, gave invaluable assistance in the final stages of my revisions by reading the entire manuscript and making suggestions that, much to her surprise, I sometimes heeded. My wife Carol also read the manuscript with a critical yet friendly eye, but that is the least of the reasons why this is dedicated to her. For the patience and skills of typists Becky Cox, Janis Pittman, and (especially) Suzie VanKrey, I am truly grateful. I am also grateful indeed for the sensitivity with which the completed manuscript was edited by Sandra Eisdorfer of the University of North Carolina Press.

Earlier versions of parts of chapters 4 and 5 appeared in *Papers on Language and Literature* (Winter 1982) and the *Journal of Modern Literature* (March 1983). A portion of chapter 6 was first published in a different form in the *Journal of the American Academy of Religion* (December 1982). Parts of chapters 1 and 7 originally appeared in the *Journal of Religion* (January 1982). Permission to reprint this material has been kindly granted by the editors and publishers involved.

Transfiguration

Chapter One A Prefiguration
Poetic Metaphor and the Languages of Religious Belief

Human reason has this peculiar fate that . . . it is burdened by questions which, as prescribed by the nature of reason itself, it is not able to ignore, but which, as transcending all its powers, it is also not able to answer.
—Immanuel Kant

Philosophizing leads to frontiers where its own language ceases while art seems still to speak. [Yet] the music that goes beyond all we can say will finally drive us back to words; and the sight of art, to thoughts.
—Karl Jaspers

Much modern and "postmodern" thought has proceeded from the assumption that the powers and limits of the human mind, whatever they may be, are directly correlated with the powers and limits of human language. Accordingly, inquiries into the nature of rationality and imagination, beauty and the arts, or morality and religion have to a large extent consisted in the study of signs, symbols, and semantic systems.

This book constitutes one such study, the central purpose of which is to examine issues relating the theory of literature and metaphor to the analysis of religious experience and reflection. Specifically, the succeeding chapters are meant to provide extensive support for the claim that the varieties of experience and reflection important to religion have an intrinsic connection with poetry and poetics—a connection best understood when one pays special attention to metaphor (broadly conceived) and to poetic metaphor in particular.

The topics, arguments, and conclusions of this study are variations on themes as old as formal philosophical and religious inquiry. But scholarship in every area touched on here has undergone a period of exceptional fermentation in recent decades. Whole movements in philosophy and in religious studies have flourished, withered, or revived with astonishing and rather disconcerting rapidity.[1] Simultaneously, the fields of literary criticism, semantics, and semiotics have undergone striking transformations, reflecting such influences as structuralist, poststructuralist, and neo-Marxist thought.[2]

Given the frankly experimental character of some of this recent intellectual activity, one cannot be surprised that the results are often confused and confusing. But more important, if not more surprising, is the fact that previously hidden connections between seemingly disparate fields of inquiry have come to light. As regards the present study, this means we may now be in a position to see more fully the ways in which languages of religious belief are related to metaphoric modes of thought and speech. At the same time, we may be able to gain fresh insight into the still larger question of how it is that human beings, through their many different kinds of language, come to discover and imagine those realities fundamental to the various faiths by which they live: religious faiths or secular, traditional or nontraditional, communal or private.

Because the argument I develop in the following pages moves through a number of stages, each of some complexity, it will be useful at the outset to give a kind of prefiguration of what is to come as well as a brief explication of my methods and terminology. As I have already indicated, this inquiry is intentionally bifocal. Whereas the early chapters focus on the theory of metaphor and poetic art, the latter chapters focus on the theory of experience and religious reflection. These two foci merge at a number of points, however—most notably in the study of T. S. Eliot's *Four Quartets*, which comprises the three middle chapters and is expressly designed to refine and exemplify the theories expounded before and after.

The keen scholarly interest that metaphor has generated for some time now is bound eventually to abate. But at present no one undertaking an examination of the relation between poetry and religion can easily avoid the topic of metaphoric language, nor can he or she expect to cover the topic in the space of a few pages. In a 1958 essay, Paul Henle could still plausibly maintain there was "little new to be said on the subject of metaphor."[3] But Warren Shibles's mammoth bibliography on metaphor, published in 1971, contained a great many entries of recent origin.[4] Since then the number of publications treating metaphor and related subjects has increased almost beyond belief.

Needless to say, the sheer volume of publications would be smaller if scholars had reached a complete consensus as to the character and function of metaphor. Yet significant areas of agreement do exist. Few contemporary theorists question the thesis that metaphor, far from being a mere ornament, plays a crucial role in language of almost every kind, from the scientific to the aesthetic. Many, following Aristotle's lead, view metaphor as the central figure of speech and thought. As Jonathan Culler remarks, "Today metaphor is no longer one figure among others but the figure of figures, a figure for figurality."[5] Likewise, the majority of writers agree that the meaning of "live" metaphoric expressions is so bound to the specific properties of the metaphoric medium that a fully adequate paraphrase or substitute is in principle impossible. Finally, many students of metaphor are convinced, as I am, that its unique semantic properties are correlated with equally unique epistemic and pragmatic potentials. From such a perspective, metaphor is seen as having the capacity to provide highly significant transformations of language, thought, and experience—transformations of a kind not duplicated by other linguistic strategies.

The very recognition of the importance and pervasiveness of metaphor raises difficult questions, however. Is there any discourse that is *not* metaphoric, at least in origins? Having categorized figurative language as essentially metaphoric, are there no important discriminations left to make among rhetorical tropes? What is the function of "dead" metaphor? And how does metaphor—live or dead—function in ordinary thought and practice as well as in relation to specialized conceptual enterprises like science, law, metaphysics, and theology? Some of these questions I can address only briefly in a book of this sort, whereas others lie entirely beyond anything I consider explicitly. Certainly I make no attempt to survey the whole range of answers offered by current scholarship. The reader wanting more complete discussions of any of these issues is urged to consult the bibliography, taking special note of recent collections of essays[6] and of Paul Ricoeur's comprehensive study *La Métaphore vive* (the English translation of which bears the misleading title *The Rule of Metaphor*).[7]

My own goal is not so much to proffer or reject theories of metaphor in general as it is to give a more adequate account than others have of the dynamics and value of specifically poetic metaphor—including whole literary works seen as extended metaphors. From the start, I stress how poetry's semantic creativity is linked to its essential interdependence with other modes of language and experience. In this way I lay the groundwork for later conclusions concerning the relation of poetic metaphor to religious languages and belief.

In view of the trajectory of my argument, one might expect Paul Ricoeur's theories to figure most prominently in the discussion. And obviously, having studied with Ricoeur and felt considerable sympathy with his aims, I have both consciously and unconsciously kept his work in mind. Yet my views of metaphor, metaphysics, and theology finally differ from Ricoeur's at a number of critical points. Furthermore, Ricoeur has never applied his theories to an analysis of the kind of literary art with which I am primarily concerned. I therefore take a different route. Content on the whole to treat the theories of Ricoeur and several other thinkers as reference points, I begin with a critique and extensive reformulation of the ideas of a philosopher intimately acquainted with literature and literary criticism—namely, Philip Wheelwright.

Wheelwright's overall stature is not, of course, equal to that of Ricoeur—or of Heidegger or various analytic philosophers, for that matter. Some of his most interesting claims are never supported with rigorous argumentation or systematic exposition. In addition, they are often embedded in a polemic against logical and semantic positivism that now seems somewhat dated. Yet Wheelwright's failures are unusually illuminating, and I believe his insights can be put to better use than anyone has realized.

Wheelwright's confusions and weaknesses are instructive because they reflect his close but ambivalent association with the so-called New Criticism dominant at mid-century in England and North America. If this kind of literary criticism had by now been replaced by alternatives free of all its defects, then a critique of Wheelwright would be superfluous. But in point of fact many of the typical New Critical dilemmas and confusions, particularly with regard to poetic structure, language, and purpose, repeatedly recur in the often brilliant attempts made in the last two decades to go beyond or to circumvent the New Criticism.[8] To see where Wheelwright fails in his own effort to transcend the limitations of such criticism is thus also to see how today's critical theories can be strengthened.

More significant, to the extent that Wheelwright succeeds, his success has neither been duplicated nor fully appreciated. This is not to say his work has been totally misunderstood or neglected. Every student of metaphor is familiar with Wheelwright's name, and his ideas continue to be discussed with respect even outside literary critical circles, whether in biblical studies of the nature of parable and symbol[9] or in philosophical studies of language such as those provided by James Edie[10] and Paul Ricoeur.[11] Yet no detailed and careful examination of Wheelwright's "semantics of poetry" has ever appeared in print. As a consequence, no one has seen or explored some important implications of his theories of poetic assertion, metaphor, and cognition.

My reading of Wheelwright is one I admit he might at points consider a misreading. And the conclusions I draw from his claims are not always ones he would either recognize or welcome. They have been deduced, as a deconstructionist would quickly note, from what Wheelwright leaves unsaid as well as from what he plainly does say, and they sometimes undermine other of his claims. If I myself am glad to accept and build on these "subversive" conclusions, it is only because I have certain goals in mind that Wheelwright never would have pursued. In the end, however, this is the only way I have seen to reach the more important goals of his and so indeed to move beyond some of the limitations of the New Criticism.

To the extent to which my strategy succeeds, it establishes a standpoint from which to see poetic (that is, literary) wholes as extended metaphoric structures having the capacity to augment, transfigure, and reinterpret meanings already a part of language and experience—meanings vital to the self as it seeks a comprehensive meaning in the patterns of existence as a whole. Whereas Wheelwright sometimes succumbs to the New Critical temptation to see poetry as an autonomous and ineffable object mediating a sense of reality essentially beyond the reach of reason and conceptual discourse, the present theory sees the transfigurations of poetry as semantic creations that, for all their uniqueness, are inevitably taken up into further language and experience, there to be reinterpreted in conceptual modes that can themselves generate further poetic and imaginative exploration. On this view, not only does the symbol (or metaphor) give rise to thought—as Kant, Jaspers, and Ricoeur all insist—but thought in turn gives rise to symbol, which itself returns, transfigured, to thought and life.

This understanding of poetic language and of language as a whole runs counter to the tendency of many modern thinkers to regard our multiple human worlds—linguistic and otherwise—as discrete spheres with distinct and totally autonomous meanings and rules.[12] Similarly, it suggests that Kant's clear-cut distinctions between the modes of reason and judgment do not completely match the operations of the mind, since in some contexts the claims of reason can apparently qualify, and be qualified by, the claims of taste. The thoughts we reasonably conceive influence the aesthetic metaphors we imagine, with the converse being equally true. Even if such relations seem illicit, they can no longer be ignored.

To envision a dynamic interrelationship between different modes of language and thought is not, however, to deny they are indeed different. I do not take metaphoric and conceptual kinds of discourse to be interchangeable, as though they were identical in semantic shape. Accordingly, I would not suggest that their most significant meanings are to be discovered using identical methods of interpretation. Nor would I argue that metaphoric and conceptual modes of meaning have the same overall purposes, even if it is true that certain basic structural patterns recur in both poetry and science, for example, or in both myth and history. The theory put forward here is therefore incompatible with the ideas of those structuralists who hold that all linguistic phenomena are not only fundamentally but also most importantly permutations of a limited number of structures underlying all the constructions of consciousness and serving essentially equivalent functions (such as the mediation of binary oppositions).[13] This is not to reject every use of structuralist methods, of course, but merely to oppose a form of structuralist ideology.[14]

Finally, my theory of metaphor has implications with regard to the perennial question of the relation of language to "reality." Phenomenologists, structuralists, deconstructionists, and analytic philosophers have all stressed, though in different ways, that human experience is linguistic to the core. Without language, they suggest, we would simply have no worlds to ponder, inhabit, or even escape. Some who say this mean merely that no particle of experience as humans know it could so much as exist for us apart from at least rudimentary language, much of it nonverbal. With this I concur. But where the "linguisticality" of experience is interpreted to mean that language is closed in on itself, so that—in Foucault's words—it has "nothing to say but itself, nothing to do but shine in the brightness of its being,"[15] there the so-called postmodern consciousness occupies territory alien to mine. It seems to me more plausible to suppose the dialogue between (or among) languages exists at all only because of an impetus from experience never quite said. I thus agree with Whitehead that there is not simply the clearly sayable and knowable on the one hand and the completely unsayable and unknowable on the other. Contrary to the import of Wittgenstein's closing aphorisms in the *Tractatus*,[16] there is also the partially sayable, the partially knowable: "the hint half guessed, the gift half understood," as Eliot puts it. And there is the process of coming to say and coming to know. Indeed, because nothing experienced can ever completely be said or known in any or all of the dialects native to the self, it is all the more important to attend to the interplay between various modes of discourse, thought, and experience. Doing so, one never sees around language, but one can see through its many levels to what motivates it and may yet be said more fully and clearly. One also comes to realize how interconnected and yet distinctive our symbol systems are and how those systems together extend and enrich our sense of ourselves, of our social world, and of the whole.

This, then, is the thrust behind the theory of metaphor and language elaborated here. But that theory and its ramifications take shape only gradually in the chapters to come. After the groundwork is laid in my critique of Wheelwright, the three subsequent chapters undertake a study of T. S. Eliot's *Four Quartets* intended to flesh out and extend the literary theoretical ideas already considered at an abstract level.

There is ample precedent for approaching the *Quartets* from a theoretical point of view even while offering an interpretation of the work that can be considered on its own merits. F. R. Leavis, for example, devotes almost half of *The Living Principle* to a discussion of the *Quartets* intended to show—among other things—that poetry is genuinely a medium of thought.[17] In a similar way, Paul Hahn utilizes *Four Quartets* to demonstrate the validity of his "reformation of New Criticism."[18] Again, in this connection, it is significant that F. O. Matthiessen's study of T. S. Eliot bears the subtitle *An Essay on the Nature of Poetry*.[19] Nor should it pass unnoticed that Hans Osterwald uses other works by Eliot to elaborate a Jakobsonian account of the role of metaphor and metonymy in language and literature.[20] And, finally, it is surely pertinent that Philip Wheelwright himself endeavors to support his theories by examining, in the concluding pages of *The Burning Fountain*, certain features of the *Quartets*.[21] It would thus seem I am in good company in judging that *Four Quartets* provides valuable material for either evaluating or formulating a theory of poetry.

The reasons for this are not hard to find. Although *Four Quartets* is not, in its combination of reflective seriousness and lyrical beauty, entirely typical of modern verse, this cycle of poems nevertheless stands as a major and influential achievement and the crowning work of an important poet. The kinds of poetic qualities it exhibits can, moreover, be shown to be fairly representative of a large number of other poems, including—in the modern period alone—many by major poets like Rilke, Stevens, and Yeats. If *Four Quartets* is in some ways exceptional (perhaps especially in its balancing of intellectual and "affective" components), this simply calls attention to traits common to all literature but frequently less conspicuous in other contexts. No work, of course, can exemplify every major characteristic of every kind of literary art. Because of its lyrical nature, for instance, *Four Quartets* minimizes the dimension of narrative. Yet one can discern in the work something at least analogous to narrative. There is, at any rate, a definite progression and "representation of action" within each of the *Quartets* as well as within the work as a whole, and this requires us to respond to the work partly as a temporal and sequential entity.

Still another feature of the *Quartets* makes it a logical choice for a study such as this. Given the poem's reliance on mystical, philosophical, and theological sources, one can scarcely avoid confronting one of the questions I have indicated I most want to confront: What is poetry's relation to religious experience and reflection and to theology in particular? But to deal adequately with this question we must of course look not only at *Four Quartets* but also at the dynamics of human experience and religious reflection. Accordingly, I next turn from poetry proper to one major way of conceiving the character of experience and its relation to poetic, theological, and metaphysical thinking. It is at this point that the theories of Alfred North Whitehead become relevant.

If Wheelwright's theories have not been given their due on account of their casual exposition and lack of rigor, Whitehead's seem to have suffered from the opposite difficulty. The ideas of Whitehead that most interest me here are in fact often deeply enmeshed in a complex and forbidding philosophical system. As a result, they have yet to receive the attention they deserve.

To be sure, it is encouraging that Whitehead's work appears no longer to be solely the property of logicians, metaphysicians, or even "process" theologians. Epistemologists and phenomenologists like Calvin Schrag have begun to recognize its significance. And some recent studies begin to meet the need pointed out by Schrag when, in 1969, he wrote: "It is unfortunate that the metaphysical scaffolding of [Whitehead's] speculative cosmology has virtually eclipsed his seminal insights into the dynamics and texture of experience. What is sorely needed in Whitehead scholarship today is a reexamination of his philosophy in light of his theory of experience." [22]

Lyman Lundeen's book *Risk and Rhetoric in Religion* is one such study. Although it is not intended to satisfy Schrag's specific desideratum, Lundeen's is a thoughtful exposition of Whitehead's broader reflections on experience, language, symbolism, and the nature of metaphysical and religious thinking. [23] Stephen Franklin's "Speaking from the Depth" also deals with these and similar topics while analyzing in far greater detail the role Whitehead's philosophy of language plays in his metaphysical system. [24] Both works thus supplement in important respects Bernard Loomer's "The Theological Significance of the Method of Empirical Analysis in the Philosophy of A. N. Whitehead" (1942), which remains the best discussion of Whitehead's views on the value of "contingent" experience for metaphysical reflection. [25] Finally, Bernard Meland—among others—has creatively utilized the aspect of Whitehead's thought concerned with the less clearly conceived elements of life experience and the more poetic elements within language. [26]

Nevertheless, no writer seems to have given a truly satisfactory account of just how the conceptual language of philosophy and theology is, in Whitehead's account, related to the language of poetry and how poetry is related both to prior language and to nonlinguistic experience. This deficiency would perhaps be unremarkable were it not for the fact that Whitehead himself was emphatic in stating not only that certain realities enter human consciousness primarily as symbols and as the sort of "intermediate representations" generally offered by literary art but also that these realities are precisely those whose apprehension forms the basis for religious and metaphysical claims, thereby permitting existing conceptual schemes to be criticized and transcended.

We thus have every reason to examine with care Whitehead's ideas as to poetry's relation to reflection, theological as well as metaphysical. In my own effort to do so, however, I deliberately avoid much of Whitehead's technical jargon, just as he himself often does when setting forth his epistemological and methodological premises or treating topics not explicitly dealt with in his metaphysics. This means that I am necessarily prevented from specifying precisely what Whitehead's metaphysical justification may be for holding certain views of language and experience, but it also happily means that the validity of those views may no longer be presumed to be contingent on the validity of the particulars of the metaphysical system he espoused.

Despite their intrinsic value, Whitehead's claims cannot provide a proper terminus for our inquiry. Whitehead, after all, was writing at a time when the basic presuppositions behind the best of the current theories of poetry and metaphor were just being formed. Then, too, Whitehead was obviously more interested in metaphysics than in religious reflection per se; he had no keen awareness of the particular constraints and special ends the theologian must keep in mind. His notion of the languages of religious belief was, furthermore, prejudiced toward intellectual, conceptual discourse. My aim is consequently to reshape Whitehead's argument and to carry it further than he was able to—partly by reference to such other thinkers as Stephen Toulmin, Paul Ricoeur, and David Tracy.

In the final portion of this study, as elsewhere, I trust my discussion will not be construed as having only to do with traditional religious belief and practice, let alone with a belief and practice that is exclusively Christian. Many of the implications of my arguments can in fact fully be appreciated only if viewed within the larger context of religious and cultural studies as a whole. Nevertheless, I have chosen to conclude by giving special attention to questions of language and belief as they have been posed for contemporary Christian theology. For this I make no apology, because it is this form of religious reflection that has been forced to confront most directly certain thorny linguistic and religious issues endemic to modern Western thought and now springing up in non-Western contexts as well.

Not that Western theologians have devised any all-encompassing solutions. Their theologies at the moment exist in a state of considerable confusion. For one thing, there is no unanimity as to the role theology can and should play among the various languages of religious belief and modes of religious practice. Most theologians would probably still accept Anselm's venerable description of the theological task as "*fides quaerens intellectum.*" But theological ideas of how faith is to seek understanding differ widely these days, as do ideas concerning the nature of the understanding that faith seeks. There is also considerable dispute as to what medium is most viable for theology. Should theology's idiom be conceptual, propositional discourse or should it be story? Autobiography or kerygmatic proclamation? Visual embodiment or political action? Thus Thomas Altizer speaks for many when he states: "Theology today is most fundamentally in quest of a language and mode whereby it can speak."[27] I cannot attempt to resolve all these controversies concerning the status and function of theological discourse. But I do ally myself with those who argue that an im-

portant place remains for a form of religious language that strives un-
abashedly to be conceptual and nonpoetic; that is, for a language designed
to articulate and support in precise, systematic, and reasonable ways the
fundamental affirmations of faith. This kind of language seems to me most
distinctively theological, retaining a unique place among the languages of
religious belief.

Granting this much, I challenge the claim of those theologians who argue that theology, precisely as a conceptual mode of discourse, can provide
the fullest possible understanding of faith—who hold, in other words, that
theology itself can constitute faith's most adequate, appropriate, and understandable expression. Because one of the strongest arguments for such
a view of theology is provided by a "process" theologian (Schubert Ogden), I take pains to dispute the argument partly on the basis of Whitehead's own "process" theories. At the same time, I criticize the opposite
view, which regards poetry and poetic metaphor as having the final word
in the realm of religious expression and understanding. This alternative, I
claim, gives us an equally distorted picture of human language, faith, and
understanding. Taking a kind of *via media*, I maintain that the metaphoric
language of poetry and the conceptual language of theology are best understood as existing in a dialectical or dialogical relationship. And I propose the concept of "transfiguration" as one fruitful way of envisioning the
manner in which the dual semantic procedures of metaphoric and conceptual discourse together explore, imagine, and give utterance to the realities
fundamental to the languages of religious belief.

It will become apparent that I am using the terms "transfiguration" and
"languages of religious belief" in a somewhat unusual fashion. Likewise, it
will soon be evident that the terms "conceptual language" and "metaphoric language" have, in the present context, a rather different relation
from what one might suppose. In concluding this overview, therefore, I
wish to comment briefly on this terminology.

Like many other theorists, I have found it convenient and useful to refer
to certain kinds of language as "conceptual" and to contrast these with
other kinds of language called "metaphoric." But, in contrast to a number
of theorists, I do not see metaphoric meaning as entirely lacking in the
logic and clarity of conceptual discourse, nor do I see conceptual meaning
as entirely devoid of metaphoric ambiguity and "tension." If we are to
speak of an absolute opposition, I believe it must be with reference to
strictly hypothetical, limiting cases that, following Wheelwright, we might
term pure "steno-language" and pure "verbal music." Consequently, with
reference to actual discourse, I use the terms "conceptual" and "metaphoric" to denote procedures of language whose means, and possibly
ends, are only relatively distinct.

In the following pages I prefer to speak of "languages of religious belief" instead of "religious language." There are two reasons for this. First, the use of the plural "languages" is consistent with my conviction that religious belief comes to expression in many different modes of discourse, none of which is completely interchangeable with another and each of which requires, in some measure, a distinct method and vocabulary of interpretation, whether it be historical, speculative, logical, or some other. (Poetry can, for my purposes, be considered one basic—though varied—language, existing as it does within the single realm of metaphoric fiction.)

My second reason for wanting to speak of "languages of religious belief" instead of "religious language" has to do with the word "belief." By "belief" I mean two things at once: a state of conviction as well as an orientation of trust. "Belief," as I use the word, thus denotes both "belief that" and "belief in." Although many actions and practices of a religious sort may well move one beyond belief, in a narrow intellectual sense,[28] they nevertheless entail belief to the extent to which they involve some degree of judgment about, and/or commitment to, what is deemed real and true. And it is poetry's relationship to (other) languages involving "belief" in this larger sense that is my chief concern here. By contrast, contemporary studies of "religious language," reflecting in part the influence of the later Wittgenstein, have often treated the languages of faith as "language games" to which "belief that" is either irrelevant or inconsequential. This has undeniably led to some stimulating studies of the pragmatics of religious discourse, but it has not entailed any large concern for what I regard as an intimate connection between linguistic action and intellectual conviction.

My usage of the term "transfiguration," though by no means commonplace, bears a family resemblance to many other usages one encounters. As might be expected, the religious import of the term as I use it is more than hinted at in the gospel narratives of Jesus' transfiguration, where the true nature of Jesus' identity and mission is described as having suddenly been revealed and confirmed through a transformation of his appearance. But I am also using the word "transfiguration" in a much more general sense to refer to any transformation of a phenomenon that is, in addition, a transformation of the significance to be ascribed to the phenomenon. For example, one changes the pattern of mere vocal sounds in a certain way and they are transfigured into speech. Writers have often used the term in this way with reference to art, as is apparent from the title of Arthur Danto's recent book, *The Transfiguration of the Commonplace: A Philosophy of Art.*[29] When applied specifically to literature, my use of the word is similar to Leo Spitzer's when he writes: "[Poetry] consists of *words*, with their meaning *preserved*, which, through the magic of the poet who works with a 'prosodic' whole, arrive at a sense-beyond-sense; and . . . it is the task of the philologist to point out the manner in which the transfiguration just mentioned has been achieved."[30] But I attribute this semantic transformation not to "magic" but to metaphor, the linguistic paradigm of transfiguration with which our study both begins and ends.

Chapter Two Poetry and Reality
A Critique of Philip Wheelwright

The lord whose oracle is at Delphi neither speaks nor conceals, but gives signs.
—Heraclitus, trans. Philip Wheelwright

To a remarkable extent Philip Wheelwright's studies of poetry all manifest one central concern: to arrive at a fuller understanding of poetry's capacity to embody and reveal aspects of reality that elude other kinds of linguistic expression.[1] Likewise, all of Wheelwright's studies employ remarkably similar approaches. In each one, his procedure involves contrasting the languages of poetry, myth, and religion with the languages of ordinary communication, logic, mathematics, and science.

However subtly drawn or variously explained, the distinction Wheelwright makes between these languages invariably comes to this: the latter languages (which collectively constitute what he calls "steno-language") are forms of discourse whose meaning is purportedly restricted to, and exhausted by, their precise empirical and logical content; whereas the former languages (which Wheelwright groups together under the rubric of "depth" or "expressive" language) are semantic forms that either exclude or in various ways move beyond logical and narrowly empirical conceptualization. It is Wheelwright's basic thesis that this fundamental semantic difference between "steno-language" and "depth" language has a direct bearing not only on the *way* in which either language is able to speak of reality, but also on *what* it is that either language is able to say. This means, according to Wheelwright, that the world mediated through "steno-" discourse is never just the same as the world mediated through poetry and myth. And it means that one's sense of reality is continually shaped by the kind of language one inherits or chooses as one attempts to articulate one's perceptions and experience.[2] Thus, when one is in the process of choosing a language to describe the world, one is to some extent also choosing a world to describe. This is why, for Wheelwright, ontology ("the study of the major ways in which anything can be said to really *be*") is inseparable from semantics ("the study of meanings and of how they can be expressed and communicated").[3]

The claim that language and reality are intimately related is, of course, one that a great many modern thinkers would support, whether they be linguists (like Benjamin Whorf),[4] neo-Kantian philosophers (like Ernst Cassirer),[5] existentialists and phenomenologists (like Martin Heidegger and Paul Ricoeur),[6] or cultural anthropologists (like Clifford Geertz).[7] It is also one corroborated in an intriguing way by recent studies in the neuropsychology of the left and right hemispheres of the brain.[8] But if it is true that the semantic properties of one's language significantly affect one's sense of reality, then Wheelwright's thesis that steno-language and depth language represent a basic semantic duality is one that raises in a most acute manner the question of whether, how, and to what extent these two modes of language are interrelated. For it is clear that human beings, at least in the modern West, inevitably use both steno-language and depth language. If, therefore, these two kinds of language are in the end utterly unrelated—or perhaps even antithetical—in their expressions of "what is," then a kind of ontological schizophrenia would seem to be an unavoidable aspect of Western sensibility.

Wheelwright himself appears, at several points in his work, to be headed toward just such a schizophrenia (metaphorically speaking). Yet, as we will see in this chapter, aspects of his semantic theory, and especially his discussions of metaphor, provide solid theoretical grounds for believing that such a fate is avoidable. They do so by indicating how the seemingly absolute dichotomy between steno-language and depth language is better understood as a duality permitting degrees of difference, overlapping, and mutual influence between the two semantic modes. My reformulation and extension of Wheelwright's "semantics of poetry" will therefore build on these specific features of his semantic theory while criticizing Wheelwright for failing clearly to recognize the implications of such a theory for philosophy or theology, or in fact for the interpretation of poetry itself.

The Language of Plain Sense

Wheelwright's own procedure indicates that the best way to approach the semantics of expressive language is through an examination of the traits of steno-language, the language of "plain sense."[9] But, because Wheelwright's assessment of steno-language is very much affected (albeit often negatively) by the views of other modern thinkers, we will do well to survey the relevant features of his intellectual background—using, as much as possible, Wheelwright's own perspective.

From Wheelwright's point of view, any satisfactory account of the nature and significance of steno-language can ill afford to ignore the fact that educated minds in the West have increasingly come to associate knowledge and genuine insight with conceptual discourse and it alone, whether this discourse be considered reliable only when rooted in rational ideas and principles (as in the Enlightenment) or whether it be deemed reliable primarily when rooted in empirical "facts" (a common twentieth-century assumption).[10] It is significant, furthermore, that ever since Kant—and especially since the demise of the grand metaphysical schemes of British and German idealism—the particular kind of conceptual discourse found in natural science has, to an extent probably without parallel in the history of semantic systems, become *the* language of "truth."[11] In the field of philosophy this development can be attributed in part to the rise of critical philosophy and its debunking of "naive" metaphysics. But the ascendancy of scientific discourse is even more directly correlated with the growth of the empiricist tradition, with its reliance on precise concepts derived from the "plain facts" of perception.[12] Although the dominance of the scientific concept of truth can be said to have reached its culmination in logical positivism (about which more will be said shortly), it is still discernible even if positivism per se has nearly died out.[13]

What makes this "triumph" of scientific language and thought so noteworthy, in Wheelwright's opinion, is that it has meant, among other things, that modern Westerners have inherited a dominant mentality that inevitably splits the world of experience into a strict dichotomy between "objective" facts and "subjective" values, "rational" ideas and "irrational" feelings. As a result, it has also meant that Westerners have found it increasingly difficult to ascribe cognitive value to those central ethical and religious claims that earlier theologians, philosophers, and even the Enlightenment rationalists had sought to justify.[14]

Wheelwright's own theory of semantic and ontological duality was from the very beginning specifically designed to combat the strict dichotomy described above, so as to avoid the negative consequences entailed for religion, morals, and other spheres of human value.[15] In order to do so, however, his theory had to confront head-on the contrary ideas of one school of modern thought in particular: the logical and semantic positivists. This was imperative because positivism, more than any other major philosophical movement, widened the split between "steno-" and "expressive" language into a veritable chasm; and it posed such an immediate threat to nonscientific modes of inquiry like metaphysics and ethics that a philosopher with Wheelwright's interest in language and values could scarcely afford to ignore its arguments. Nor, for that matter, can any study of Wheelwright's work—though, for our purposes, a short review of the tenets and literary influence of the positivist movement will be adequate.

The most outspoken proponents of logical positivism in the early decades of the twentieth century were a group of philosophers who called themselves the Vienna Circle. This Circle, closely allied with Berlin's Society for Empirical Philosophy, included such philosophers as Moritz Schlick, Rudolf Carnap, Kurt Gödel, Otto Neurath, Friedrich Waismann, and Herbert Feigl. Outside the Circle there were other significant figures either formally or informally associated with the logical positivist movement, the most distinguished of these being the young Ludwig Wittgenstein[16] and, later, A. J. Ayer.[17] For the most part mathematicians and philosophers of science, these thinkers all wished to set philosophy on a solid scientific and logical foundation. To this end, they advanced the semantic theory that the meaning of a statement is its method of verification. It was agreed, furthermore, that, according to this "verifiability principle," only two forms of expression could be judged to be strictly meaningful: synthetic propositions (that is, those propositions that are scientific, and so empirically verifiable) and analytic statements (those that are tautologous, or true by logical necessity).[18]

Although the positivists' primary intention in formulating their verifiability principle was to demonstrate the basic unintelligibility and irrationality of metaphysics and traditional philosophy, it was at once evident that acceptance of the positivists' criterion for meaning would lead to the conclusion that religious, moral, and poetic assertions are all meaningless or at least cognitively empty. For none of these forms of what Wheelwright calls "depth" language could pretend to be capable of verification in a narrowly empirical sense; yet neither could such language be represented as uttering pure tautologies. Thus, if the positivists were right, the only content or "meaning" one could possibly assign to such language was an emotive one, its function in that case being to express or to inculcate affective states.

Given their antihumanistic stance, the positivists were not likely to win many friends among lovers of art and literature. As early as the 1920s, however, I. A. Richards began advancing, on the literary front, a theory of language that Wheelwright was quite justifiably to call "semantic positivism." Richards's presentation of his ideas, moreover, was so articulate and forceful as to make it almost inevitable that Wheelwright would come to see Richards as his major opponent in the area of the semantic analysis of poetry.[19]

It is true that Richards was never, strictly speaking, a logical positivist; his thinking and terminology were more dependent on the theoretical framework of experimental psychology than on formal philosophy of any kind. And his overt intention, in contrast to the positivists', was not to champion the language of science, logic, and mathematics. Far from it. As one who would later be identified with the "New Critics," Richards was a humanist whose sympathies lay with Matthew Arnold and the belief that human culture is dependent on poetry and artistic expression for its essential vitality. He even went so far as to claim, in a sort of *Credo* found in *Science and Poetry* (1926), that poetry can save us by "preserving us or rescuing us from confusion and frustration."[20]

But Richards, unlike Wheelwright, did not imagine that poetry provides one access to a higher form of knowledge, or really to any form of knowledge at all. Instead he contended that poetry's chief value is the purely affective one of "releasing or organizing our impulses and attitudes." In defense of his position, Richards made much of the idea that only empirically verifiable statements are genuine (that is, have a truth value); and from this he deduced that poetry consists not of real statements but of emotive "pseudo-statements." Such "pseudo-statements," Richards acknowledged, do appear to make cognitive claims, but their real purpose, he insisted, lies in eliciting emotional rather than intellectual assent.[21]

It is apparent, then, that Richards agreed with the essential points of the positivists' semantic theory per se. Both the semantic positivism of Richards and the logical positivism of the Vienna Circle described language in terms of an absolute dichotomy. Both pitted science against poetry, reason against emotion, cognition against valuation. Consequently, even if Richards himself preferred poetry to truth, his theories provided ammunition for those positivists whose concern for truth caused them to do battle against any elevated concept of poetry.

Such theories raised questions Wheelwright could not circumvent. And the fact that the positivist interpretation of the duality of language was antithetical to Wheelwright's own helps explain the way Wheelwright would frame his response, as well as the passionate rhetoric he would sometimes use.[22] It also helps explain some otherwise inexplicable inconsistencies in Wheelwright's analysis of steno-language—an analysis to which we can now turn our attention.

We have seen that Wheelwright ordinarily defines steno-language as conceptually precise, logical discourse. This relatively neutral description of steno-language contrasts markedly, however, with the far more negative impression left by much of his rhetoric and some of his analysis. Whereas Wheelwright describes expressive language as "alive," "fluid," "open," "organic," "imaginative," and "deep," he describes steno-language as "dead," "block-like," "closed," "static," "inert," and "stereo-typed."[23] Even the term "steno-language" is hardly a neutral one; as Wheelwright points out, the Greek prefix "steno" means "closed" or "restricted."[24] Wheelwright's coolness toward steno-language is also betrayed in his statement that "steno-language *by definition* represents the negative limit of expressive language, its absolute minimum" (Wheelwright's emphasis).[25] Even if Wheelwright is not intending here to provide a complete definition, he is nevertheless implying that steno-language is little more than the semantic residue left when language is deprived of all expressive or "poetic" properties. This impression is only reinforced by an analogy in which Wheelwright likens expressive language to sound and steno-language to silence.[26]

Once again it seems we are to think of steno-language as merely the ab-
sence of expressive language—as not only a limiting case[27] but also a case
of pure limitation or deprivation. Silence, after all, is not only the limit of
sound; it is the utterly negative limit.[28] Should we still somehow miss the
point, Wheelwright can be explicit indeed, as when he declares that the
steno-expression of reality is a "thin piping" that compares to an attempt
to score the Eroica Symphony for two flutes.[29]

By this point one cannot refrain from asking whether Wheelwright sees
even the steno-languages of logic, science, and mathematics as simply what
is left when language is deprived of poetry, and thus as "inert" and "closed"
semantic systems indistinguishable from discourse that is merely trite, cli-
chéd, or incoherent. If our answer is based on the evidence found in the
parts of Wheelwright's discussion we have just examined, we must admit
that this indeed seems to be the case. But since such a view of certain
highly sophisticated forms of steno-language is patently absurd, we should
be prepared to acknowledge that Wheelwright may sometimes have in-
dulged in exaggerating the negative features of steno-language, and doubtless because the positivists had gone to the opposite extreme.

In any case, it is of vital interest to this study to observe that an entirely
negative view of steno-language is incompatible with much of Wheelwright's semantic theory (and even—as we shall see—with his analysis
of expressive language). Elsewhere, for example, Wheelwright makes a
valuable distinction between steno-language closed by "default" and steno-
language closed intentionally, by "stipulation."[30] The former kind, a result
of habit, carelessness, or imaginative failure, shows neither intellectual precision nor imaginative creativity, and it is susceptible of useless ambiguities. Hence, it is of no great worth. When language is limited by stipulation, however, it is created for a specific purpose. Its semantic properties
leave as little as possible to the imagination, but only so that the intellect
will not be distracted from conceptual, logical pursuits. Far from being
merely the negative limit where all poetry ceases, "steno-language at its
best"[31] exhibits positive traits peculiar to it alone.[32]

Paramount among these is the fact that the overall structure of a work of
steno-language follows the shape of logical argumentation. Because such
argumentation proceeds by consecutive reasoning devoid of intentional
ambiguity or significant affective appeal, its basic semantic units are pure
propositions: sentences that are entirely declarative and internally coherent
(not self-contradictory) and whose truth is "a function of the potential evidence on which it rests."[33] Propositions, in turn, must consist of semantic
indicators that are unequivocal, their meaning fixed and definite. These
"steno-signs," as Wheelwright calls them, must be so arbitrary or conventional as to be capable of being interchanged with any other steno-signs

stipulated as synonymous. ("Rosa rubiginosa" and "Rosa eglanteria" are, in botany, completely interchangeable terms for the sweetbriar rose.) [34] Finally, a steno-sign must have a referent that is either a logical universal or an existential particular—either the sort of entity referred to by the noun "man" or the sort referred to by the name "John."

Now what Wheelwright goes on to say about this rigorously controlled form of steno-language reveals that we cannot take his more negative evaluations of steno-language to be his final word. For Wheelwright declares that "steno-language is a *must*, expressive language is a *can* and *may*"—by which he means to state emphatically that in human society the use of steno-language is not optional. [35] Wheelwright openly acknowledges that not only the sophisticated languages of science and mathematics and law depend on unambiguous systems of steno-signs, but so do what he calls the important but ordinary transactions of the "marketplace." [36]

Having seen that Wheelwright ascribes considerable worth to certain kinds of steno-language, however, we must not lose sight of what he understands to be the price paid whenever steno-limits are imposed on discourse. Although Wheelwright addresses this question at length in *The Burning Fountain*, [37] one of the most succinct statements of his position appears in *Metaphor and Reality*, where he writes:

> While logical language is manifestly of very great importance for situations and types of question to which it legitimately applies, its powers of reference are limited. . . .
> Intelligibility is manifold. It can be simplified in an effort to be widely understood, and it can be confined with scientific responsibility to the kind of thing that publicly sharable experiments and observations are capable of indicating. In either case, however, something is left out. [38]

It is evident that what Wheelwright believes is left out of steno-language and thought is not merely affect or aesthetic decoration but, more importantly, a dimension of the intelligible world.

The basis for this belief is already to be found in *The Burning Fountain*. [39] There, leaning heavily on Heraclitus and the post-Kantian Mexican philosopher and politician José Vasconcelos, Wheelwright argues that one side of human experience consists of an orderly array of rationally comprehensible, law-abiding events and facts. This is the domain of what Kant described as the cognizable world—the world of causes and effects, substances and attributes, and measurable units of time and space. Because steno-language "serves the conceptual object," it is seen, in Wheelwright's analysis, as the appropriate and adequate linguistic response to this orderly, quantifiable, rational world.

Yet, Wheelwright declares, we are also aware of aspects of the world that defy precise conceptualization. In our experience we encounter not only clear and distinct empirical or logical entities but also "subtly blended qualities, dramatic oppositions," feelings and values, persons and presences—elusive but undeniable realities that evoke, among other responses, the attitudes of awe or love or even hate. This "tensive" world of interrelated phenomena, Wheelwright contends, exceeds the grasp of narrowly empirical concepts and of Kantian categories of understanding and hence is not amenable to interpretation through semantic procedures addressed to the intellect alone. To the extent that such a world of experience can be known and assimilated at all, it must be by means of language that can create and represent something of the "vitalistic" synthesis of sensation, thought, and feeling that lies at the threshold of human rationality. Obviously a language of this kind must move beyond the limits of plain sense.

Expressive Language

Wheelwright's views of "expressive" or "poetic" language are in many ways similar to the views of the so-called New Critics, whose theories of literature were so influential in Anglo-American criticism of the mid-twentieth century.[40] Both Wheelwright and the New Critics stress what they believe to be the unique semantic characteristics of poetry (that is, literary art): its essentially metaphoric or symbolic character, its reliance on paradox and creative ambiguity, its resistance to paraphrase. Both parties are fundamentally concerned with the poem itself rather than with the literary history to which it belongs, or the life and genius of its author, or the edifying or pleasurable effect it has on its audience. Lastly, Wheelwright and most of the New Critics are alike in rejecting positivism and in insisting that poetry bodies forth a special kind of knowledge. It is little wonder, then, that several historians of the New Criticism have seen Wheelwright as one of the New Critics' chief philosophical allies.[41]

But if the New Critics and Wheelwright share a common interest in the language of poetry and in defending poetry against any attempt (positivist or otherwise) to undermine poetry's autonomy, the semantic theories undergirding their respective defenses of poetic art are by no means identical. For what the New Critics claim in their classic utterances is essentially that poetry's semantic properties are so exceptional as to warrant viewing a poem more as a self-contained verbal object than as a mode of representation or assertion. Indeed, as Murray Krieger points out, they seem to be arguing that poetry is not only autonomous but supreme in being so:

"The poet does violence to the principles of discourse in order to achieve in his poem a unique and closed system of discourse which can break through the inherent incapacities of all non-poetic uses of language."[42] The irony is that the New Critics' emphasis on the superiority, autonomy, and uniqueness of poetic discourse left them hard pressed to explain how the "closed" semantic system of poetry could have real cognitive value. As a result, their theoretical stance unwittingly lent credibility to the positivists' contention that between conceptual, verifiable discourse and all poetic discourse there is a great gulf fixed.[43]

Wheelwright's semantic analysis of poetry is not entirely free from the mystifications and internal contradictions that plagued New Critical theories of literature. Nonetheless, it does have the distinction of resting squarely on the assumption that there exists a complex and extremely important array of connections between the language and world of steno-discourse and the language and world of poetic art. Exactly what Wheelwright believes these connections to be is perhaps most fully illumined by his theory of metaphor, which we will shortly examine. But considerable light is also cast on the subject by Wheelwright's more general discussion of the major features of expressive language, as contrasted with the steno-linguistic traits we have already discussed.

In *The Burning Fountain* Wheelwright states that seven of the most important traits of expressive language are "referential congruity," "contextual variation," "plurisignation," "soft focus," "paralogical dimensionality," "assertorial lightness," and "paradox"—all of these being linguistic procedures by means of which the "semantic plenitude" of such language is achieved.[44] Despite the peculiarity of some of the terminology, we can readily decipher Wheelwright's main points.

"Referential congruity" refers to the fact that there is an intimate connection between what is said in a poem and the poem's way of saying it, the properties of each semantic unit of a poem being so completely congruent with the poetic meaning that any rewording, paraphrase, or translation could at best only approximate the sense of the original. This explains why "O my luv is like a red, red rose" could not satisfactorily be replaced by the conceptually equivalent statement, "My love is like a very red rose." Here connotation is as important as denotation.

Nor is there, in poetry, any such thing as a fixed meaning. Rather, every semantic unit within a poem is susceptible of "contextual variation." This is true because the subtleties of meaning essential to poetry are the product of the interaction between and among the poem's constituent parts and not of a mere accumulation of ordinary meanings, an assemblage of discrete, inorganic semantic blocks. For example, the word "rose" at the conclusion of *The Divine Comedy* means something quite different from what it does in the final line of *Four Quartets* or in the Robert Burns verse quoted above. In each case the context is a major factor in the meaning.

In every one of the above instances, moreover, the word "rose" has multiple meanings; it exhibits the trait of "plurisignation." This word is also perceived in "soft focus," in that one cannot eliminate from it certain creative, controlled ambiguities that prevent one from sharply focusing on a single meaning.

Even in cases where the semantic units of a poem are sharply focused, however, they are seldom organized strictly according to the canons of logic. The progression from the octave to the sestet of a sonnet, for example, will often violate the laws of excluded middle, noncontradiction, and identity, substituting for them the "logic" of image, sound, idea, and mood. Images like the rose, moreover, may have symbolic overtones that allow them to function simultaneously as particulars and as universals. More often than not such illogical procedures overtly contradict common sense in order to arrive at a deeper sense. Hence, Wheelwright speaks of "paralogical dimensionality" and "paradox" as primary traits of expressive language.

Finally, there is "assertorial lightness," by which Wheelwright apparently means two things, the first having to do with the *way in which* poetry is declarative and the second having to do with the *degree to which* it is declarative.[45] With regard to the former, Wheelwright argues that a poetic assertion differs from a pure steno-proposition in that its declarative component is invariably combined with nondeclarative sentential functions: the interrogative, exclamatory, hortatory, or acquiescent. Whereas a steno-proposition simply and plainly asks to be affirmed, a poetic assertion unites its assertorial function with that of eliciting various kinds of affective responses and of shaping the reader's attitude toward what is to be affirmed. As a result, the assent finally elicited by a poetic assertion is a complex response conditioned by the particulars of the poetic context and acknowledging that the poetic claim being advanced is never completely abstract and general.[46]

But if poetic assertions are relatively "light" because of their special *manner* of being declarative, they are also "light" because of the lesser *degree* to which they are declarative. This does not mean that poetic assertions are confined to the status of sheer hypothesis or of mimesis devoid of any declarative intent. As Wheelwright says: "A first postulate of the poeto-statement is that it may have any degree of statemental character, ranging between the extremes of fully realized statement, or proposition, on the one hand, and mere pseudo-statement, or phatic collocation, on the other."[47] By and large, however, poetic assertions tend to be gentle, tentative, or conjectural; however didactic in intent, they generally propose possibilities to be pondered, or distinctive and alternative ways of envisioning things, rather than dogmatic and definite answers. In other words, poetry "courts" reality rather than assaulting it.[48] And in this way, too, it is "lighter" than steno-language.

This last point obviously has what Wheelwright would term "ontological implications," or implications concerning the relation between poetic language and reality. These we will later want to explore. At present, however, we need to ask a question more pertinent to the sphere of semantics: If the seven semantic traits just discussed are truly the main "expressive traits" to be found in language, and if Wheelwright believes (as I have implied and shall argue he does) that the properties of steno-language are to some extent intrinsic to language even in its most "expressive" forms, is it not puzzling that not a single word, sentence, or work of pure steno-language exhibits any of the "expressive traits" mentioned? For this seems to imply that, as language becomes more expressive—more softly focused, paradoxical, plurisignative—it has less and less in common with steno-language. In that case, the properties of steno-language would actually be antithetical to those of expressive language.

This potential objection can be answered if we look closely at what Wheelwright means by "expressive traits." What Wheelwright says at the beginning of his discussion of these traits is that they are the main traits that *differentiate* expressive language from steno-language.[49] This wording is well worth noting. If I say that the traits that differentiate jazz from other music are improvization, popular melodies, syncopated rhythms, a preponderance of minor thirds and sevenths, and so forth, I have not denied that jazz has much in common with other music; nor have I denied that, without some very ordinary musical traits like major thirds and rhythmical pulse and instrumental timbre, jazz could not exist at all. Certainly I have not said that the forms of music in which the "jazzy" traits are most predominant are necessarily the purest or the best jazz. Similarly, Wheelwright does not mean that expressive language has nothing in common with steno-language; for he says outright that the differentiation between steno-language and expressive language "is by no means absolute but admits of the most varied and subtle degrees, disguises, and overlappings."[50] (This statement, incidentally, implicitly rejects the analogy in which Wheelwright likens steno-language to silence and expressive language to sound; for silence cannot "overlap" or "disguise" itself as sound, or vice-versa.) Again, Wheelwright does not wish to suggest that the relatively "steno-" properties found in poetry play merely an incidental part in poetry's dynamics. He declares, rather, that expressive language transcends ordinary language not by sheer opposition but by "an imaginative enlargement which presupposes a common language as its initiating base of operations."[51] Finally, Wheelwright would never argue that the most paradoxical, plurisignative, softly focused, and lightly assertive poem is necessarily the most expressive one. On the contrary, he maintains that when expressive language approaches the point of completely excluding the traits of steno-language, it becomes markedly less expressive rather than more so.[52]

Expressive language would therefore appear to be a compound created out of two contrasting kinds of elements—the "closed" and the "open." Soft focus is neither sharp focus nor a total lack of focus; assertorial lightness is neither weightiness nor weightlessness; multiple meaning is neither univocal meaning nor infinite meaning; and so on. Each is a mixture of conceptual ingredients and the ingredients of what Wheelwright calls "verbal music." As Wheelwright says: "We may regard the strictly logical use of language as one pole [of discourse], the purely evocative, unreferential use as its opposite pole, and poetic language as swinging airily between them, never quite reaching either, on pain of losing either its poetic or linguistic character."[53]

From all this we may conclude that, even if Wheelwright is reluctant to give steno-language its due, his theories assume that steno-meanings are positive ingredients in expressive language itself. We have yet to see, however, just what semantic possibilities are created when language incorporates and transcends the semantic procedures of steno-language. For this we must scrutinze more closely the linguistic principle that Wheelwright conceives to be the epitome of expressive language—namely, metaphor.

The Language of Metaphor

In Wheelwright's view, the semantic structure of metaphor is paradigmatic of the semantic structure of expressive language in general, including poetry. It should be pointed out, however, that it is not until we come to the relatively late book *Metaphor and Reality* that we find Wheelwright consistently pointing to metaphor as the primary vehicle for that process of semantic transformation which he had for some time considered to be essential to all expressive language. Twenty years before, in his essay "Poetry, Myth, and Reality," Wheelwright was satisfied simply to declare that the meaning of language is somehow mysteriously transformed when discourse taps the depths of "mythological consciousness."[54] Compared with that early essay, *The Burning Fountain* was quite sophisticated, focusing much more precisely on metaphor and related semantic processes expressive of ontological depth; yet, interestingly, the book is subtitled *A Study in the Language of Symbolism*—thus making symbolism rather than metaphor the pivotal concept. Moreover, despite the fact that Wheelwright states in this book that metaphor is the essence of poetry and the single most important element in all expressive language,[55] he does not maintain this position with complete consistency. Thus, in this same work, Wheelwright also suggests that the "metaphoric way of imagining" is complemented by an "archetypal" or "emblematic" way that operates according to different principles.[56] By the time Wheelwright came to write *Metaphor and Reality*, however, he was prepared not only to assert that "imaginative language is basically metaphoric,"[57] but also to back up that assertion by treating symbols, poems, and myths all as metaphoric forms of language.

It is probably evident by now that Wheelwright's concept of metaphor is broader than the grammarian's—broad enough, in fact, to seem in itself somewhat metaphorical. Traditional grammar and rhetoric have regarded metaphor as simply a special kind of trope stating an identity between two entities that cannot literally be equated.[58] Wheelwright, by contrast, sees metaphor as operative in any mode of predication or semantic synthesis in which meanings creatively interact, carrying across (as the Greek *meta-phora* suggests) from one semantic domain to another. This, Wheelwright admits, is to subject the word to some "semantic stretching,"[59] but he believes the stretching is justified; for it serves to point out what makes for effective metaphor as traditionally defined and to specify the larger semantic and imaginative processes to which the best metaphors of every kind give access.

According to Wheelwright, the processes by means of which metaphoric transformation takes place can be explicated in terms of two different principles that overlap and unite in an almost infinite variety of ways. The first principle, which Wheelwright calls "epiphor," is operative when there is an intrinsic, recognizable similarity between the referents of the terms of a nonliteral comparison or identification, as when Shakespeare writes, "All the world's a stage."[60] The latter principle, which Wheelwright calls "diaphor," is at work when there is a suggestive juxtapositioning and synthesis of seemingly unrelated and incongruous semantic elements the referents of which can indeed be perceived as belonging together, but primarily by virtue of their having been metaphorically linked—as in Gertrude Stein's line, "Toasted Suzie is my ice-cream." In either case, however, the metaphoric expression results not only in a transformation of the ordinary meanings of the terms employed but also in a transformation of ordinary thought, an innovation in meaning that could only have been achieved through the specific expression employed. To see how this comes about, we will take a closer look at both epiphor and diaphor.[61]

We begin with Wheelwright's observation that epiphor is the dominant feature of that form of metaphor referred to by Aristotle where, in the *Poetics*, he writes: "A metaphor is the transfer [i.e., *epiphora*] of a word belonging to something else, a transference either from genus to species, from species to genus, from species to species, or according to an analogy."[62] Wheelwright, however, gives one or two new twists to Aristotle's concept of epiphor. In the first place, Wheelwright stresses that epiphoric metaphors can be created not simply by the substitution of a particular word that does not "belong" for one that does, but also by the substitution of much larger semantic units for their literal equivalents, allegory apparently being a prime example of this. (Like many New Critics, however, Wheelwright is not favorably disposed toward allegory, as it is not sufficiently diaphoric to meet his criteria for imaginative invention.) In the second place, Wheelwright considers the fact that lexical norms are transgressed in epiphor to be less interesting than the fact that, in epiphor, the whole procedure of steno-thought is subtly altered. The best epiphoric metaphors lead, as Aristotle says, to "an intuitive perception of the similarity of dissimilars," but their goal, finally, is not to cause one merely to recognize literal similarities. That is, the ultimate aim of poetic metaphor is never to discover a simple likeness that, upon its discovery, one can say outright. It is rather to hold the similar and dissimilar together in a creative tension that reveals a new truth, a new identity, that cannot be reduced to a matter of literal similarity, however surprising or unexpected.[63]

Yet the fact remains that an epiphoric transformation of language and thought is predicated on recognizable similarities, the more abstract or less familiar phenomenon often being probed and elucidated by comparison with the more concrete and familiar. When Edgar says in *King Lear* that "ripeness is all," he is, as Wheelwright points out, likening an intangible spiritual condition to a well-known state common to gardens and fruits; and though, presumably, the truth about the spiritual condition is by no means exhausted by a literal account of how it is similar to botanical ripeness, the recognition of that truth is sparked by the comparison of the less palpable condition to the more palpable.[64] Furthermore, the aptness of this comparison cannot only be "felt" or "intuited" but also intellectually discerned and rationally defended. Indeed—to draw a conclusion perfectly in keeping with Wheelwright's analysis, if not with his emphasis—it is apparently a mark of epiphor that the clever or perhaps profound "fit" between the terms compared can be, in large part, conceptually explicated, or at least conceptually interpreted. And this means that, however surprising or resistant to full paraphrase, a metaphor that is predominantly epiphoric will retain a strong relation to steno-language and thought; it will exhibit a rational, analogical foundation.

Whereas epiphor is rooted in discernible (if surprising) likenesses, diaphor creates new meanings through (that is, *dia*) the sheer juxtapositioning of unlike, heterogeneous elements. Consider, for example, the following:

> The apparition of these faces in the crowd;
> Petals on a wet, black bough.

These two lines, which together constitute the whole of Ezra Pound's poem "In a Station of the Metro," create an arresting effect. But here, Wheelwright claims, "the association of ideas is based not on similarity but on emotional congruity."[65] In other words, the poem is diaphoric. Whatever similarity one sees between faces in the underground and petals on a bough is an "induced" likeness, one that is "presented" rather than "represented." The unity of the poem is not a unity of logic and ideas but a unity of aesthetic effect, derived from such coherent poetic devices as the assonance between "crowd" and "bough" and the succession of three stressed, monosyllabic words that, in the last line, produces a feeling of closure.

Naturally a poem that is predominantly diaphoric will almost entirely elude paraphrase and rational analysis. In extreme cases it will even result in near-nonsense, as in much of Gertrude Stein. Hence it is evident that the semantic movement of diaphor is toward the purely nonreferential and irrational pole of language that Wheelwright describes as a sort of verbal music.[66] This being so, diaphor can be characterized as the component of poetry and metaphor that is diametrically opposed to the norms of steno-language.

Now if diaphor represents the more intuitive and affective resources of "verbal music," just as epiphor represents the more conceptual resources of steno-language, it follows—although again Wheelwright stops short of saying so directly—that the metaphoric unification of diaphor and epiphor creates a field of interaction between "steno-" properties and "musical" properties. Here we have further confirmation that poetic language is never divorced from steno-language, but joined with it in a creative, transforming dialogue; for, as Wheelwright declares, we can see "the two processes, epiphoric and diaphoric, as intimately related aspects of poetic language and as mutually contributing to the power and significance of all good metaphor."[67] To some extent, that is to say, every effective metaphor involves an epiphoric reaching out of the old to the new and a diaphoric combining of the fresh and unexpected with the ordinary.

Wheelwright makes it quite clear, however, that when metaphor unites the epiphoric with the diaphoric, or the more definite and rational with the more indeterminate and affective, this is not a simple process of mixing strictly compatible semantic elements. Indeed, the complex way in which these elements interact clearly exemplifies what Wheelwright means by the important concept of "metaphoric tension." But in speaking of "tension" Wheelwright is not referring to an absolutely antithetical relationship in which the epiphoric sense and the diaphoric sense necessarily seek to cancel each other out, nor to an inevitable, direct clash between the "steno-" or literal semantic thrust and the "expressive" or nonliteral; he is rather referring to a dynamic quality correlated with semantic vitality and energy. "Tensive" language is, above all, language that is "alive" and thus capable of incorporating ambiguities, multiple meanings, and thoughts and feelings that are not completely clarified or resolved.[68] At its heart is semantic metamorphosis.[69]

Keeping in mind that it is semantic metamorphosis that constitutes, for Wheelwright, the heart of metaphor, we should have little difficulty comprehending why Wheelwright would see metaphor at work in a variety of linguistic contexts. Not only is it the case that all the "expressive traits" that we have seen Wheelwright single out obviously exhibit a metaphoric dimension, by virtue of their combining relatively "steno-" and relatively "musical" properties, it is also true that particular linguistic forms like similes, symbols, and poems—none of which possess the structure of grammatical metaphor—all can be seen to function in a genuinely metaphoric manner. To take the simplest example first, we can now hardly be puzzled to find that Wheelwright thinks it misleading to consider Burns's line "O my luv is like a red, red rose" a mere simile while calling "My love is a red rose" a true metaphor.[70] In the so-called "metaphor" little semantic transformation occurs; no feeling and only minimal insight is generated concerning the relation of love to roses. Consequently, the conjunction of the subject and predicate by means of the copula "is" seems either contrived or merely stereotypical. In Burns's simile, by contrast, the simple addition of the phatic "O" and the repetition of the adjective "red" are enough to create a pulse of feeling, a rise of tensive energy, appropriate to the subject matter. This slight alteration of the pattern of common speech is sufficient to alert the reader to nonconceptual meanings and to create a total meaning for the sentence that cannot exactly be duplicated in literal discourse.

Wheelwright's reasons for regarding expressive symbols as metaphoric are somewhat more complex, though related. Whereas a steno-symbol (a "sign") like the mathematician's π simply stands for an abstract concept, and does so in a predetermined and definite way devoid of semantic tension or innovation, an expressive symbol like Keats's Grecian urn stands for some larger aspect of life experience for which there can be no precise intellectual concept.[71] Inevitably, then, an expressive symbol must communicate by embodying or imaginatively representing the nonconceptual (as well as certain conceptual) properties of the reality to which it refers. But how can this occur? First, Wheelwright says, it is a fact of the human psyche that if a symbol belongs to a special class of signifiers like "fire," "night," "tree," or "bridge," it naturally tends to call forth personal, cultural, or even crosscultural "depth meanings." The empirical reality for which the term ordinarily stands is already invested, by human experience, with nonempirical and nonconceptual meanings. (The same holds true for certain story patterns, such as those that recur in myths.) Second, Wheelwright points out, even when a symbol is a mundane term like "urn" or "blackbird," it can function expressively if placed within a semantic context like a poem, because there the strictly conceptual sense is displaced or transformed by a general expressive tenor in which the matter-of-fact concerns of daily discourse are plainly not predominant. (Witness Wallace Stevens's "Thirteen Ways of Looking at a Blackbird.") In any case the symbol becomes a tensive and metamorphic form of predication, not only standing for a particular empirical reality but transforming it into a representation of something larger and possibly more significant. To the extent that an expressive symbol is a kind of analogy or model, bearing a clearly discernible resemblance to that which it symbolizes, it is epiphoric. To the extent that it is evocative and allusive, merely suggesting its symbolic status and hinting at the qualities of that to which it "refers," it is diaphoric.[72] Either way, the symbol discovers and creates meanings, functioning as a kind of condensed and concealed metaphor.[73]

If Wheelwright really considers expressive symbols to be metaphoric, what are we to make of the fact that, in *Metaphor and Reality*, Wheelwright describes what seems to be a progression from metaphor to symbol (and then from symbol to archetype and myth)? Doesn't this suggest that metaphor is but one form of expressive language, and distinct from symbol? Actually Wheelwright's intent here is to distinguish between particular *kinds* of metaphoric language; he is, as Paul Ricoeur explains, attempting to establish a "hierarchy of metaphors":

> At the lowest level [Wheelwright] finds the dominant images of a particular poem; then the symbols that have "personal" significance and permeate an entire work; next, the symbols shared by an entire cultural tradition; then those that link the members of a vast secular or religious community; and finally, at the fifth level, the archetypes that hold meaning for all of humanity, or at least a major part of it.[74]

Although these various modes of expressive language vary widely in their breadth of appeal, the metaphoric process is common to all.

Keeping in mind how Wheelwright justifies his claim that expressive symbols of all kinds are essentially forms of metaphor, our final task in analyzing Wheelwright's semantics of expressive language will be to determine on what basis he can regard as a metaphoric assertion the more complicated semantic structure constituted by a complete poem.[75]

If Wheelwright is to support this understanding of poetry, he must, of course, first be able to show that a poem does indeed make some kind of assertion; and this is something that both I. A. Richards and the New Critics had questioned—Richards contending that poetry affords nothing but "pseudo-assertions," and the New Critics arguing that a poem is self-intentive and nonreferential. Because the latter argument is succinctly summed up in Archibald MacLeish's well-known dictum that "A poem should not mean / But be,"[76] the contrary thrust of Wheelwright's semantic theory is conspicuous in his declaration that, even in "their most purely poetic usage," words "not only *are*, they also *say*."[77]

Many of Wheelwright's reasons for making this counterclaim against the New Critics and Richards alike have already been discussed in the course of our analysis of his idea of assertorial weight. Wheelwright rejects Richards's thesis that the function of poetic statement cannot be both emotive and cognitive; he discounts the New Critical assumption that poetry is a nonreferential verbal object; and he disputes Richards's and the New Critics' common contention that poetic statements neither invite nor elicit belief, and are consequently not real assertions—Wheelwright's reply being that such statements always invite a complex response, part of which includes various kinds and degrees of assent. In all these ways Wheelwright lays the groundwork for seeing entire poems as assertions of some kind.[78]

This is not to say, however, that Wheelwright believes the "total assertion" made by a work of poetry is of exactly the same species as the "partial" or "component" assertions internal to it, or that its assertorial function is as evident as that of a steno-proposition. For one thing, a "total assertion" is often extremely complex. Whereas many of its component assertions may be explicitly metaphoric, others may be relatively plain; the whole, furthermore, may differ in assertorial weight from its parts.[79] Nevertheless, a poem in its entirety will generally posit realities and possibilities in such a way as to invite a measure of assent. It asserts—however lightly.

What makes the total assertion of a poem metaphoric is less the expressive quality of its constituent semantic units than the mimetic/metaphoric function of the whole.[80] Poems do not simply refer to reality, they also "imitate" reality (or realities) in creative ways. By subjecting phenomena to stylistic "distancing," "perspectival" interpretation, fresh combination, and various kinds of intensification, the "total assertion" of a poem reshapes experience even as it represents it.[81] Thus poems become creations that do not so much duplicate as transform the ordinary world. To the extent that the new worlds bodied forth by these "total assertions" are representations, they are implicit assertions concerning "what is." But, as is essential to their imaginative vitality, they are also modifications of "what is" and presentations of what has reality only within the poem itself. In short, the total assertions of poetry are creative transformations of language and experience. Establishing a dynamic relation or balance between imitation and transformation, assertion and mere presentation, they display the essential ingredients of metaphor, namely, epiphor and diaphor.

This is the heart of Wheelwright's analysis of metaphor and of poetry as metaphor.[82] It is not the end point of his reflections on poetic language, however. The semantics of poetic metaphor is, for Wheelwright, intrinsically connected with ontology. If poetry is the locus of a basic, transformative interaction between thought and feeling, "steno-" semantics and purely "expressive" semantics, it is precisely for this reason that, in Wheelwright's eyes, poetry can transcend the steno-linguistic and the rational, thereby disclosing realities to which steno-discourse is blind.

Poetry and Ontology

The Burning Fountain opens with a revealing passage in which Wheelwright—borrowing from an Estonian legend—states that, of all the human languages, only the poetic can imitate the god of song and so strive to "sing the full song" of reality.[83] This statement is accompanied by the judgment, noted earlier in this chapter, that the majority of human utterances, being steno-linguistic, are mere "thin pipings." The reader thus deduces from the very beginning that what is at issue in Wheelwright's distinction between steno-language and poetic or expressive language is not just whether both forms of language are legitimate and meaningful semantic procedures but also whether the world or "reality" is not in certain important respects more fully disclosed through one than it is through the other.

Consequently, it may strike one as somewhat disingenuous of Wheelwright to caution his interpreters, at a later point in the same book, that the distinction he is making between expressive and steno-language is semantic only, entailing no epistemological or ontological judgments.[84] I, for one, am convinced that this statement cannot be taken at face value. What Wheelwright must mean is that at this particular stage of his discussion he will *treat* the distinction as though it were a purely semantic one, thus "bracketing off," as he says, the significant but potentially distracting question of the truth-status of these forms of language.[85]

In any case, we are now examining a phase of Wheelwright's discussion in which the question of truth-status is certainly no longer bracketed, truth here being defined by Wheelwright as "that which ought, by one criterion or another, to be assented to."[86] What we now want to know is how Wheelwright can claim—as he most assuredly does—that poetic metaphor constitutes a "deeper" use of language than is found in literal, rational discourse. Indeed, we must ask how he can claim that poetic metaphor is true at all.[87] For it may seem that such language involves the very sorts of "category mistakes," illicit comparisons, and unwarranted associations that must muddle perception and confuse thought even when producing a desirable aesthetic effect.[88]

In trying to answer these questions, Wheelwright has us look not only at the internal dynamics of metaphor but also at the dynamics of the human mind and imagination. This is necessary, he believes, because "we must recognize and make room for whatever fresh, unexpected, and unpredictably diverse modes of synthesis may find expression when the mind operates at levels and at moments of highest poetic intensity."[89] But in order to recognize the essential features of these "poetic" levels of mental intensity and awareness, we must, according to Wheelwright, be prepared to question some common philosophical assumptions concerning what we rather vaguely term "emotions" and "feelings,"[90] and to reconsider their role in cognition.

One such questionable assumption—held by I. A. Richards, among others—is the notion that language cannot simultaneously be emotive and cognitive. Wheelwright challenges this assumption in two ways. First he shows that its truth is not dictated by logic. (The opposite of "emotive" is "nonemotive," not "cognitive" or "referential.")[91] Then he points out that the assumption is actually contradicted by fact. (It is undeniable, for example, that when an honest person shouts "Fire!" in a theater, an authentic emotion accompanies this communication of vital factual information.)[92] Wheelwright concludes that the emotive and referential aspects of communication should be seen as independent variables existing on different semantic axes and so as capable of coexistence.

The second assumption Wheelwright finds questionable is the idea that the cognitive content of a nontautological statement (whether it be emotional or not) is nothing other than the statement's precise empirical "cash value." According to this assumption, which lies at the core of positivist and empiricist philosophy, such affective properties as a statement might possess can have a cognitive function only to the extent that they can be translated into conceptual, scientifically verifiable propositions. (The cry "Fire!" can certainly be understood as a condensation of one or more verifiable propositions.) It is quite significant that Wheelwright, in attacking this assumption, modifies his earlier thesis that reference and emotion must exist on separate semantic axes. Without denying that these two components of language do generally function independently even when they function simultaneously, Wheelwright now argues that the special form of language found in poetry and expressive metaphor "means, refers, awakens insight, *in and through* the emotions it engenders," and that "where an appropriate emotion is not aroused the full insight is not awakened."[93] Now if Wheelwright is to hold that a particular kind of language refers and awakens insight "*in and through* the emotions it engenders," he cannot very well maintain that in this instance the referential axis of meaning is independent of the emotive. And in fact this is precisely what Wheelwright is here wishing to deny. His point is that poetic metaphor must be emotive in order to refer as it does; if it were emotionally neutral and devoid of "tension," like a scientific statement, it might be cognitive but it could not engender cognition of the particular realities to which it does in fact give access.

Wheelwright in this way plainly disputes not only the semantics but also the epistemologies of positivism, empiricism, and rationalism.[94] All these philosophies hold in one form or another that the route to truth is via clear and distinct ideas. All in some way accept the Cartesian compartmentalization in which "affective" language and mental states are labeled "subjective" while the "hard facts" of sense-data and the concepts of reason are given "objective" standing.[95] Wheelwright, by contrast, regards the world of nonquantifiable emotions, values, and imaginings as no more self-evidently subjective than the world of scientific data and logic, the human mind being necessary for the apprehension of either. Accordingly, the forms of language that articulate perceptions of the former world cannot be dismissed as irrelevant to the attempt to say and know "what is."[96] If it is the legitimate function of steno-propositions to serve the "conceptual object" and to be true to the dimensions of experience that can be known with precision and clarity, then it is the equally legitimate function of poetic metaphors to serve the "phenomenological" object[97] and to be true to the ambiguities and "living insights" that arise out of one's encounter with experience prior to exhaustive conceptual interpretation.[98]

To argue that the world(s) to which expressive language refers and gives shape need not be accorded lower ontological status than the world(s) of logic, mathematics, and science is already to make a large philosophical claim. But Wheelwright does not stop with this declaration of "separate but equal." He goes on to insist that expressive language discloses "depths" missed by other discourse. Apparently he believes the adjective "deep" is uniquely appropriate to describe expressive, metaphoric language because such language glimpses realities one is bound to experience as related to one's fundamental sense of self, others, the whole, and the holy.[99] These very realities are the most significant and elusive, never fully encompassed by any thought or language. It is expressive language that lets one sense how deep and inexhaustible they are even as it brings them into view. The same cannot be said of the usual language of sociology, geography, logic, and other fields of steno-thought.

At the very center of Wheelwright's epistemology and/or ontology, therefore, is the thesis that poetry can indeed, in Murray Krieger's words, "break through the inherent incapacities of all non-poetic uses of language."[100] But if this is Wheelwright's claim—a claim Krieger rightly associates with the New Critics—then it is important to ask whether, according to Wheelwright, poetic insights are at all amenable to any kind of systematic, reflective interpretation (be it theological, ethical, metaphysical, or some other). That is, we must consider whether he believes it possible for certain kinds of steno-language to refer, at least in a mediate way, to the sort of "depth" reality to which poetry gives utterance. For if Wheelwright does not consider this a possibility, then, in the end, his New Critical (and neo-Kantian) inclinations win out, and he leaves us with an ontology that sees human reality sharply divided between the world of expressive language and the world of steno-language. In that case, certain important implications of his semantic theory will not have been followed out at the level of his ontological reflection.

In some respects Wheelwright obviously does acknowledge the possibility of a kind of conceptual reflection that would in some measure take into account the "depth" insights of poetry. In practice, for instance, his own philosophizing makes extensive use of ideas and images drawn from T. S. Eliot's *Four Quartets*. (This reliance on Eliot—often unacknowledged and extraordinarily subtle—is perhaps most evident in Wheelwright's essay "Poetry, Myth, and Reality" and in the analysis of "threshold existence" found in *The Burning Fountain*.) In *The Burning Fountain*, moreover, Wheelwright calls his ideal for ontology a "metapoetical ontology," by which he appears to mean a philosophical attempt to discern and describe reality as it is expressed through the poetic imagination.[101] Indeed, *Metaphor and Reality* contains a tentative effort to adumbrate just such an ontology by exploring "the possibility of what, as distinguished from a metaphysics, may be called a *metapoetics*."[102] It would seem, then, that Wheelwright must believe one can express nonpoetically something of the truth of poetry.

When one looks more closely at the content of Wheelwright's "metapoetics," however, one notices that his ontology is limited to describing reality in terms scarcely more abstract and rational than those of the poetic medium from which its insights are said to be derived. This is not to say that he reaches no general conclusions, but it is to say that those general conclusions all emphasize that reality largely eludes rational generalization! When Wheelwright states, for example, that the reality poetry makes manifest meets us as a Thou, as Presence, and as Mystery, he is insistent that this reality defies "explanations, theories, and specific questionings," since these are appropriate only to the world of objects rather than persons.[103] (Buber's influence on Wheelwright seems undeniable here.) Again, when Wheelwright speaks of the reality disclosed through poetry as "coalescent," he does so partly to say that the logical distinction between particulars and universals does not strictly apply to its features.[104] Finally, although Wheelwright declares that "metamorphosis, the continual passing of one qualitative state into another, is a primary ontological fact,"[105] he inadvertently raises doubts as to whether he thinks even this philosophical judgment is truer than any other, for he states in the same context:

> Reality, as distinguished from the intellectual artifacts that often usurp the name, is neither object nor subject, neither matter nor mind, nor can it be limited to *any* other philosophical category; it is That to which every such category tries to refer and which every philosophical statement tries to describe, always from an intellectual point of view and always with ultimate inadequacy.[106]

This statement, along with the others mentioned above, strongly implies that if philosophy is to be at all true to the revelations of the poetic medium, it must resist the temptation to systematize or to rationalize (that is, to determine which ontological facts are "primary") and must be content merely to acknowledge and report—albeit feebly—the ways in which reality is "imperfectly glimpsed" through expressive language.[107] Confirmation that this is indeed what Wheelwright means to say is provided when Wheelwright argues that conceptual, philosophical thinking cannot criticize or analytically compare, let alone integrate, the extremely heterogeneous visions of reality presented by various major works of poetic art. Thus, according to Wheelwright, one is obliged to view the different perspectives on reality offered by Shakespeare, Proust, Dostoyevsky, and Kafka as all true—though none absolutely so, and none in the same way that scientific or practical thinking is true.[108] In sum, Wheelwright here disowns any endeavor to give a coherent account of "depth" reality, claiming that "if we are willing to seek philosophical insights in and through the testimony of poetic diction and artistic forms, examining and responding to such insights in their fullness as they are presented—then a kind of basic, irreducible pluralism results."[109]

Interestingly enough, Wheelwright's adoption of a radical ontological pluralism is closely correlated with what in this connection evolves into an astonishingly strict semantic dualism. For, in formulating his ontological reflections, Wheelwright advances the semantic thesis that the assertions of poetry, although "contextually true," cannot be generalized; their truth, being embedded in their poetic form, is concrete rather than abstract—which is to say that they are in this respect quite unlike steno-assertions.[110] Wheelwright's reasoning here seems to be that, were poetic assertions to any extent general and abstract, they would not only compete with one another but also compete with the assertions of science and, possibly, with those of religion. "Irreducible pluralism" would then be threatened and, along with it, the autonomy of poetic art.

I think it is fair to say that these developments in the ontological phase of Wheelwright's thought do not provide a satisfactory capstone for his work. There is, to be sure, a sense in which ontological pluralism suits Wheelwright's needs. It at least makes room for religious and poetic truth. It also reinforces Wheelwright's unblinking and welcome recognition that "we cannot hope ever to be perfectly right,"[111] all truths being to some extent limited and contextual.[112] But, when his pluralism goes to the extreme of picturing all truths as equal and as essentially incomparable, it is inconsistent with Wheelwright's basic convictions. What Wheelwright wishes most to affirm is that certain ontological facts are *more* profound and *more* fundamental than others. He wants to reserve the right to say that metamorphosis and personhood are more basic ontological facts than stasis and inert being; that, in his words, "such-or-such is more real, or more deeply real, than something else."[113] This, however, is the one kind of judgment for which an extreme pluralism or relativism has no room.

What is more important, Wheelwright's brand of pluralism is connected with a semantic dualism more consistent with the New Criticism than with the semantic theories spelled out elsewhere by Wheelwright. It may insure the autonomy of poetry to claim that poetic assertions have no general implications and that every poetic truth is sui generis, but this necessarily means that poetic assertions are all totally and equally unrelated to steno-assertions, and it thus flatly contradicts certain premises of Wheelwright's semantic theory as a whole. Similarly, to declare that poetic assertions are beyond criticism and that their truth is strictly contextual may shut off debate as to whether particular poetic assertions are true; it may even permit one to declare, without fear of rebuttal, that poetic assertions are *invariably* deep and true. But if poetic assertions are thus true simply by virtue of their being poetic, their specific assertorial content is irrelevant and they should, after all, be classified as "pseudo-assertions." In that case, however, the laurels should go to I. A. Richards.

It is worth reiterating, therefore, that the above claims run counter to many of Wheelwright's central convictions and certainly to his practice. In actuality Wheelwright makes comparative judgments. He calls *Four Quar-*

tets "perhaps the most fully pertinent single poem in our moment in history," for example.[114] He argues that the "best utterances" of poetry are on the same lofty plane as those of myth and religion, engendering in the reader a sense of the sacred and transcendent; and this implies that some other poetic utterances are less than the best and less profoundly true.[115] Lastly, as I have gone to some pains to demonstrate, Wheelwright's theories concerning the semantics of poetry repeatedly show how the traits of expressive language—and particularly of poetic metaphor—never entirely exclude the traits of steno-language. Thus Wheelwright's semantic theory hardly supports the idea that poetic truth is completely contextual, completely without general implications, or completely resistant to conceptual interpretation. What it does support we can now begin to consider.

Wheelwright and Beyond

Writing in 1970, Morse Peckham lamented what he took to be the probability that "the notion of poetic language now most widely held by professional critics and literary scholars" is the idea that "poetry is a means of discovering a 'truth' which is accessible to no other way of thinking, and that the technique of such [poetic] thinking is metaphor."[116] Apparently Peckham had in mind theories like Wheelwright's. And what he found most disturbing was the attempt to place poetry's language and truth-claims in an unassailable position, separate and superior. A related objection lies behind Paul Ricoeur's judgment that Wheelwright's work, despite coming close to adumbrating a tensional conception of truth like Ricoeur's own, is naive in supposing that "the semantics of metaphorical utterance contains ready-made an immediate ontology, which philosophy would then have only to elicit and to formulate."[117] Thus, according to Ricoeur, the "dialectical inclination" of Wheelwright's theory is "dissipated by the intuitionist and vitalist tendency that takes him finally into the metapoetics of the 'What Is.'"[118]

Although I have criticized these very aspects of Wheelwright's thought, I have argued that a truly dialectical conception of language and reflection can in fact be deduced from Wheelwright's work if one is willing to remove certain inconsistencies and to pursue some of his ideas to conclusions his New Critical inclinations caused him to overlook. Much of my attempt to make good on that claim will come in my examination of *Four Quartets*, in the course of which I will apply my own reformulation and extension of Wheelwright's theories. My aim at the moment is to establish as clearly (and yet as briefly) as possible how Wheelwright's theories either are, or could be modified so as to be, relevant to current thinking about the basic issues that we have raised and that are fundamental to the rest of our inquiry.

Among the largest of these issues is the question of poetic assertion and reference—a question Charles Altieri has recently described as "at once the oldest and the least resolved in literary theory."[119] As we have seen, Wheelwright argues against the New Critical view that literary art is a closed, nonreferential, or self-referential kind of language. Far from dying out with the New Criticism, this view has persisted in an amazing variety of forms—a number of them continental in origin.[120] To be sure, the contrast between "referential statements" and literary "pseudo-statements" drawn by certain New Critics (and particularly by I. A. Richards) is now seldom made using those terms. But Barbara Herrnstein Smith is right when she claims we can discern its ghost or reincarnation in "a number of more sophisticated formulations offered in recent years by literary theorists and linguistic philosophers of various persuasions." The contrast can be seen

> [in] the distinction drawn, for example, between "judgments" and "quasi-judgments," or the one between "reality language" and "mimetic language"; or the contrasts made between texts with "engaged-designative meanings" and those with "disengaged-gestural meanings"; we have heard, and still hear, of the difference between "illocutionary utterances" and "imitation illocutionary utterances" and, most recently, have been presented with the difference between "serious speech acts" and "nondeceptive pretended speech acts."[121]

Unfortunately, Professor Smith's own constructive proposal does not break the pattern. For she contrasts "natural" discourse (which refers and denotes) with the fictive or poetic *representation* of discourse (which inherently refers to and denotes nothing, although it can be *used* to denote and refer). The former, she says, comprises "actual utterances"; the latter comprises "purely possible utterances."[122] Such a distinction, however helpful in certain respects, still isolates the language of poetry from any sort of intrinsic referential function.[123]

But all these ways of denying literature a genuinely referential dimension seem mild when compared with the conclusions reached by some of the current poststructuralists and reflected in Robert Scholes's observation: "Once we knew that fiction was about life and criticism was about fiction—and everything was simple. Now we know that fiction is about other fiction, is criticism in fact, or metafiction. And we know that criticism is about the impossibility of anything being about life, really, or even about fiction, or, finally, about anything."[124] The self-referential function the New Critics ascribed to poetry is now being ascribed to language as such, which is seen—in an ironic reversal of Heidegger—as the prison-house of being.

In this context, Wheelwright's theory that poetry is partly (if often only implicitly) assertion and that poetic assertions exist on a continuum of declarative weight and seriousness, stands out as refreshingly straightforward and as gratifyingly close to the assumptions poetry itself invites readers to make. It goes far toward placing the language of literature in dialogue with other modes of discourse without denying the integrity and uniqueness of each mode. When followed to its logical conclusions, moreover, Wheelwright's theory allows us to respond to a literary work as both assertion (or even argument) and representation, as both fictive creation and ontological disclosure. In this way we are better able to see poems as complex wholes addressing the whole self of the reader. Nevertheless, when we come to applying Wheelwright's theories we will find it necessary to reconsider the nature of the "total assertion" made by a poem, to determine more precisely the underlying structure and purpose of such an assertion, and to recognize hierarchies of assertions within a poem as a totality. We will need, in addition, to look more closely at the way in which the assertorial function of literary art is related to its other functions.

A second point of obvious importance in Wheelwright's work is his thesis that an entire poem, precisely as a whole assertion and representation, is essentially metaphoric. Although not completely original, this seminal idea has implications commonly overlooked by various kinds of criticism (including the New Criticism) that have focused on the metaphoric and "literary" properties of the semantic units internal to a poem while ignoring traits unique to a poetic work as a whole. Wheelwright's own discussion of "expressive traits" in language shows that he too tends to stress "literary language" as opposed to the literary *use* of language. But his overall theory by no means demands such an emphasis. In fact, it in principle encourages examination of the properties unique to the kind of metaphor constituted by a poem in its entirety. Wheelwright would thus have little reason to quarrel with Paul Ricoeur's statement: "From one point of view, the understanding of metaphor can serve as a guide to the understanding of longer texts, such as a literary work. . . . From another point of view, the understanding of a work taken as a whole gives the key to metaphor."[125] What this implies remains to be seen.

Wheelwright's understanding of the duality of language, and of the role steno-language plays in that duality, is a third aspect of his thought deserving special comment. Having already criticized certain features of Wheelwright's account of steno-language in particular, I want to stress here its more positive features and implications. But first I want to examine one respect in which Wheelwright's view of steno-language and its connection with poetry must be questioned still further.

Because Wheelwright's chief preoccupation is with the "live" and innovative metaphors characteristic of poetry, he neglects what we might term the "steno-metaphors" of everyday language. As a consequence, his picture of ordinary discourse and thought is oversimplified. This becomes obvious when one considers the argument of the recent book by George Lakoff and Mark Johnson entitled *Metaphors We Live By*.[126] Claiming that "the essence of metaphor is understanding and experiencing one kind of thing in terms of another,"[127] these authors argue that even our unexceptional activities and ways of talking are permeated and structured by metaphors. We habitually experience and talk about arguments as wars or as buildings. We regard and refer to our minds as machines, ideas as food, time as money, life as a story, love as a journey or an investment. Whole networks of concepts and phrases are organized in terms of these and other basic metaphors.

From Wheelwright's point of view all such "metaphors" are simply a form of steno-language. They are conventional, predictable, reasonable, and "dead." Although their medium shapes their message, the message they convey could just as easily take another shape.[128] Wheelwright's is an important point. But what Wheelwright overlooks is that these so-called dead metaphors, or steno-metaphors, are active in certain ways uncharacteristic of steno-language as he describes it. They are not governed entirely by Aristotelian or other philosophical logic; they are at least marginally ambiguous and polysemous. And yet they are not merely symptoms of sloppy thinking. Their widespread and perhaps unavoidable use demonstrates, therefore, that one of the most deeply engrained and ordinary habits of the human mind is to think and talk double: "to understand and experience one kind of thing in terms of another." Because this metaphoric duplicity occurs (albeit at a low level of "tension") even in our "plain" speech, it is apparent that Wheelwright underestimates the extent to which the metaphors of poetry draw on and maximize a potential already latent in steno-discourse.[129]

With this observation we are brought up against the jarring possibility that Wheelwright's whole idea of steno-language or plain speech is a fiction. At the moment, a number of thinkers influenced by poststructuralists like Jacques Derrida[130] would indeed be inclined to say that metaphor is coextensive with language itself. For example, J. Hillis Miller writes: "All words are metaphors—that is, all are differentiated, different, deferred. Each leads to something of which it is the displacement in a movement without origin or end."[131] Steno-language, he implies, is only metaphor in disguise.

At the very least, Wheelwright himself would have to acknowledge a degree of plausibility in W. V. Quine's more modest claim that "it is a mistake . . . to think of linguistic usage as literalistic in its main body and metaphorical in its trimming. Metaphor, or something like it, governs both the growth of language and our acquisition of it. What comes as a subsequent refinement is rather cognitive discourse itself, at its most dryly literal. The neatly worked inner stretches of science are an open space in the tropical jungle, created by clearing tropes away."[132] But whereas Quine assumes that to some extent tropes *can* be cleared away, Hillis Miller appears not to allow for that possibility at all. For this reason Wheelwright would doubtless maintain that Hillis Miller's position is simply untenable. Unless some kind of language could be less tropological than some other kind, metaphor simply could not exist. It would have nothing to work with. And even if it could somehow exist as the only form of language, metaphor could then never be recognized as such.

This, I think, is essentially what Wheelwright would argue and it is what I myself take to be true. But now we need to notice what Wheelwright would probably *not* argue, even though this second kind of argument— perhaps best expressed by Paul Ricoeur—is likewise intended to challenge views such as those of Derrida and Hillis Miller. In summarizing ideas he shares with many other theorists, Ricoeur declares: "A word receives a metaphorical meaning in specific contexts, within which it is opposed to other words taken literally. The shift in meaning results primarily from a clash between literal meanings."[133] Like Wheelwright, Ricoeur is pointing out that metaphor cannot exist apart from language that can with reason be taken literally; metaphor depends on there being discourse in which sense and reference are at least relatively determinate. But in two major respects Ricoeur and Wheelwright differ. The first, having to do with the "clash between literal meanings," is one to which we will shortly return. The second, which we now consider, has to do with the status of literal concepts, especially in speculative philosophy.

In *The Rule of Metaphor* Ricoeur repeatedly acknowledges that literal and conceptually precise discourse arises, as Quine suggests, from a metaphoric matrix. The semantic innovation of metaphor is not itself a conceptual gain, Ricoeur says, but it is nonetheless the condition of possibility for speculative and conceptual thought.[134] Yet, once in existence, the resulting language of literal concepts and philosophical abstractions is fundamentally different from the metaphoric. "The speculative [and conceptual] fulfills the semantic exigencies put to it by the metaphorical only when it establishes a break marking the irreducible difference between the two modes of discourse."[135] Indeed, Ricoeur says, the difference between metaphoric meaning and literal concept (or speculative idea) is basic and distinct even though it may sometimes seem infinitesimal—and even though nonreductive "interpretation" as such is a "composite" mode of discourse that "functions at the intersection of two domains, metaphorical and speculative."[136] Restricting metaphor to a preconceptual and prereflective role, Ricoeur maintains that "the conceptual order is able to free itself from the play of double meaning and hence from the semantic dynamism characteristic of the metaphorical order."[137]

That there is a real and important difference between poetic metaphor and the language of philosophical or everyday concepts is something Wheelwright would readily affirm. And I myself, unlike Wheelwright, would say Ricoeur is justified in placing a high value on the critical and highly reflective steno-discourse of philosophical speculation and conceptualization. But Wheelwright might well retort that Ricoeur's belief in the sheer univocacy of the semantic procedures of such philosophical discourse seems unwarranted. I would second this, although I would add that Wheelwright, for his part, seems not to recognize that speculative concepts are not the only ones that retain a degree of indeterminacy and semantic tension. At any rate, Wheelwright never perceives that even the most precise scientific and logical assertions are less than perfectly steno-linguistic and less than completely determinate in meaning. If a deconstructionist like Hillis Miller errs in seeing the domain of metaphor as virtually boundless, Ricoeur and (in a different way) Wheelwright err in seeing it as clearly circumscribed. Neither side allows for the possibility that, as I want to argue, all actual linguistic strategies exist on a continuum along which one can observe differentiation but no absolute distinction.

Ricoeur's particular refutation of the deconstructionists, moreover, seems to involve a paradox we surely can do without. On the one hand, as we have seen, Ricoeur holds that literal concepts originate in metaphor— which means that, theoretically, at least one metaphor could, and must, have existed prior to any completely literal conceptualization. On the other hand, however, Ricoeur insists that metaphoric meanings invariably originate in the clash between literal concepts—which means (contradictorily) that *no* metaphor could even theoretically have existed prior to some literal conceptualization(s). Ricoeur's clear-cut distinction between metaphoric discourse and discourse that is nonmetaphoric (literal or conceptual) is therefore problematical.

What could be most helpful here is the idea, not so far from certain of Wheelwright's notions, that we can best think of language as bounded by two *purely hypothetical* limits that are polar opposites. At one hypothetical pole is pure steno-language, characterized by absolute conceptual clarity, logical validity, and completely determinate truth value and meaning. (As we will see with Whitehead, even the language of logic and mathematics can only approximate this limiting case.) [138] At the other hypothetical pole is "verbal music," or language whose meanings are entirely felt rather than conceived, whose connections are purely aesthetic and organic, and whose truth or reference is related to nothing other than the medium itself. (Even the most abstract forms of art, when perceived by a thinking human being, can only approximate this state.) All actual discourse falls somewhere in between these two poles. In every semantic situation, therefore, one can detect at least some minimal interplay or dialectic between the powers of definite rational conceptualization and the powers of imaginative presentation or free fabrication. No metaphor is completely prereflective or preconceptual and no literal statement is completely devoid of semantic creativity and ambiguity. Although the aims of rational conceptualization and metaphoric imagination may differ, the means are intimately and intricately related, and the aims themselves are capable of significant connection. Thus the dialectical movement within language as well as within thought is not between completely different semantic modes but between two poles of influence that coexist in every moment of meaning. What we call metaphor—the union of epiphor and diaphor—is the strategy for maximizing in one semantic situation the dialogue that is always at least minimally present in thought, writing, and speech.

This brings us to the fourth and final aspect of Wheelwright's thought needing our attention here—namely, his analysis of the dynamics of metaphor per se and of its capacity to disclose realities that steno-language by nature either misses or reduces. In this connection the crucial insight lies in Wheelwright's thesis that epiphor and diaphor are very different but related principles of semantic metamorphosis united within metaphor—the one principle closer to steno-language, the other closer to "verbal music."

Because the ways in which diaphor and epiphor interact can be seen to be almost infinitely varied, Wheelwright's use of the term metaphor as a figure for metamorphic language in general seems warranted. Although further examination of differences between the metaphoric strategies designated by the traditional rhetorical analysis of various tropes could be immensely helpful in understanding some of the major means by which metaphoric transformations take place,[139] the capacity to see affinities between all these ways of creating meaning is a notable gain.

Wheelwright's analysis of the interaction between diaphor and epiphor is also useful in that it corroborates and augments the "interaction" and "tension" theories of Max Black[140] and Paul Ricoeur, indicating how metaphor creates meanings not yet within any lexicon while generating insights not yet located on any conceptual map. Wheelwright's own notion of semantic "tension" deserves special comment, however. As we have seen, Wheelwright characterizes the interaction between epiphor and diaphor as "tensive" in nature. For Wheelwright, moreover, this semantic tension in-cludes—at least by implication—many of those traits that writers like Ricoeur have singled out in their own discussions of metaphoric tension: the interaction between clarity and ambiguity, focus and frame, lexical meaning and surplus meaning, similarity and difference, logic and affect, assertion and hypothesis, idea and image, sound and sense, and fiction's simultaneous "it was" and "it was not."[141] But it is significant that Wheel-wright does not mean exactly the same thing by "tension" that Ricoeur, Monroe Beardsley, and others do. In Ricoeur's vocabulary, for exam-ple, "tension" refers to a semantic dissonance or conflict that, in meta-phor, forces the literal level of meaning to "self-destruct" in "absurdity."[142] Metaphoric meaning, he says again and again, emerges from the "ruins" of literal sense.[143] Ricoeur takes the existence of the initially destructive func-tion of metaphoric tension as a clear indication that metaphoric discourse serves "neither to improve communication nor to insure univocity in argu-mentation, but to shatter and increase our sense of reality by shattering and increasing our language."[144]

By contrast, the metaphoric "tension" Wheelwright talks about is, as we have noted, primarily positive—like the tension of a tuned string. It de-notes semantic vitality and energy. There is nothing in this or in his analy-sis of epiphor and diaphor to suggest that the creative metaphor must in-evitably "shatter" its connections with ordinary meaning, logic, reference, feeling, and so forth. The highly diaphoric metaphor *can* do this, to be sure, and in doing so it can turn our prior ways of being and understand-ing upside down. But Wheelwright explicitly rejects any undue emphasis on the "destructive" function of metaphoric tension.[145] And my own in-ference from Wheelwright's theory is that metaphor can build on prior language, life orientation, and understanding, and can do so without first destroying it. In point of fact, a tensive metaphor need not be literally false.[146] When T. S. Eliot writes in *Four Quartets* that "home is where one starts from," the statement is literally true and *must* be so if the metaphoric meaning is to be grasped.[147] In other words, the first order of reference is not in this instance really suspended, even though it may be somewhat am-biguous. What makes the assertion metaphoric, and recognizably so, is the relatively trivial character of the literal level of meaning together with the immediately perceptible overtones of a further and more interesting sense and reference—overtones generated in large part by a resonant poetic con-text in which the logic of conceptual reflection and argument interacts with the logic of sound and image, cadence and connotation. Ordinary thought and discourse are not "shattered" here; they are used, challenged, complicated, affirmed, and finally transfigured.

In pursuing such ideas, one finds that Wheelwright's theory of metaphor does provide, after all, seminal insights for understanding some of the myriad ways in which the dialectical processes of poetic metaphor exploit and create linguistic resources, serving both to form and transform the reader's sense of self and world. Perhaps in spite of himself, Wheelwright also manages to suggest how the world disclosed through poetry is in various ways related to the world open to conceptual reflection. Thus, at a moment in which the threat of positivism and the counterinfluence of the New Criticism have both waned, we can perhaps best honor the spirit of Wheelwright's enterprise by reflecting in a more careful and tempered way than he does on the ontological implications of his own semantic analysis. One way of doing so is to explore connections between poetry and formal religious thought that Wheelwright glimpses but barely examines[148] and to ask in particular how poetry's interpretations of reality are either potentially or actually related to the formal and informal articulation of religious beliefs. A significant step toward this goal will be to determine how Wheelwright's theories, as I have reformulated them, can be modified further, applied, and extended in the analysis of a major work of poetic and religious art, Eliot's *Four Quartets*.

Chapter Three
Poetic Transfiguration

Four Quartets (I)

> *See, now they vanish,*
> *The faces and places, with the self which, as it could, loved them,*
> *To become renewed, transfigured, in another pattern.*
> —"Little Gidding": III

No one has better summarized the overarching purpose of T. S. Eliot's *Four Quartets* than Helen Gardner when she writes: "It presents a series of meditations upon existence in time, which, beginning from a place and a point in time, and coming back to another place and another point, attempts to discover in these points and places what is the meaning and content of an experience, what leads to it, and what follows from it, what we bring to it and what it brings to us."[1] It is true that Dame Helen does not here explicitly state the religious concern of *Four Quartets* with the problem of the redemption of temporal existence. Nor does she allude to the distinctively Christian aspect of the *Quartets'* response to the problem, which is epitomized in Eliot's use of the doctrine of the Incarnation. Instead, she employs the general language of human reflection on the limits and possibilities of life in time. This does not, however, betray the spirit of *Four Quartets* as a whole, because common human experience is its point of departure and return.

Even so, the *Quartets* assumes that reflection on the human experience of time does, in the nature of the case, ask for the kind of completion that a religious and, finally, Christian conceptuality confers. So the cycle of poems moves from one mode of meditation to another, from one language to another. The first vision of the pattern of temporal existence is gradually transfigured through the process of poetic exploration. Secular experience is revealed in a new light; it is not abandoned but illumined, so that

> . . . the end of all our exploring
> Will be to arrive where we started
> And know the place for the first time.
>   (LG:V)[2]

Ultimately, my goal will be to indicate how such a poetic transfiguration of experience is related to the dynamics of formal religious and metaphysical reflection. But my immediate aim is to examine the poetic strategies employed by Eliot to bring about the fuller, transfigured vision of time finally disclosed in *Four Quartets*. Here I make use of key elements of my critique and reformulation of Philip Wheelwright's semantics of poetry. It should be noted, however, that the cogency of those semantic theories will be demonstrated more by such adequacy as my poetic analysis as a whole may exhibit than by a step-by-step substantiation of my theoretical claims.

Because a detailed examination of the entirety of *Four Quartets* is clearly out of the question, the first stage of my analysis will focus on the development of the motif of the special moment in the rose-garden, first encountered in section I of "Burnt Norton." Starting from the premise that Hugh Kenner is basically correct when he claims that the revelation in the Burnt Norton garden is "so rich in its promise that the whole of *Four Quartets* exfoliates from it," [3] I initially center my discussion on the passage from "Burnt Norton" descriptive of the rose-garden "revelation" and then gradually move outward in perspective in order better to perceive Eliot's progressively Christian interpretation of the experience. In tracing the "exfoliation" of a single poetic motif, I am for the moment intentionally taking an approach consonant with New Critical notions of poetic structure, because Wheelwright shares most of these notions. But I intend later to show the importance of constructing a more adequate concept of the total structure of those expanded and complex metaphors we call poems.

The Rose-Garden

As early as 1942, Leonard Unger discussed in some detail the evolution of the rose-garden motif throughout Eliot's poetry, tracing its ancestry from Eliot's French poem of 1920 "*Dans le Restaurant*" through *The Waste Land*, "Ash Wednesday," and the play *The Family Reunion*, to its subtle exposition and development in *Four Quartets*.[4] That this motif occupies a special place in Eliot's poetry is plain. We would be mistaken to attribute to it an invariable meaning, however. Even the fairly explicit interpretation it receives in *The Family Reunion*—a play closely related to *Four Quartets*—cannot serve as an unambiguous gloss on its usage elsewhere. In point of fact, the rose-garden passage in "Burnt Norton" I is one of the most elusive in all Eliot's poetry:

> Footfalls echo in the memory
> Down the passage which we did not take

> Towards the door we never opened
> Into the rose-garden. My words echo
> Thus, in your mind.
>   But to what purpose
> Disturbing the dust on a bowl of rose-leaves
> I do not know.
>   Other echoes
> Inhabit the garden. Shall we follow?

. The poetry guarantees that we shall. In this way begins the first of many explorations and travels concerning each of which the poetic voice will ask, "But to what purpose?" The *Quartets* are nothing if not meditative explorations raising a basic question as to the ultimate reason for moving or exploring at all. The answer to the question emerges slowly, by "hints and guesses," out of patterns of emotion and thought, image and idea. Its final configuration, apparent in the beautiful coda that concludes the entire cycle, is a transfigured one: namely, that, drawn by Love,

> We shall not cease from exploration
> And the end of all our exploring
> Will be to arrive where we started
> And know the place for the first time.

The exploration into the rose-garden is undertaken, then, with the intent of arriving where we started, at our beginning (though we will not yet know the place). Accordingly, our first step is a step backward in time. The "deception of the thrush," we are told, summons us "through the first gate, / Into our first world."[5] Already, one should observe, common sense begins to be baffled. If our route leads through the passage "which we did not take" and "towards the door we never opened," how could the garden that is its terminus really ever have been our habitat? It is certainly not exclusively ours now:

> There they were, dignified, invisible,
> Moving without pressure, over the dead leaves,
>
>   .   .   .   .
>
> And the bird called, in response to
> The unheard music hidden in the shrubbery,
> And the unseen eyebeam crossed, for the roses
> Had the look of flowers that are looked at.
> There they were as our guests, accepted and accepting.
> So we moved, and they, in a formal pattern,
> Along the empty alley, into the box circle,
> To look down into the drained pool.

There can be no doubt that the poetry here creates a metaphoric tension between its world and the one Wheelwright calls the world of "steno-awareness." The invisible, dignified presences mentioned in the poem go permanently unnamed—a fact that heightens the reader's sense of the sur-real; and, strangely, they move without pressure as they cross over dead leaves. It is equally strange that the bird that first summoned "us" calls out in response to music "we" cannot hear but can locate as hidden in the shrubbery. Finally, it is at least odd that "we" can tell from the look of the roses that an unseen eyebeam has crossed over to them.

Eliot is presenting the reader with events and actions radically different from the ordinary. Only against the ground of our ordinary experience do we recognize the figure of the extraordinary, however. Although the scene defies in several ways the reader's notions of natural laws, it is described in terms of phenomena the reader associates with the everyday, natural world: sound, sight, motion, motivation. It is, in fact, just because the "first world" is both like and unlike our own usual experience of the world that the events and images Eliot employs are able to resonate within the reader's mind.

Thus it is that the poetry provides a metaphoric context for its subse-quent depiction of how the fictive "we" and the invisible guests come to stand before the empty pool. This action, although not clearly motivated, does not seem to the reader to be completely arbitrary; for "we" move with our guests in what Eliot calls a "formal pattern." If "we" are depicted as devoid of specific expectation, the sensitive reader nonetheless receives the impression of "our" having been led to that point by a purpose yet to be revealed.

> Dry the pool, dry concrete, brown edged,
> And the pool was filled with water out of sunlight,
> And the lotos rose, quietly, quietly,
> The surface glittered out of heart of light,
> And they were behind us, reflected in the pool.
> Then a cloud passed, and the pool was empty.
> Go, said the bird, for the leaves were full of children,
> Hidden excitedly, containing laughter.
> Go, go, go, said the bird: human kind
> Cannot bear very much reality.

Eliot presents this special moment in the rose-garden in such a way that the oddly dessicated unreality surrounding "our" entry into "our first world" acts as a foil to the vision in the pool. In contrast to the world ini-tially encountered, the world of the vision is enchantingly full, radiant with a quiet ecstasy. Before the moment of vision, the reader was scarcely aware of live roses in the garden, attending rather to images of dead leaves, autumn heat, an empty alley, invisible presences, and a drained pool with brown edges. Now the pool is filled with water, a lotus rises, the water's surface glitters "out of heart of light" (as if in touch with the light's inner being). "They"—the guests—are no longer invisible but are actually reflected in the pool, and the leaves will momentarily be full of children, a sure sign of life. So it is that "we" have come upon something that the reader is invited to believe would satisfy desire and that seems, as the bird says, reality itself. Then the bird commands "us" to go: "human kind / Cannot bear very much reality."

The rose-garden passage is a highly suggestive exposition of what will be varied and developed throughout the *Quartets*. It metaphorically presents an experience the full implications of which will only gradually become clear; it is therefore meant to intrigue the reader, stimulate the imagination, and set a poetic exploration in motion. This passage seems, moreover, explicitly to make several assertions that, as Wheelwright would be quick to point out, are marked by varying degrees of assertorial weight. Specifically, we are forced to assume that the idea of the "deception" of the thrush is asserted lightly in comparison with the idea asserted by the thrush itself when it states that "human kind cannot bear very much reality." Otherwise the thrush's assertion would be merely a deception, which is plainly not the intent of the larger assertion being advanced by the poem as a whole. The thrush's explicit statement seems, in turn, more ironic and more lightly asserted than the implied assertion it contains—the assertion that the vision in the garden was in some way a vision of reality. This, I believe, is the heaviest (or at least the most "ontologically serious") assertion of all, and one that is supported by the subsequent poetry. Yet it remains to some extent ambiguous, indefinite, and open-ended. In fact, the feeling of poetic closure at the end of the entire rose-garden passage is, at most, tentative. And this indicates that, in order to understand the full significance of this passage, we must consider the larger poetic structure.

For one thing, we cannot ignore the fact that the passage we have focused on up to now is but the second half of a two-part exposition, being the lyrical complement of the relatively abstract reflection that opens "Burnt Norton." The intellectual, prose-like quality of that introductory section has often been noted. There are few tropes, the rhythm is irregular, and the thought progression is close to that of logical discourse.

> Time present and time past
> Are both perhaps present in time future,
> And time future contained in time past.
> If all time is eternally present

All time is unredeemable.
What might have been is an abstraction
Remaining a perpetual possibility
Only in a world of speculation.
What might have been and what has been
Point to one end, which is always present.

Wheelwright describes this opening as "four statements of a formal metaphysical character," differing from steno-thought largely in that they are elliptical. (The reader must supply connectives in order to bring the meanings of all four "into logical consistency.") [6] If rational discourse were necessarily incompatible with poetry, we would be obliged to judge Eliot's opening to be a poetic failure.[7] The "poetry" as such would not begin until the rose-garden passage. Even if we were to take the tack of dismissing the opening passage as "pseudo thought" or "thought for the sake of emotion," we would have to admit that thinking is required if the reader is to discern the meaning of these "pseudo assertions." The most sensible approach to the poem's opening seems to be simply to recognize that Eliot has presented in genuinely intellectual terms a problem intrinsic to the poetry and having, as will become apparent, a direct bearing on the reader's interpretation of the rose-garden passage.

To say that the problem posed in the opening passage of the poem is presented in intellectual terms is not to say, however, that the intellect will be found adequate in itself to discover a solution. Having confronted in the first lines the possibility of determinism and of time's unredeemability, the reader is directed by line 10 to regard the present moment as an "end" toward which "what might have been and what has been" point. At this juncture discursive reason begins to falter. Up to now the poetry had given it a map of temporal experience the coordinates of which excluded the possibility of envisioning a meaningful outcome to its exploration of time. On that map the "end" spoken of in line 10 could be nothing more than a dead end: a terminal Now in which "all time is eternally present" in a frozen simultaneity of potentiality and actuality. The idea of something's *pointing* to an end, however, inevitably suggests the possibility of a purpose and meaning to that end. The first interpretive framework therefore begins to dissolve and the focus of reflection to shift. One begins to realize that the chief question guiding this search for the "end" that is always present is not whether time is free or determined, simultaneous or sequential. It is more subtle, imbued with regret for the "perpetual possibility" of "what might have been" and motivated by a desire to approach the genuine purpose of the present moment. Thus, as will be true throughout the *Quartets*, the main impetus for striving for an adequate understanding of time becomes not so much a craving for a lucid, rational scheme as a craving for redemption. As this becomes apparent, we can see that the introductory speculative concepts of "time," "possibility," and "redemption" have been highlighted and ordered in such a way as to make possible a double interpretation of the "end" that is "eternally present." For now it is evident that the very terms that, when read one way, portray history as endless futility, have an ambiguity that will permit a diametrically opposed reading to emerge—a reading in which our "end" will be our spiritual beginning, in which our "possibility" will be the redemption of time through the Incarnation, and in which the present will not only be "always" but also "eternal," in a religious sense.[8]

It is this level of meaning that begins to be confirmed in the context of the rose-garden passage. We can now realize that the latter passage is metaphorically juxtaposed with the philosophical opening in what Wheelwright would term a basically "diaphoric" manner. The opening conceptual reflections affect the reader's response to the minimally conceptual description that the rose-garden passage offers. Because reflective thought has strained the intellect and impelled it toward a reassessment of experience, the reader brings to the rose-garden urgent questions. And we can be sure that these questions give a sharper focus and more definite significance to the images of the rose-garden passage than could otherwise be possible. Because we now see the garden in the context of a quest for time's redemption, we feel justified in associating this garden of "our first world" with Eden (though perhaps an Eden after the Fall, since it has a formal, civilized plan, and death is present in the leaves). Because we have confronted the introductory question of the interrelationship between past and present time, we also feel justified in associating the place with childhood (eventually we even hear the laughter of children). In spite of its historical locus as the garden at Burnt Norton—a country house in Gloucestershire, England—the place assumes an almost primordial aura as a location toward which one might at any time begin to journey. As Eliot writes in "Little Gidding" I,

> If you came this way,
> Taking any route, starting from anywhere,
> At any time or at any season,
> It would always be the same.

Above all, this is a place one comes upon without purpose, but "from which the purpose breaks."

In the garden at Burnt Norton what breaks forth is, of course, the special moment of vision. Its full significance cannot yet be grasped by the reader or by the "we" of the poem, but the experience itself has an immediate and powerful effect. Having in mind the questions raised in the philo-sophical introduction, moreover, the reader will not be unaware of a la-tent, larger significance. The sudden filling of the pool with water, the sunlight, the lotus, the heart of light, the children—these will seem to be-token an experience of fulfilled purpose, meaningful time, and of commu-nion with a higher order of reality than is revealed to ordinary perception.

In asking the nature and significance of the experience described, how-ever, the reader cannot isolate one specific answer. The answer appropriate to the moment is to be found in the web of associated thoughts and feel-ings the poem has spun out. In Wheelwright's terms, the focus of the po-etic passage is soft, the meaning contextualized, the signs plurisignative, the thoughts "paralogical" and paradoxical, and the assertions light. Yet this does not mean there is no focus whatever, no paraphrasable content, thread of reason, or weight of assertion. The metaphor Eliot fashions by implicitly equating the garden of the poem with other gardens, real or imagined, is not simply verbal music. In asserting that the garden is "our first world," the poem establishes boundaries for appropriate response: a subject for thought and a focus for feeling. And in describing the special moment in the garden, it does more than invite the reader to engage in free association; it insists (lightly) that the reader be attentive to both physical and mystical implications. This creative balancing of the poem's metaphorical tensions—setting the reader's mental processes to work fol-lowing hints and guesses as to the import of vaguely coherent semblances of experience—is the source of the unique power and quality of the poetry. It is this that is humanly engaging. To refuse to enter the sphere of the poetic metaphor either by dissolving its rational fibers into a fog of amor-phous emotion, or else by petrifying its emotive fluidity into a rigorous conceptual scheme, is simply to refuse to read the poem for what it is. My adaptation of Wheelwright's theories, by contrast, permits a reading that is responsive to the poem's true dynamic, because we are thereby allowed to take seriously the interaction between genuinely intellectual and emotional components.

Wheelwright's concept of plurisignation allows, furthermore, for a ret-rospective reinterpretation of the rose-garden scene in terms of yet more definite—and definitely more religious—meanings than those the reader could first perceive clearly. As the poem progresses, new levels of signifi-cance are exposed and old meanings altered. Thus we must consider the rose-garden passage from the standpoint not only of the prior poetic struc-ture but also of the subsequent. For example, the "still point of the turning world," described in "Burnt Norton" II, comes to be identified as the source of the garden's graced moment. And the death-like emptiness to which "we" descend in "Burnt Norton" III suggests that taking the "way up" through special moments like that in the garden also entails taking the "way down" into a state that is the opposite of the plenitude experienced in the rose-garden. This third section of the poem is, in turn, followed by a meditation offering yet another perspective on the rose-garden experience:

> Will the sunflower turn to us, will the clematis
> Stray down, bend to us; tendril and spray
> Clutch and cling?
> Chill
> Fingers of yew be curled
> Down on us? After the kingfisher's wing
> Has answered light to light, and is silent,
>   the light is still
> At the still point of the turning world.

Prayer-like, this is a passage of delicate beauty and of lyrical, tentative affirmation. It is filled with the sort of hidden symbolism first encountered in the rose-garden scene, but it is more specifically Christian in the images it employs. Given the nature of the preceding poetry, the reader should be alert enough to detect this and, short of constructing an allegory, place the images conceptually as well as emotionally. Consider the flowers mentioned here, for instance, which are no longer rose and lotus but sunflower and clematis. Because the sun has been identified with the center of things, with the still point, the flower of the sun may be taken to be a sign of Godly grace. As many have pointed out, the clematis can likewise be seen as a Christian symbol, for it is known as "Virgin's Bower," its blue hue being "Mary's color."[9] The other images are similarly suggestive of Christian symbolism. The yew, long a symbol of death as well as eternity, may point to the necessity for death or a spiritual "end" to come before birth or a spiritual beginning; and the kingfisher (Halcyon) is mythologically associated with a tale of burial and resurrection through divine intervention, so that it may be seen as a disguised emblem of Christ, whose light answers in earthly form the light that abides at "the still point of the turning world."[10]

These suggestions of the Christian language of redemption remain faint. Eliot chooses not to use the specific name "Virgin's Bower," as he might have in the context of the later quartets. Likewise, in "Burnt Norton" V he does not, after addressing the problem of the limitation of words, specifically name Christ as the incarnate Word that could withstand the assaults of desert temptation. By the end of "Burnt Norton" a pattern has emerged, nevertheless; and the reader is necessarily mindful of the Christian story when a recapitulation of the major themes begins, ordering them in such a way that one finds in them a new meaning. The secular tone has been taken up into a religious one that "restores the meaning" that was always present but not to be discerned apart from a death of the ordinary mode of experiencing and perceiving.

This process of the restoration and discovery of meaning is evident, moreover, in relation to the rose-garden passage in particular. From the point of view of the conclusion of "Burnt Norton," the elements of this passage take on additional significance. Again in keeping with Wheelwright's notion of plurisignification, previously hidden meanings are brought into the foreground as the reader becomes aware of their larger context. The reader will now feel more certain, for example, that the rose is there functioning (as it does in a whole tradition of European literature) as an emblem of both profane love and mystic ecstasy.[11] The lotus, similarly, can now be taken to imply both a physical and metaphysical consummation of experience, the latter being identical with spiritual enlightenment.[12] Whereas water is to be associated with spiritual birth and with a death leading to that birth, sunlight (both fire and light) can now be understood as the physical and divine source that illumines, purifies, and unifies—as we shall see in the concluding lines of *Four Quartets*, which point to the eschatological time when

> . . . the tongues of flame are in-folded
> Into the crowned knot of fire
> And the fire and the rose are one.

The plurisignification of the *Quartets* operates, therefore, at several levels. It both alludes to and represents three basic dimensions of experience. The first is the dimension of ordinary awareness, which Eliot characterizes as distraction or empty calculation and which Wheelwright regards as intimately connected with steno-language. The second is the dimension of depth-awareness, which is exemplified by the special moment in the rose-garden as that moment is confronted in its original ambiguity. The third is the explicitly religious (and, ultimately, Christian) dimension of awareness, exemplified by the transfiguration through which the special moment becomes a moment of revelation. It is in this last dimension that the Incarnation is understood as the reality undergirding an affirmative orientation toward temporal existence.

Both of the latter dimensions of experience rely on what Wheelwright calls "depth" or "expressive" language for their articulation. But the entire structure of *Four Quartets* is built on the assumption that the language of general depth-awareness only hints at the Reality disclosed more fully through "expressive language" that is, at root, Christian. For this reason the language of *Four Quartets* must be understood as depth language committed to a particular view of reality. As such it points to depth experiences common to all human lives and utilizes their latent power in order to part the veil of ordinary awareness and complacency. It then guides the reader to a recognition of the truth—or at least the seriousness—of the Christian interpretation of time and life as partially glimpsed in those moments of awareness. Thus it is by no means arbitrary that Eliot at first prevents the reader from grasping the full significance of such passages as the one depicting the special moment in the rose-garden. He is constructing a poetic metaphor of how, even in our depth experiences, "we had the experience but missed the meaning" (DS:II) and of why, in Eliot's view, we must be "undeceived" of our prior understanding (EC:II).[13] The whole exploration embarked upon by the *Quartets* is an approach to the meaning missed in experience. As such, it poetically "imitates" a meditative analysis and self-examination of the kind that Eliot regards as preparatory to hearing the Christian kerygma.

The specifically Christian dimension of the understanding of existence offered in the *Quartets* is not entirely evident, however, even by the conclusion of "Burnt Norton." Granting that "Burnt Norton" was originally conceived as a self-contained poem,[14] we nevertheless must observe that the resolution it proposes with regard to the problem of time is equivocal at an emotional as well as at an intellectual level. To be forced in the end to pronounce "ridiculous" the "waste sad time / Stretching before and after" the special moment in the rose-garden (BN:V) is to be forced to hover at the brink of despair, regardless of the supposed efficacy of the Incarnation. Consequently, I believe that what motivated Eliot to develop a whole cycle of related poems was something other than a wish to work out technical possibilities in the construction of "musical" poetry.[15] It seems to me altogether likely that what most motivated Eliot was a desire to make a poetic journey from the rose-garden of "Burnt Norton" to its transfigured counterpart in "Little Gidding," that is, to the moment of "midwinter spring." But if this is so, one is obliged to consider the nature of the whole cycle of poems in order fully to comprehend the place of the rose-garden experience in Eliot's essentially Christian interpretation of temporal existence and so to appreciate the range of the poetry's resources for the disclosure of reality or realities.

The Rose-Garden Transfigured

In "Burnt Norton" the experience in the rose-garden is something that—however intriguing and moving both for the speaker in the poem and for the reader—is at first fully understood by neither. Its religious overtones gradually become more prominent as that poem progresses, but the ultimate significance of the experience—its significance as a kind of "incarnation" of the primary Incarnation, for example—is merely hinted at. In Wheelwright's terms, we can say that in "Burnt Norton" the metaphor of the rose-garden is to a large extent diaphoric; its meaning is intuited more than it is understood, felt more than apprehended.

It should also be said that, to the extent that the rose-garden experience *is* the subject of reflection and interpretation in the context of "Burnt Norton," it appears to be mostly a private experience divorced from a historical community and the needs of daily life. The time before and after the special moment seems indeed "waste" and "sad" (BN:V). Thus reader and speaker alike are initially tempted to look to the rose-garden experience as a refuge from time and a source of redemption, and yet they are simultaneously forced to acknowledge that such an experience could never, in itself, suffice. It is much too transitory, too fugitive.

Only from this perspective, I believe, can one adequately understand what Eliot earlier meant by the "deception of the thrush" (BN:I). That deception is, I think, to be comprehended as residing in the fact that "we" are deceived into looking to the isolated rose-garden experience for a solution to the problem of time posed in the beginning lines of the poem. Momentarily it seems we have discovered an earthly paradise beyond the concerns of time. What we find instead, however, is "what might have been"— a kind of paradisiacal bliss—but what also can never be for more than a brief moment. It cannot last, not only because we do not morally deserve it, but also because the garden is not the true abiding place for human beings, even saints. This becomes increasingly clear in the later quartets as the larger Christian framework of interpretation becomes more firmly established. But even in "Burnt Norton" the bird's cryptic parting words inform us that "we" do not here belong in the immediate presence of the reality we momentarily envision.[16]

In "East Coker" there emerges a different sense of what one is looking for when one seeks the redemption of time. Moments of epiphany such as that in the rose-garden are no longer dwelt on with such feelings of nostalgia, regret, and sadness as they were in "Burnt Norton," for it now appears that their isolated intensity is but a beginning point:

> Home is where one starts from. As we grow older
> The world becomes stranger, the pattern more complicated
> Of dead and living. Not the intense moment
> Isolated, with no before and after,
> But a life-time burning in every moment
> And not the lifetime of one man only
> But of old stones that cannot be deciphered.
>
> (EC:V)

Thus our "first world"—symbolized by the paradisiacal garden of Burnt Norton—not only can never fully be ours; it also can never be a fruitful point of departure unless we recognize its connection with death and with those who have gone before. This realization casts a revealing light on the closing lines of "Burnt Norton," which seem to summon us to a perpetual pursuit of the timeless rose-garden moment:

> Sudden in a shaft of sunlight
> Even while the dust moves
> There rises the hidden laughter
> Of children in the foliage
> Quick now, here, now, always—
> Ridiculous the waste sad time
> Stretching before and after.

These lines stand in marked contrast to the above passage from "East Coker," which continues:

> Love is most nearly itself
> When here and now cease to matter.
> Old men ought to be explorers
> Here and there does not matter
> We must be still and still moving
> Into another intensity
> For a further union, a deeper communion
> Through the dark cold and the empty desolation. . . .
> (EC:V)

It is necessary to journey beyond here and now, through the dark cold and empty desolation, because, as Eliot goes on to say in the last line, only in reaching one's "end" does one discover a "beginning." And this, I take it, is what is meant in "East Coker" III as well, where Eliot writes:

> The laughter in the garden, echoed ecstasy
> Not lost, but requiring, pointing to the agony
> Of death and birth.

With this in mind it is quite impossible to interpret the speaker's desire for "a lifetime burning in every moment" (EC:V) as a desire perpetually to experience, here and now, the pure bliss of the rose-garden. The idea of burning, to be sure, is commonly associated with love and ecstasy, so that the vision of the rose-garden rapture is naturally summoned to mind at this point and its apparent desirability considered. But it is summoned in order to be reappraised. We now see that the hope that this sort of burning intensity might be prolonged indefinitely is childish, being based on a wish to remain at the "beginning." Hence, the reader is driven to find a second and more profound level of understanding of Eliot's meaning. Here the connotations of "burning" that have to do not only with love but also with fire, purgation, and even consumption become predominant. And the framework for this new understanding is that established in "East Coker" IV, where the images of roses and burning are associated with "purgatorial fires / Of which the flame is roses, and the smoke is briars."

The concept of purgatory should be sufficient to alert the reader to the fact that the poem will not advocate the seemingly pointless self-humiliation and contrived agonies characteristic of certain varieties of asceticism. Ascetic Eliot may be, but here at least he posits an ultimately life-affirming goal to be attained through self-denial, that goal being a "deeper communion" in which the whole of the human community—"not the lifetime of one man only"—is involved. Indeed, Eliot points to a further union in which (as "Little Gidding" will say) "All manner of thing shall be well . . . / And the fire and the rose are one" (LG:V).

It should require little theological sophistication to recognize in these themes of death and communion an ever clearer poetic expression of certain central Christian doctrines and at least a partial interpretation and elucidation of insights but dimly adumbrated in "Burnt Norton." In the earlier poem the significance of the water and fire encountered in the rose-garden vision was a matter of conjecture, their relation to spiritual birth and death being only lightly asserted and only softly focused. But in "East Coker" there is an unmistakable echo of the New Testament teaching that he who would save his life must lose it. Again, in "Burnt Norton" the lotus and light of the rose-garden could have been interpreted as betokening a secret and even slightly cloying sexual-mystical union. The images of "East Coker," however, are designed to remind one of the communion of the saints and of the agape that Christians are commanded to have one for another. Finally, it is worth recalling that in this later poem—Eliot's "Good Friday lyric"—the chief references to the rose-garden experience frame a lengthy passage in which allusions to Christ, the church, Adam, sin, grace, and the eucharist could hardly be plainer. ("East Coker" IV has in fact been accused of being an unabashed and not particularly subtle allegory.) It is not unreasonable to conclude, therefore, that in "East Coker" the meaning of the rose-garden theme is intended by Eliot to coalesce with a Christian interpretation of temporal life and its possibilities.

Yet in "East Coker" Eliot makes no attempt imaginatively to depict any human experience that would both be comparable to the rose-garden experience and yet reflect this new level of insight. Nor does he proceed, as he will in "Little Gidding," to offer concrete metaphors of the ultimate Christian hope of the eschatological consummation of history. He is in fact emptying the reader's consciousness of images of what to hope for, love, or have faith in. "Wait without thought," he writes, "for you are not ready for thought" (EC:III). The thoughts, images, and feelings conjured up by the poetry almost all relate to the bondage of ordinary time and life and to spiritual poverty. Because no positive metaphor of the truth—and certainly no conceptual scheme—is offered the reader, the only real and positive Christian insights the reader can feel in possession of consist in an awareness of limits and a consciousness of merely the *words* for what under other conditions might be perceived as saving realities: namely, the "wounded surgeon" (Christ), the "dying nurse" (the Church), the paternal care of which we shall "die" (God's grace), and the "old stones that cannot be deciphered" (the human community). The dominant imagery of sickness, decay, and death strongly colors, in fact, those very references to love, communion, and "beginning" that I earlier discussed as the means by which Eliot reinterprets in Christian terms the meaning of the rose-garden experience. I therefore believe it accurate to say that "East Coker" establishes merely the Christian *context* of interpreting significant experience. The Christian *content*, although certainly alluded to, largely remains to be revealed in the later poems. Without that content, "East Coker" conveys little more of the Christian kerygma than Good Friday would if it were contemplated apart from Easter.

"The Dry Salvages" supplies much of the positive content missing from "East Coker." Indeed, this poem provides the fullest conceptual articulation of the meaning of Incarnation to be found in any of the *Quartets*. Thus it is most assuredly not simply to be dismissed as a parody of a true reconciliation between the opposites of time and eternity, darkness and light, and so on—although Hugh Kenner has made an ingenious argument to this effect.[17] However disappointing "The Dry Salvages" may have been to the majority of critics and readers (myself included), it carries forward the argument of *Four Quartets* and cannot well be ignored.

That this is true can easily be seen in relation to this poem's treatment of the rose-garden theme, to which Eliot turns in "Dry Salvages" II. Actually what Eliot is dealing with in this passage is the phenomenon of special moments in general, but what he says is naturally applicable to that paradigmatic special moment constituted by the rose-garden experience:

> The moments of happiness—not the sense of well-being,
> Fruition, fulfilment, security or affection,
> Or even a very good dinner, but the sudden illumination—
> We had the experience but missed the meaning,
> And approach to the meaning restores the experience

In a different form, beyond any meaning
We can assign to happiness. I have said before
That the past experience revived in the meaning
Is not the experience of one life only
But of many generations. . . .

In part these lines are indeed a recapitulation of what Eliot had "said before" in "East Coker." Whatever one is to make of the "moments of happiness," he again declares, they should not be regarded as ends in themselves.
Rather, they are to signify and to illumine. As one approaches their meaning, one realizes that, in order to make sense of them, one must somehow
make sense of all experience, historical as well as current; and this, of
course, involves reckoning with the suffering inherent in temporal existence as well as with the more pleasant realities of private ecstasy or creaturely comfort.

None of this should surprise the reader who has pondered "East Coker."
What does surprise and even shock one is the speaker's subsequent judgment that, because the approach to the meaning of the experience of sudden illumination must take into account the experience of many generations and the vicissitudes of history, it leads to the discovery that, in time,
agony is no less enduring than joy:

. . . the moments of agony
(Whether, or not, due to misunderstanding,
Having hoped for the wrong things or dreaded
      the wrong things,
Is not in question) are likewise permanent
With such permanence as time has.

This statement amounts to a major reinterpretation of the meaning of the
rose-garden experience; for it would be hard to imagine a more radical rejection of the notion that moments of transcendent happiness could ever
be sufficient to redeem time. If agony is no less enduring than happiness,
there is no justification for assuming that even extraordinary happiness can
compensate for the grief and guilt inevitable in life, or that such happiness
is somehow more "real" than suffering. What the poem implies is that
somehow both happiness and suffering at once abide and are transitory, in
the same way that time itself at once preserves and destroys. This is apparently a fact of existence not to be eradicated by other-worldly mysticism. In
short, time must be taken seriously. Thus, according to the speaker, to approach the meaning of moments of special happiness is to realize that the
product of such moments is not, finally, "happiness" at all, as that state is

normally envisioned. Indeed, it is to perceive that, to the extent that time is real, the "waste sad time" before and after moments of sudden illumination likewise is real, and the vestiges of such time abide.

In spite of the conversational tone ("I have said before"), the vocabulary of common speech, and the semblance of steno-reasoning, Eliot's writing here is subtly elliptical and surprisingly difficult. The difficulty of the passage is magnified by the fact that the reader by now expects the poetry to begin trying to "make sense" of time and so expects to find, following the poetry's negations, a "nevertheless" or a "yet" or an "although" to ameliorate the pessimism and to introduce some sign of a Christian "answer." But, as we have seen, when Eliot at last reaches a point of saying, "Now, we come to discover," it is only to demolish another false hope and false answer. Even the promising lines "And approach to the meaning restores the experience / In a different form" terminate in the sobering conclusion that the restoration of the form does not result in greater happiness but in a cognizance of "primitive terror" (DS:II). One begins to wonder whether the poetry has not, in its firm resolve to avoid false hope, succeeded in undermining even the grounds for Christian hope and faith.

The concluding section of "The Dry Salvages" reassures us that this has not been the poet's aim. Here one finds Eliot's most comprehensive statement as to the meaning of such moments as that in the rose-garden. To begin with, this passage makes it clearer than ever that experiencing the moment in the rose-garden is different from fully apprehending "the point of intersection of the timeless / With time." The latter "occupation," given to the saint, is nothing less than the devotion of one's whole life to the Reality disclosed in the primary Incarnation. (And even this "occupation" is not an affair of perpetual rapture but of "a lifetime's death in love.") Such an apprehension is more than most of us are capable of:

> For most of us, there is only the unattended
> Moment, the moment in and out of time,
> The distraction fit, lost in a shaft of sunlight,
> The wild thyme unseen, or the winter lightning
> Or the waterfall, or music heard so deeply
> That it is not heard at all, but you are the music
> While the music lasts. These are only hints and guesses,
> Hints followed by guesses; and the rest
> Is prayer, observance, discipline, thought and action.

But our general inattention, our failure to approach the meaning of the moments "in and out of time," does not mean that we are in no way illumined by such moments. Despite the fact that the rose-garden vision provides but a hint as to its own significance, that hint qualifies as a lesser vision or secondary incarnation of the same Reality to which the saint's life is devoted:

> The hint half guessed, the gift half understood,
>   is Incarnation.
> Here the impossible union
> Of spheres of existence is actual,
> Here the past and future
> Are conquered, and reconciled. . . .

To respond rightly to this hint would be to obtain, as Eliot goes on to say, freedom from the enslavement of past and future alike. It would be personally to appropriate the reality of the reconciliation effected through, and symbolized by, the Incarnation. And although that aim is, for most of us, "never here to be realized," the actuality of the Incarnation means that, regardless of our meager success, our limited lives can and do nourish "the life of significant soil." In other words, paradoxically enough, even those of us who are not saints—that is, those of us for whom the rose-garden experiences are but random events only half understood—we too, having "gone on trying," can count our time as graced and redeemed.

Exactly what all this means is not entirely clear. No one, to my knowledge, has supposed that Eliot ever fully develops a conceptually cogent and comprehensive soteriology, and he certainly does not do so here. But the following and final quartet does not add a great deal conceptually to what one already can comprehend of the meaning of Incarnation and redemption. The central "doctrines"—whether those of Eliot, Christianity, F. H. Bradley, or all three—have all by now been expounded, their "steno-" content explicated insofar as the poet deems this explication necessary, and the result is substantial. Certainly one has a clearer conception of what is meant by the earlier, enigmatic declaration in "Burnt Norton" II that "only through time time is conquered."

But it must be said that, even if the intellect is now partially satisfied, the imagination is not. Hugh Kenner may be indulging in hyperbole when he writes that "there is nothing in the last three-quarters of *The Dry Salvages,* not the materials handled, the mode of ideation, nor the process by which instance yields formulation, that is beyond the scope of a sensitive prose essayist."[18] Yet there is a good deal of truth in what he says. "The Dry Salvages" is poetry that frequently approaches the status of informal steno-language. And because it lacks the conceptual coherence of formal theology or philosophy, the predominance of fleshless thoughts and words, and therefore of bare musing, is all the more apparent. The reader is left hungry for imaginative nourishment (if not for further conceptual enlightenment). However provocative it may be to have Incarnation named as the reality to which the rose-garden experience points and as that event in time that conquers time, reconciling past and future, still the full import of this naming is not transmitted poetically. The "music" of the poetry is neither adequate to, nor unified with, the thought.

Nonetheless, one might plausibly argue that this effect is not entirely unintentional, its function being to prepare for "Little Gidding." Eliot is willing to prolong the "way down," extend the reader's sense of darkness and deprivation, and include a lengthy section of quasi steno-language within the metaphor of the work as a whole, because he knows that a different kind of poem is to follow.

In any event, it is not until "Little Gidding" that one encounters the full transfiguration of the rose-garden motif. Here, in the opening lines, Eliot describes a scene that completely qualifies as a counterpart to the moment in the rose-garden. This is the moment of "midwinter spring" experienced on the road to Little Gidding, the site of the ruins of an Anglican religious community founded by Nicholas Ferrar in 1625. In describing this latter moment, Eliot uses an overarching metaphor of a paradoxical season of life-in-death that is at once appropriate to the Christian proclamation of the reality of Easter and Pentecost and adequate to the reader's general sense of what might serve as a suitable symbol for the redemption of time. Drawing on the central imagery of the preceding poems, Eliot transforms it in such a way as to suggest how, having put aside one's former "sense and notion," one might discover the ultimate purpose behind one's temporal quest. It is an altogether remarkable passage, deserving to be quoted in full:

> Midwinter spring is its own season
> Sempiternal though sodden towards sundown,
> Suspended in time, between pole and tropic.
> When the short day is brightest, with frost and fire,
> The brief sun flames the ice, on pond and ditches,
> In windless cold that is the heart's heat,
> Reflecting in a watery mirror
> A glare that is blindness in the early afternoon.
> And glow more intense than blaze of branch, or brazier,
> Stirs the dumb spirit: no wind, but pentecostal fire
> In the dark time of the year. Between melting and freezing
> The soul's sap quivers. There is no earth smell
> Or smell of living thing. This is the spring time
> But not in time's covenant. Now the hedgerow
> Is blanched for an hour with transitory blossom
> Of snow, a bloom more sudden

> Than that of summer, neither budding nor fading,
> Not in the scheme of generation.
> Where is the summer, the unimaginable
> Zero summer?

David Perkins, in his excellent essay "Rose-garden to Midwinter Spring: Achieved Faith in the *Four Quartets*," has already compared in some detail this opening passage of "Little Gidding" with the rose-garden passage in "Burnt Norton."[19] In point of fact, several of his observations are pertinent to my own line of inquiry.

As Perkins notes, there are several striking similarities between the rose-garden passage and that concerning midwinter spring. The descriptions of both the rose-garden and the winter landscape yield what Perkins calls a "brief intimation" of transcendent reality, and, in so doing, both use a nexus of water, flower, and light imagery. Furthermore, in both passages the light referred to is described as reflected from various forms of water (an element that, in the *Quartets*, is often a symbol of time). Because light—especially that of the sun—is associated in this poetry with eternity, we have in each case a depiction of a moment "in and out of time" and thus an emblem of the intersection of the timeless with time.

Perkins also correctly observes, however, that the differences between the passages are significant. First of all, the light symbolism itself is used with a different effect in each. In "Burnt Norton" one has the impression that the vision is not only quite fleeting but also in some way illusory. The illumination, moreover, is physically restricted: the space filled by the light is no larger than a pool. But in "Little Gidding" nothing suggests that the vision may be an illusion, and here the whole landscape reflects the light, doing so with overwhelming intensity. In Perkins's words, "The difference is, perhaps, between gazing at the 'heart of light' and being virtually in it."

The flower symbolism likewise is used differently in the two passages. On the one hand, the lotus and rose of "Burnt Norton" immediately suggest a joy that is to some significant degree natural, sensual, and even sexual—a joy that is youthful and therefore sadly inaccessible to one in the "waste" years to come. On the other hand, the flowering of the hedgerow in "Little Gidding" connotes a purity and chilling beauty not so immediately appealing to the "natural" self that has not "put aside sense and notion." The petals, after all, are of snow, and to one's natural mind they seem fragile and transitory. Yet the state of radiant illumination created by the scene declares that they partake of a time not our time, being

> . . . a bloom more sudden
> Than that of summer, neither budding nor fading,
> Not in the scheme of generation.

Finally (though Perkins fails to take note of this particular difference), the general setting of the two visionary scenes is dissimilar in a revealing way. To be sure, both locations are, as it were, waste places: one is an autumn garden with dead leaves, dry heat, and a drained pool, the other a barren winter landscape in "the dark time of the year." But one should not overlook the fact that the first is a garden adjacent to a house whereas the second is at the end of a "rough road" and near to a chapel graveyard. Even though Eliot makes it clear in "Burnt Norton" that it is the wrong time of year to expect fresh-blossoming flowers and water and a light that renews rather than oppresses, the place itself is nevertheless one where a person given to nostalgia might at least come to *recall* such phenomena; it is where one could expect to feel at home and could want to reenter "our first world." In "Little Gidding," by contrast, the place and time speak of death. The site is that of a historic religious community, now largely in ruins. Marked by a tombstone and the "dull façade" of a chapel, it is to be found at the end of a journey, and when one no longer knows what to expect. The Christian irony, then, is that the vision in the rose-garden is the one that turns out to be elusive and in some sense illusory; the garden itself is discovered to be a place from which one must be expelled. Little Gidding, by contrast, is where one ultimately discovers one's purpose. Whereas the rose-garden could offer one but a moment "in and out of time"—a moment "unattended" because not understood—the place of apparent death offers one a genuinely timeless apprehension of time's meaning: "Here, the intersection of the timeless moment / Is England and nowhere. Never and always" (LG:I). The first place therefore corresponds to that beginning in which is one's end, the second to that end in which is one's beginning. "He who would save his life must lose it."

All of which further supports the conclusion that "Little Gidding" restores the rose-garden moment in a different form, taking up the theme of ineffable joy and modulating it into the new key of religious faith. Instead of being burdened with "an intense nostalgia for something that never happened," as Perkins says of the vision in the rose-garden, the new vision is riveted on something evidently real and immediate that stands as a true point of illumination. In Perkins's words: "The meaning has been discovered. The kindling illumination taking place is framed within Christian theology—it is 'pentecostal'—and the protagonist recognizes its significance. . . . It is the moment of baptism or rebirth, a crossing from the merely natural realm into a dimension of religious faith."[20] We should notice that the religious faith here incipient is social as well as private in nature; its symbols include the church at Little Gidding and the history associated with that whole community. Although this development of a social and historical dimension of faith had of course been anticipated by both

"East Coker" and "The Dry Salvages," its positive implications neverthe-less have not until this point in the poetry been given imaginative form.

This last observation points to a final, crucial feature of the poetry, al-though it is one that Perkins acknowledges only implicitly. With the mo-ment of "midwinter spring," the reader, as well as the poetic speaker, has truly arrived at a point of potential illumination because it is now and only now that the reader has a concrete metaphor embodying the major themes of the *Quartets* and of what Eliot believes to be the heart of the Christian understanding of time and eternity. The reader, of course, may not person-ally experience at this juncture a moment of actual religious vision (Eliot would be the last to claim that his poetry could guarantee such an experi-ence), but the poem does guide the reader's intellect, imagination, and sensibility to recognize in the passage we have examined a moving and profound likeness to such an experience. In other words, the sensitive reader is likely to feel that what has been glimpsed in "Burnt Norton," ago-nized over in "East Coker," and talked about in "The Dry Salvages," has become an imaginative reality in the poetry of "Little Gidding." When, therefore, the final section of the poem again alludes to the rose-garden we encountered so early in *Four Quartets*, it is indeed as though we "know the place for the first time":

> Through the unknown, remembered gate
> When the last of earth left to discover
> Is that which was the beginning;
>
> .   .   .   .
>
> And all shall be well and
> All manner of thing shall be well
> When the tongues of flame are in-folded
> Into the crowned knot of fire
> And the fire and the rose are one.

On that note of promise the cycle of poems closes.

In discussing the nature of the poetic transfiguration intrinsic to *Four Quartets*, we have by now given considerable evidence as to the validity of Philip Wheelwright's central claims concerning the semantics of poetry. As Wheelwright has led us to expect, the seriousness with which the reader is required to entertain the assertions of this poetry clearly prevents us from speaking of these assertions as merely "pseudo" or purely emotive. The en-tire progress of the *Quartets* from the moment in the rose-garden to the moment of midwinter spring entails serious reflection on the insights la-tent within various conceptions of, and attitudes toward, temporal exis-tence. Thus, for example, when the poem finally asserts that "the hint half guessed, the gift half understood, is Incarnation," the reader naturally

forms some sort of judgment as to the assertion's validity, not only in relation to the rest of the poetry but also in relation to extra-poetic experience.
Any attempt to read *Four Quartets* as verbal music making no demands on
one's capacity for thought and evaluation would consequently be tantamount to a refusal to read the poem that Eliot actually wrote. Nor could
any greater adequacy be ascribed to theories that would treat the poetic
thought as "real" but as nevertheless existing, in the end, for the sake of
inducing an emotion devoid of intellectual substance. Such theories confuse the poetry's transformation—and even rejection—of ordinary thought
with a purely romantic indulgence in mere mood and feeling.[21]

And yet, as Wheelwright would insist, *Four Quartets* is not a steno-
argument to which feeling and connotation is incidental. We have seen
that the passage in "Little Gidding" describing the midwinter spring conveys, through its affective and sensory images, something approximating a
total awareness of the meaning of the pilgrimage undertaken in *Four Quartets* as a whole, and an awareness that far exceeds whatever one could have
known from the relatively disembodied statements in "The Dry Salvages,"
even though the latter convey most of the essential "information."

This observation, in turn, makes all the more plausible the thesis that
poetry is best regarded as a form of metaphor. For it can be argued that the
semantic units internal to *Four Quartets*—ranging from nearly literal statements to nearly nonsensical interludes—combine to create a complex metaphor equating the fictive meditation of the poetic speaker with the actual
process of approaching the purpose of temporal existence, of struggling to
apprehend the moment of the intersection of the timeless with time, and
of faithfully continuing the struggle even if the goal is "never here to be
realized." We do not find in the poetry a literal presentation of this process
in all its dimensions; poetry, after all, is not life. But we do find the essential ingredients of the process represented in a condensed, "tensive" form
that speaks to the reader's sensible self and does so more and more clearly
as the poem progresses. Indeed, the movement of the poem from lesser to
greater clarity can itself be described in the terms Wheelwright applies to
metaphor. Beginning as a metaphor in which diaphoric elements complicate and diffuse the assertorial content, *Four Quartets* becomes a metaphor
increasingly epiphoric in character, so that it culminates in an identifiable
perspective (Christian) and a definite—though still tensive—assertion that
time is in the end redeemed.

But having established this, we find ourselves compelled to raise semantic and meta-ontological questions for which Wheelwright has provided
only minimal and, to some extent, misleading answers. Wheelwright argues that one's experience of an extended metaphor such as *Four Quartets*
will inevitably challenge, invigorate, and deepen one's ordinary ideas and

feelings, and he maintains that the poetry's semantic transformations can transform and shape one's sense of reality. For this reason, he argues, poetry can be said to provide a basis for developing a "meta-poetic ontology"—that is, a view of reality based on reality's poetic embodiments. Wheelwright, however, is in this connection using the term "ontology" in a highly restricted sense. What he is referring to is not a philosophical and conceptually coherent articulation of a fundamental sense of reality mediated by poetry or by a given poem, and still less a metaphysic that would presume either to unify or to select among the multiple visions of reality disclosed through poetic metaphor. I think it is accurate to say that the fundamental sense of reality Wheelwright believes poetry as a whole conveys is the sense that reality as humans can know and express it is not at all unified and not at all amenable to systematic expression. In fact, therefore, the only "ontology" Wheelwright sees as warranted by a sensitive response to the worlds of literary art is one that sees reality as irreducibly plural. His reason for maintaining this is that he believes poetic assertions concerning reality are all different, yet all in some way true, and all strictly beyond comparison and criticism, being concrete and particular rather than abstract and general.

Even disregarding the fact that it is difficult to reconcile the above claims with Wheelwright's belief (expressed elsewhere) that some poems are "deeper" and "more pertinent" than others, and with his conviction that certain ontological facts are, after all, "primary"—"facts" like transcendence, personhood, and metamorphosis, for instance—the particular conclusions Wheelwright reaches in the context of formulating his ontology are now surely to be considered suspect. For they are canceled out if one accepts those semantic theories of his that have been confirmed so far by our study of *Four Quartets*. We have validated, for example, Wheelwright's insight that poetry can incorporate to a significant degree the assertorial properties of steno-language and hence (to some degree) the capacity to hold out a particular view of reality as in certain ways more truthful than another. My reading of *Four Quartets* indicates, in fact, that one cannot fully appreciate the unique quality of the reality claims intrinsic to it if one insists from the start that they must be "irreducibly particular." To regard Eliot's poetic assertion that "only through time time is conquered" as a statement necessarily devoid of general significance, and therefore as narrowly and only "contextually true," is clearly to misrepresent the poetic intent and to shut oneself off from the poem's full ontological import. One is not asked to decide in a clear-cut fashion whether the *Quartets'* understanding of the possibilities of temporal existence is true, or even if it is true to Christianity, but one is asked to take that understanding seriously. In order to do that, one must be able to assent to the possibility that this particular expressive language is deeper or more comprehensive than some other. That is, if one is to make a sensitive and serious response to the work, one must take seriously the generality of the work's insistence that not all approaches to the reality of time and eternity—and not even all "deep" approaches—are equally true. This is something Wheelwright's meta-poetic ontology will not allow him to do, but it is also something that, by using his semantic theories, we ourselves certainly may do.

This will become still more apparent as I spell out in a more precise fashion how the semantic principles we have seen to be operative in *Four Quartets* fit into the work's larger dynamic structure of metaphoric assertion, interpretation, and even argumentation. Our further examination of this aspect of the poetry will support my own extension and modification of Wheelwright's semantic theories and, at the same time, will provide a surer basis for understanding how poetic transfigurations of language and experience can generate insights of intrinsic worth to formal religious and metaphysical reflection.

Chapter Four The Dynamics of Poetic Structure

Four Quartets (II)

Words, after speech, reach
Into the silence.
—"Burnt Norton": V

Having followed the evolution of the rose-garden theme from its first appearance in "Burnt Norton" to its transfiguration as the midwinter spring in "Little Gidding," we can undertake a more thorough examination of certain essential aspects of the structure of *Four Quartets* as a whole. My goal, therefore, is to look carefully now at the design and primary poetic purpose of the five-part sequence common to all of the poems in the cycle and crucial to the structure of the entire work. If, in doing so, I continue to be indebted to Philip Wheelwright's semantic theories, I also continue to extend and modify these theories, pursuing their implications even when I am led to conclusions very different from Wheelwright's own. Thus, I alter the picture Wheelwright gives of poetic wholes and their structure. I suggest that the *Quartets* in some sense actually theologizes. And I maintain that, even though the poetry does (in Eliot's words) "after speech, reach / Into the silence," such silence is not what Wheelwright would sometimes have us believe—namely, a mute but knowing sense of reality totally beyond critical reflection and conceptual analysis. Silence of this kind, encompassing the internalization of the poetic transfiguration of experience, eventually leads back to words. The poetic itself can then be transfigured in a different sort of speech: a philosophical or perhaps theological "raid on the inarticulate" that is somehow both more and less than the poetry and silence from which it emerges. Although I conclude with this last point, at present I intend to show in what way the basic structure of the *Quartets* permits this work simultaneously to embody religious beliefs and assertions and yet to move beyond theology, or formal religious reflection, to reach into the silence.

"Approach to the Meaning": Poetic Representation

It has been the general consensus of criticism that no interpretation of *Four Quartets* and of its inner dynamics can afford to ignore the five-part form common to all the poems in the cycle. Whether described in musical terms or in terms of thematic or symbolic patterning, this aspect of the poetic structure has been recognized as crucial to the meaning and effect of each quartet.[1] Furthermore, it is a peculiarity of *Four Quartets* that the kind of progression found in this five-part sequence, and thus incorporated by each poem in its own distinctive way, is also characteristic of the cycle of poems as a whole. This means, however, that what the reader or critic most needs to note is not that the poetic form has exactly five parts (obviously the cycle itself has only four) but that it indeed constitutes a sequence containing, and perhaps representing, a definite progression the nature of which deserves investigation.

With this observation we have hit upon the chief weakness of many otherwise excellent studies of the *Quartets* and the chief reason why most such studies can be of little help to us at this point in our inquiry. Any number of critics have described with great acumen various features of each of the poems in the cycle: the major ideas; the thematic, rhythmic, or "musical" patterns; the imagery; and the literary, philosophical, and theological sources. All have naturally noted that the various features of the poetry are organized into a five-part form in which the poetic materials are spun out and interwoven in a variety of ways. But these same critics have not been notably successful in determining how this "form" is integrally related to an overall poetic purpose and so actually formative of some kind of coherent progression. In short, they have not talked about how the elements of the poetry are basically *formed* but merely about how they are organized.[2]

In this respect Philip Wheelwright's critical practice is as inadequate as anyone else's and his semantic theory almost as undeveloped. During the course of Wheelwright's analysis of *Four Quartets*, he assumes that he can describe the essential semantic properties of the work without seeing how its parts function to create a certain kind of progression and a distinctive, unified whole.[3] Presumably convinced that the different sections of each poem simply indicate shifts in style, mood, or theme, Wheelwright gives his attention to semantic units that he regards as more essential to the poetic meaning, these being various ideas and images. The whole poem, for Wheelwright, simply results from the interrelationship between such component parts. Clearly it is not something he thinks of as in any real sense *determining* the semantic function of those parts, much as a whole piano constitutes the "end" and purpose determining how the sounding board is made and the hammers adjusted. Even when Wheelwright speaks of the *Quartets* as incorporating a structure of assertion, he does not see that structure as shaped by the intention of reaching any "conclusions"; certainly he does not see it as any form of argument and thus as informed by a rhetorical or dialectical goal and method. The poem's "total assertion" tends to be, in his view, little more than the consequence of the tensive interaction between component assertions having different assertorial weights and expressive traits. As he says: "Rhythm and ideation, song and vision, collaborate in the poetic act; and their tension motivates—perhaps even *is*—the poem."[4] If a poem is best described as only the semantic tension created by its parts, it becomes unnecessary to say why its parts are ordered in a certain way. One will only say that they constitute "a pattern of living themes," or an organic structure of symbols and images, or a network of "poeto-philosophical ideas."[5] One will want to say that a poem is all these things, but one will not say how these things are all made into a whole. And because one will not and cannot say this, one is unable to show exactly how a work like the *Quartets* in its entirety, or any poem internal to it, functions as an overall metaphoric assertion having a particular purpose and import.

Anyone very familiar with the literary criticism of the past quarter century will hear in the above critique of the critics an echo from what has often been called "neo-Aristotelian" criticism.[6] Perhaps it is no accident, then, that the essay that I think may go furthest toward providing a satisfactory account of the five-part sequence common to all the *Quartets* is one written from what is basically a neo-Aristotelian point of view. Because even the weaknesses of this essay point toward the kind of interpretation I myself eventually propose, I would like to consider the main theses of this piece of criticism.

In his article entitled "Character and Action in *Four Quartets*," William T. Moynihan argues—in terms partly derived from Eliot's own criticism—that the aim of the *Quartets* is not primarily to present a philosophy, as would be the case in a didactic poem, but to dramatize what it "feels like to believe."[7] To this end, the work depicts an action, which is an act of meditation in which the speaker wrestles with his thoughts and emotions in an attempt to "grasp the meaning of the Divine Logos."[8] The five-part form of each quartet "presents the speaker following an almost ritualistic sequence of insight, loss, searching, praying, and an ending in climactic perception."[9] In fact, Moynihan sees the spiritual exploration presented in this sequence as nothing less than a progression toward a mystical vision—albeit muted, understated, and peculiarly English. He makes his case by arguing that the five sections of each poem depict levels of awareness and action that closely resemble the five stages in the development of mystical awareness described by Evelyn Underhill in her influential book *Mysticism*.[10]

Moynihan is insistent, however, that the reader who is sensitive to the nature of these poems is not so much concerned with the content of that mystical illumination per se as with the relation of the mystical experience to the character of the speaker and how he orders his reflections.[11] The five-part sequence is not primarily one of ideas or beliefs, however mystically illumined, but of the speaker's experience of such ideas and beliefs. It seeks to convey not thought but "the emotional quality of the speaker's thought."[12]

These claims, I will grant, are not altogether new, and they may not seem especially remarkable. In some ways, therefore, it is regrettable that I have had to pass over much that is of more obvious interest in Moynihan's essay. But I believe that if we carefully assess these particular claims we will be well on our way to a better understanding of the structure and purpose of each poem in the *Quartets*, although that understanding may be, in the end, very different from Moynihan's own.

To begin with, Moynihan points out an important feature of the form of the *Quartets* when he states that the sequence within each poem presents an action in five parts. This observation is significant because it means that everything within each poem contributes to what Aristotle and his disciples would call an "imitation of an action"—or, as I will put it, a metaphoric representation. The five-part form itself is thus not simply a stylistic convention, nor is it, on the other hand, a vehicle for the direct outpouring of the poet's actual thoughts and feelings. Although the poem is written in the first person and certainly expresses thoughts and feelings Eliot himself would claim as part of his experience, there are subtle but critical differences between the poetic speaker and Eliot. The speaker is a persona, one who is intimately related to the actual poet but who sometimes knows, thinks, feels, and believes not as the actual poet does but much as the poet did in his past. Furthermore, the thoughts, the feelings, and the very world of the poem are in various ways altered, or "distanced," from their counterparts in actuality. It is as though the poem were a stage, a metaphoric world, from which Eliot speaks as an actor and to which he always refers, even when he also thereby refers to the world beyond that stage. Likewise, the parts of the poem resemble acts of a play. This does not mean Helen Gardner is wrong when she states that *Four Quartets* "presents a series of meditations upon existence in time";[13] it is only to say that here the mode of meditating is to employ a semblance, a metaphoric representation, of the act of meditation.

The second valuable aspect of Moynihan's analysis is his observation that, because each quartet is structured in such a way as to represent an action, every element within each poem qualifies the reader's perception of the character of the poetic speaker. In this way even the most abstract ideas presented in the poem are seen in relation to their meaning for the existence of a fictive being who is represented as feeling and willing as well as thinking. This again indicates that, as I have contended all along, the conceptual or "steno-" content of the poem is qualified by a context that both interprets, and is interpreted by, that content.

The third point of special insight in Moynihan's essay is his tacit recognition not only that the five parts of each poem trace a spiritual exploration but also that this exploration is the kind of quest that would in actuality encompass years of a person's life, if not the whole of it. Anyone who really could, in meditating for a mere two hundred lines or so, pass from a life of marginal belief and deep despair to a life of faith and vision would be a prime candidate for sainthood. And this, we may safely say, the poetic speaker is not. What the poem evidently presents is a metaphoric representation, rather than a literal exemplification, of an essentially religious quest.

In addition to containing these insights, however, Moynihan's essay exhibits in a revealing way the problematical status of certain theoretical and practical assumptions that my own analysis of the *Quartets* is specifically meant to challenge. The first and most important of these has to do with the question of what poetic purpose might be served by a poetic representation like that found in each of the quartets. In dealing with this question Moynihan is trapped within a theoretical framework that, if accepted, would invalidate the basic premises of the semantic theory I have been working to substantiate and amplify. For, once Moynihan has determined that none of the quartets is primarily interested in ideas in themselves, he draws the conclusion that this is poetry primarily concerned with feelings; it presents the "emotional equivalent of thought." Moynihan justifies this thesis not only by appealing to Eliot's well-known views [14] but also by relying on a kind of distinction repeatedly made by neo-Aristotelian critics— that is, the distinction between mimetic and didactic art. Moynihan plainly is arguing that the poetry of *Four Quartets* is mimetic instead of didactic. What this means, in his view, is not that the *Quartets* makes no use of ideas but that it always uses them only in order to "mime the emotional quality of the speaker's thought" rather than to reflect on actuality or to make assertions about the world beyond the poem. [15] The sole alternative Moynihan sees would be for the poem to be strictly didactic. In that case it might make use of fictions or "imitated" actions but only so as to persuade or argue more effectively. Translated into Wheelwright's terminology, Moynihan's assumption is that mimetic poetry has no assertorial weight while didactic poetry has, in the end, the same weight as a steno-proposition or logical argument. [16] Because Moynihan considers the *Quartets* to be mimetic, his analysis does not consider that the work might also function as an assertion.

Needless to say, the entire thrust of my argument in this book opposes such a dichotomy, whether set up to divide poetry from other kinds of discourse or to divide one kind of poetry from another. Indeed, having accepted and amplified Wheelwright's critique of such concepts of language, we may at this point find it somewhat difficult to see why it was ever thought necessary to make an absolute distinction between mimetic and didactic literature. Why not simply see the distinction as one of degree? Upon further reflection, however, we can see that this distinction was established in order to answer a question Wheelwright himself appears not even to consider. Put simply, the question is this: Assuming that a poem like "East Coker" must have a single, unifying purpose informing its overall structure, how could such a work include a genuinely dialectical or "argumentative" strategy as well as one that is dramatic or "imitative"? For if it did, would it not have a dual purpose, and would not the work then be divided rather than unified? The neo-Aristotelians believe that this would in fact be the consequence.

It would take us far afield to challenge this conclusion now in the depth required fully to expose its faulty foundations. Yet it is important to observe here that the neo-Aristotelians' conclusion is warranted only if one accepts their assumption that no single purpose could be served by a work that combined genuine assertion with genuine imitation and that reduced neither one to the other. This assumption is surely questionable, however. Even if one holds that a chief end of literature is cognition or insight, one might suppose, with Wheelwright and many other thinkers, that certain basic understandings derive not from linguistic structures concerned exclusively with truth but rather from structures of tentative exploration and imaginative invention. One could then argue that a synthesis of assertion and metaphoric representation (that is, "imitation") is required if such understandings are to be attained. A semantic structure that was purely mimetic or purely didactic would be seen as simply inadequate to convey insight of a certain kind.

But one need not have the cognitive dimension of literature foremost in mind in order to imagine a poetic purpose for which assertion and representation—and also thought and feeling—would be necessary and irreducible components. One need only conceive of the reader as a being who, as a whole person, is more than the sum of all the discrete activities in which the person is engaged. In other words, if one thinks of the human self as a vital unity of thought and feeling, knowing and willing, acting and imagining—as, indeed, analogous to a "purpose" informing and formed by all these modes of experience—then it makes sense that there should be a medium designed to express and address that self as a whole. It also makes sense that this medium should do so by transforming and unifying the various functions of language, these having been isolated precisely in order to let the human being carry out tasks for which that being as a whole is not needed and not wanted. Poetry, we can then speculate, is just such a medium. If this is true, then the power of poetry, or what Aristotle would call its *dynamis*, is its capacity to provide a particular engagement—sometimes playful, sometimes serious—of the whole self. The "end" of poetry, in keeping with this power, is no less definite and unified than pleasure or cognition alone. It is merely more complex.

Sketchy as it is, the above argument at least indicates a basis for disputing Moynihan's assumption that a quartet cannot be a genuine assertion if it is a genuine mimetic whole. But this is not to deny the validity of Moynihan's procedure of attending to the nature of what is represented in the *Quartets* before attempting to judge exactly what the purpose of the work might be.

There is obviously much to commend Moynihan's thesis that each quartet presents the spiritual struggle and progress of a "finite center," a human being, seeking to discover his relationship to the ultimate Center. But I think we must now question Moynihan's theory that the five parts of each quartet show the speaker progressing toward a kind of mystical union, and in fact following essentially the same steps toward such union that Evelyn Underhill discusses in her book *Mysticism*.[17] This argument is potentially seductive because it does at first appear quite plausible. Even if one realizes that the correspondence Moynihan finds between the third part of each quartet and the third stage of the mystic's progress is based on an outright misinterpretation of Underhill, Moynihan's basic claim may seem reasonable enough.[18] It is no accident, after all, that *Four Quartets* has frequently been interpreted as mystical literature.[19] It does undeniably refer to mystical experience, and it alludes to and quotes from various classics of mysticism: Buddhist and Hindu scriptures, *The Cloud of Unknowing*, the writings of St. John of the Cross, the "shewings" of Mother Julian of Norwich, and the like. Certain passages even seem to embody, through their very imagery, some kind of mystical vision. We know, furthermore—although Moynihan seems unaware of this himself—that Eliot read widely in mysticism when he was an undergraduate at Harvard and that he later made the acquaintance of Evelyn Underhill, whose book on mysticism he already knew as a landmark of scholarship on the subject.[20] It thus seems plausible that the progression represented by stages in the *Quartets* should have some connection with mysticism.

But it may be that the connection is much less direct than Moynihan and others have supposed. As Moynihan admits, the main goal of the poetic speaker's effort to order his present life and thought is never depicted by Eliot as being mystical rapture, however muted and "reserved." Nor, for that matter, is the goal that contrasting kind of union with God sought in the "apophatic" mystic tradition and described therein as a special darkness and emptiness;[21] for the phases of darkness are not seen in any of the quartets as the ultimate destination, nor as times in which the speaker is at one with God. Lastly, Moynihan (and countless other critics) would have done well to notice that the speaker in the *Quartets* is never in fact represented as having progressed beyond the third step of the ten that St. John of the Cross describes in his discussion of the ladder by which the soul ascends to God.[22] Since St. John of the Cross is the source for Eliot's lengthiest quotation from mystical literature, it should not pass unmarked that this quotation, found in "East Coker" III, is taken from a passage concerning the very first stage of the journey toward God—a stage that is prior to faith itself.

All of which suggests that perhaps the speaker in the poem is not destined to be a mystic and that the brief moments of quasi-mystical experience known by the speaker function in a different way in his life from the way they would in the life of one whose "occupation" is to "apprehend / The point of intersection of the timeless / With time" (DS:V). This thesis is further corroborated by the obvious fact that the "I" of the *Quartets* is essentially a representation of Eliot himself, who can hardly be said to have seen himself as a full-fledged mystic. The overall sequence of thoughts and feelings presented in each poem seems, therefore, to represent a development within the experience not of an aspiring mystic but simply of a thoughtful and sensitive human being and poet whose life includes moments of special and seemingly transcendent significance.

But this still leaves us with the question of just what kind of development within thought and experience these poems might represent. The very fact that there could be some question as to this, and even as to whether the sequence found in the poems is related to a sequence within life experience at all, indicates that the poetry represents its "subject" in a highly condensed and metaphoric way, rather as a postimpressionist painting might depict its "subject." One is aware of the way the medium is used before one is fully aware of what it represents. With the *Quartets*, however, one must be able to discern what is represented if one is fully to appreciate the significance of the way it is presented. Fortunately, the kind of experiential and meditative sequence that is indeed being represented in the *Quartets* begins to be evident when we carefully consider the well-known essay Eliot wrote on Pascal and published in 1931, just a few years before he began work on "Burnt Norton."[23]

"The Sequence Which Culminates in Faith"

It has been said more than once that Pascal's *Pensées* may be read as a preface to *Four Quartets*.[24] Be that as it may, I am persuaded that at least the essay Eliot wrote to introduce the *Pensées* may be read in this way. In particular, I think that Staffan Bergsten puts us on the right track when he observes that Eliot's characterization of Pascal as an intelligent believer writing of the progress of the intellectual soul seems to be a perfect characterization of the later Eliot himself.[25] But Bergsten does not go much beyond this broad statement. Furthermore, he misunderstands Eliot to be saying in his essay that Pascal is "the counterpart and forerunner of the modern Christian mystic"[26]—which is certainly not the case.

If we look beyond Bergsten to Eliot's essay itself, we will find a very different picture of Pascal's own so-called mysticism. More important, we will discover that the essay serves in at least two other respects to shed light on the action represented in the *Quartets*. First, as Bergsten hints, Eliot's portrait of Pascal in the essay bears a remarkable resemblance to his portrait of the poetic speaker—and hence of himself—in each quartet. Second, the purpose and reflective structure that Eliot attributes to the *Pensées* is, as we will see, revealingly similar to that which is exhibited by each of the quartets and by the work as a whole.

Pascal, Eliot declares early in his essay, was a man who had mystical experiences without being a mystic. But this is not unusual, Eliot says, for "what can only be called mystical experience happens to many men who do not become mystics." Indeed, something roughly analogous to such an experience sometimes occurs in literary composition when "a piece of writing meditated, apparently without progress, for months or years, may suddenly take shape and word." What Eliot finds more noteworthy than Pascal's mystical experience per se is the fact that Pascal was a person who was at once "highly passionate and ardent, but passionate only through a powerful and regulated intellect"; he was a person whose "intellectual passion for truth" was reinforced by "his passionate dissatisfaction with human life unless a spiritual explanation could be found." The rigor of Pascal's intellect, combined with the intensity of his passion for a "spiritual explanation," meant that he would at times despair of himself and others. Standing as "a man of the world among ascetics, and an ascetic among men of the world," he delivered a skeptical and disillusioned analysis of human bondage. But, Eliot insists, Pascal's skepticism should be distinguished, on account of its penetration and integrity, from the skepticism of the ordinary unbeliever, who is "lazy-minded, incurious, absorbed in vanities, and tepid in emotion, and is therefore incapable of either much doubt or much faith." Pascal's analysis of human bondage, while disillusioned, is nonetheless perceptive; indeed, Eliot says, "our heart tells us that it corresponds exactly to the facts and cannot be dismissed as mental disease." Eliot observes, moreover, that for people like Pascal the moments of despair and skepticism are "the analogue of the drought, the dark night, which is an essential stage in the progress of the Christian mystic"; thus they are "a necessary prelude to, and element in, the joy of faith."[27] In Pascal's case, therefore, we see a skepticism that neither "stops at the question" nor "ends in denial," but leads to faith and "is somehow integrated into the faith which transcends it"—a faith in the Incarnation.

· And what of the *Pensées*—those vivid and provocative fragments that were eventually to have constituted an apology for Christianity? Eliot emphasizes that Pascal wrote these not primarily as a scientist or systematic philosopher, nor even as an academic theologian constructing a work of formal apologetics, but as "a great literary artist" whose major work would, if completed, "have been also his own spiritual autobiography." It is written in a style that Eliot describes as "free from all diminishing idiosyncrasies, [and] yet very personal." Eliot acknowledges, of course, that Pascal intended for the *Pensées* to have a theological, apologetic function. Yet, Eliot claims, Pascal's first and essential aim in this crowning work was "to explain to himself the sequence which culminates in faith," and to do so with the heart as well as the head, because, for Pascal, "in theological matters which seemed to him much larger, more difficult, and more important than scientific matters, the whole personality is involved." His work would thus have universal significance not by being impersonal but by addressing at a personal level matters of universal import. Pascal could do this because he himself was, in Eliot's view, representative of a certain kind of person who is found in every age—the doubting intellectual soul—and because he used a method of exploring the basis of faith that is, on the whole, "the method natural and right for the Christian." For all these reasons, Eliot concludes, there is "no religious writer more pertinent to our time":

> The great mystics, like St. John of the Cross, are primarily for readers with a special determination of purpose; the devotional writers, such as St. François de Sales, are primarily for those who already feel consciously desirous of the love of God; the great theologians are for those interested in theology. But I can think of no Christian writer . . . more to be commended than Pascal to those who doubt, but who have the mind to conceive, and the sensibility to feel, the disorder, the futility, the meaninglessness, the mystery of life and suffering, and who can only find peace through a satisfaction of the whole being. (*Selected Essays*, [1951], p. 416)

I have quoted at length from Eliot's own words partly because they convey with such force how keenly Eliot feels Pascal's contemporary relevance and partly because they reveal the extent to which Pascal's personality and concerns, when seen through Eliot's eyes, are related to Eliot himself and the concerns embodied in the *Quartets*. One cannot help being struck by the fact that almost every major aspect of Eliot's portrait of Pascal has its correlative in Eliot's own self-portrait in the *Quartets*. In these poems the speaker, who naturally represents Eliot, is like Pascal in being passionate, "but passionate only through a powerful and regulated intellect." Like Pascal, he is an intellectual soul whose passion is for truth and for a spiritual explanation for his life and for reality as he finds it. He is ascetic, and yet a man of the world; a man given mystical experiences, but not a mystic; a skeptic, and yet one whose skepticism "is somehow integrated into the faith which transcends it." Although he is deeply convinced of human bondage and vanity and is scornful of the skepticism of the ordinary unbeliever, his despair and disillusionment do not lead him to a thoroughgoing pessimism like Voltaire's but, rather, to a state that is analogous to the mystic's dark night of the soul, this being an "essential stage" in his progress. Finally, the "I" who speaks in the *Quartets* is a literary artist who is proceeding toward the goal that Eliot considers to be Pascal's as well—faith in the Incarnation.

The parallels extend beyond this similarity between Eliot's poetic persona and his image of Pascal, however. Judging solely from what our study has shown so far, it seems at least plausible that the *Quartets* itself and each poem therein could be characterized in somewhat the same way that Eliot characterizes the *Pensées*. Every quartet appears to be a kind of spiritual autobiography, or a portion of one, having a theological component. Each one is written in a style that is "free from all diminishing idiosyncrasies" and yet is very "personal." And *Four Quartets* could surely be seen as addressing primarily the same audience to whom Eliot so fervently commends the *Pensées*. For the *Quartets*, although dealing with spiritual and theological matters, is not mystical literature "for readers with a special determination of purpose," nor devotional literature "for those who already feel consciously desirous of the love of God," nor is it simply a work for those "interested in theology." Instead, *Four Quartets* appears to address the mind and sensibility of that person "who can only find peace through a satisfaction of the whole being." I would now advance the hypothesis that it does this by exploring, in each poem, not the way to mystic union with God but simply "the sequence which culminates in faith." That, of course, is precisely what Eliot claims the *Pensées* is intended to do.

But what might that sequence be? And how might a Christian poet go about reconstructing, through the structure of a poem, the essential elements of that sequence? Almost midway through his essay on Pascal, Eliot describes what he understands to be the essence of the procedure that Pascal—and, generally speaking, any intelligent believer—uses in explaining to himself this very sequence. According to Eliot, such a person

> . . . finds the world to be so and so; he finds its character inexplicable by any non-religious theory: among religions he finds Christianity, and Catholic Christianity, to account most satisfactorily for the world and especially for the moral world within; and thus, by what Newman calls "powerful and concurrent" reasons, he finds himself inexorably committed to the dogma of the Incarnation. (*Selected Essays*, [1951], p. 408)

Even prior to examining the specific structure of any of the quartets, we can easily see that there is at least one important respect in which this kind of reflective project resembles Eliot's project of poetic exploration, or does so when looked at from Eliot's perspective. The project described above is that of someone who, from a standpoint within faith, is both reexpressing for himself and others the basis for faith in the Incarnation and also tracing the development of his own religious awareness as it has been "inexorably" drawn toward that faith. Like the *Quartets*, this project has about it a certain interesting ambiguity: its author sees the progression toward faith from a Christian point of view, but at the same time he explores it in such a way as to reexperience it in the present; he "*finds* himself inexorably committed," as though he were not already. Thus Eliot says that, in writing the first sections of the *Pensées*, Pascal is actually (again) "facing unflinchingly the demon of doubt which is inseparable from the spirit of belief" (p. 411). And so, one feels, is the author of the first section of each quartet.

It could fairly be objected that the method described above sounds too formal and intellectual to be used in literature. Certainly Eliot himself never claims this is a peculiarly literary method. But he does indicate that it is nevertheless the means by which Pascal reflects on the essential moments of his spiritual progress and is thus the skeleton upon which Pascal fleshes out his *Pensées*, a work that Eliot describes as indeed literary, and more literary than theological. Furthermore, as we have seen, Eliot explicitly informs us that Pascal's method is the one that is "natural and right" for the Christian who is meditating on the sequence that leads to faith. This is particularly significant in view of the fact that it is, after all, Eliot himself who formulates "Pascal's" method by making inferences from the relatively unsystematic arrangement of the fragments Pascal left us. Thus it is Eliot who thereby makes it sound as though Pascal's topics lead in a logical and linear sequence toward the doctrine of the Incarnation.[28] Whereas the truth of the matter is that—as one modern account of Pascal's approach makes clear—the "method" actually used in the *Pensées* is scarcely more logical and direct than the "method" of *Four Quartets* itself, when considered as a whole: "Pascal's method is deliberately not linear, and consists of converging arguments, all directed to the same end but with different starting points. In his own words: 'Jesus Christ is the object of all things, the centre towards which all things tend.'"[29] If Eliot could attribute to Pascal the method that Eliot himself formulates in his essay, we are surely justified in attributing to Eliot the capacity for using some such method in his own literary meditation on the sequence that culminates in faith.

The sequence as it is described above, however, is largely a sequence of thoughts; it is a mode of rational explanation. In what follows I intend to show that the five-part sequence found in the individual quartets includes this sequence but only as a kind of bare framework that the poetry fills out. This the poetry does by representing through image, idea, and metaphor the same kinds of thoughts and experiences that Eliot describes in his essay when he elaborates on what each stage of this sequence in fact involves and, especially, when he discusses Pascal's own personal journey toward faith. To make this evident, I will first outline the general structure of the "action" common to all the poems. I will then examine in detail how one of the quartets represents "the sequence which culminates in faith" while incorporating that sequence into a kind of metaphoric argument.

In each quartet the poetic speaker[30] begins his meditative reflection at the point where Eliot says Pascal begins—that is, by observing his world to be "so and so." In point of fact, he finds the world of his experience to be bound within the limits of time and yet also inexplicably graced by quasi-mystical moments seemingly transcendent of time. He therefore recognizes, in section I, certain basic limitations and tantalizing possibilities of human life, and at least implicitly expresses his dissatisfaction with such life "unless a spiritual explanation . . . be found." Hence, one senses from the first of each quartet that the speaker's search is not for an abstract understanding of time but for a "satisfaction of the whole being."

In section II the speaker generally meditates further on the contrast between the possibilities glimpsed in section I and his ordinary experience of life and the lives of others, these lives being characterized by vacuity, vanity, and meaningless, *ec*-centric movement. His perceptions, that is to say, are fully in accordance with what Eliot in his essay says someone like Pascal discovers when he examines the world within and about himself. Even more than before, he becomes intensely aware that the harmony of things that he can still envision and (as it were) remember has been either disrupted or lost; the still point of eternity seems at present separate from the chaotic movements of history. While the disillusioned speaker finds this condition unacceptable, it seems that no "spiritual explanation," or at least no direct way "up" from this condition of bondage, is available to him. He can only acknowledge that—as Eliot explains in reference to this stage of Pascal's awareness—"certain developments of character, and what in the highest sense can be called 'saintliness' are inherently and by inspection known to be good" (p. 408). The conviction and action that would be fully in accordance with this awareness are yet to come.

When we reach section III an important change occurs, or seems already to have occurred. After again reflecting on "human bondage" and human-ity's empty striving for self-possession and self-love, the speaker acts on a newfound religious conviction. Drawing on various religious, and indeed mystic, ways of interpreting "right action" and human possibility, the speaker now seeks to empty himself of empty self-possession and to move away from chaotic movement. He thus pursues a *via negativa*—a "way down" by means of negation, nonaction, humility, discipline, and a pro-found emptying of self, sense, and desire. Only in this way, the speaker seems to feel, can grace find one and grant the beginning of love and wisdom, the "way down" thereby becoming the "way up." Hence the speaker, like the Pascal of Eliot's essay, begins at this stage to turn toward specifically religious ways of understanding and being; but, in order to do so, he must enter a stage that is analogous to the mystic's dark night of the soul and that is an essential "moment" in his progress.

Section IV is the shortest one in every poem, but it is always of utmost importance. Here the speaker utters a kind of prayer, and in fact a Chris-tian prayer, addressed—if only implicitly—either to some person, or per-sons, of the Trinity or to Mary. (Eliot's Christianity, like Pascal's, is essen-tially Catholic, although Eliot's Catholicism is Anglican.) This prayer marks the crucial point at which the speaker turns toward not only religion but also an identifiably Christian answer to his deeply felt need. In all of the poems except "Burnt Norton," moreover, this answer is presented in its most challenging, "scandalous," and paradoxical form—one bound to be a stumbling block of apparent foolishness to anyone not prepared to abandon prior "sense and notion." Yet there is evidently a sense in which, for the speaker, this paradoxical answer most fully takes into account the world of his experience and especially what Eliot terms "the moral world within." The answer approached by the speaker is consequently not seen as totally irrational; the reasons are simply those of the heart.

The fifth and final section of every quartet shows the speaker's medita-tive journey as similar to Pascal's in leading "inexorably" and by heartfelt "concurrent reasons" toward Incarnation. At the beginning of this section, the speaker confesses the poverty of language and laments his plight as a poet trying to say what can never precisely be said and therefore having always to make yet another "raid on the inarticulate." Clearly the speaker now believes that it is only through something like an act of grace that the right word or sentence or poem is discovered at all. No final linguistic formula is bequeathed to the present by history or by the saints, but only an attitude—an "approach to the meaning"—and "hints and guesses." But, following this humble account of the limited powers of language, the speaker moves on to celebrate the reality of what has nevertheless been discovered, offering his recollection (or "recapitulation") of the major significant experiences (or "themes") that have acted powerfully and concurrently to guide his search. Inevitably they appear in a new light, radiant with heightened significance. The old pattern is seen in transfigured form. Its meaning is comprehended, however darkly, and in fact comprehended within the framework of Christian faith. Thus, even in the first two quartets, the speaker returns with fuller knowledge to the place from which his meditative journey started. But Eliot's beginning point in each successive quartet is progressively closer to an explicitly Christian understanding of things. It is especially at the end of the whole cycle, therefore, that the speaker clearly apprehends the earlier moments of special, "mystical" awareness in a new way. He sees them not as ends in themselves, nor merely as ephemeral occasions of transcendent happiness, but as signs of grace present in (while not restricted to) the natural, temporal order. In short, they themselves are recognized as minor instances of Incarnation, the reality toward which Eliot describes Pascal's own search as ultimately moving. And it is, finally, in the light of Incarnation that the speaker is able to arrive at a transfigured view of temporality and eternity and so to approach a new mode of being—one that can be patient with penultimate goals like poetic art and loving with temporal creation and, lastly, hopeful of the new time when "all shall be well." This mode of being is not so much that of the mystic and saint as it is simply that of a person of faith.

What I have described above seems, then, to be the basic "action" or "subject" represented differently in each of the quartets. This is not to say that we find a one-to-one correlation between what is depicted in each section of each poem and the steps by which Eliot's Pascal is said to move toward faith and toward an understanding of his spiritual progress. But it should be apparent that the progression represented in these poems contains the essential moments of what Eliot in his essay calls "the sequence which culminates in faith." [31] In each poem the speaker surveys the ambiguities of his experience of the world, reaches conclusions as how best to understand that experience, embraces a religious and then specifically Christian mode of response, and finally glimpses the true meaning of Incarnation. In each poem this process is described in many of the same terms used by Eliot to describe Pascal's personal experience.

That the broad outlines of this pattern can likewise be discerned in the development of *Four Quartets* as a whole should also be apparent. As we saw in chapter 3, the overall tenor of the poems changes from "Burnt Norton" to "Little Gidding." In the former poem the Christian elements are symbolically suggested rather than overtly expressed, the problematic or ambiguous perceptions of life receiving more emphasis than the hopeful and distinctly religious. With each quartet, however, the speaker's beginning point is located ever closer to the sphere of conscious faith and obedience until even the opening "vision" of "Little Gidding" has about it a quasi-Christian ambience, although it is far removed from that of devotional literature and further still from the eschatological union of fire and rose envisioned in the last lines of the poem. Considered as a whole, therefore, *Four Quartets* can be seen to represent in a highly condensed and metaphoric way the thoughts and feelings intrinsic to the "progress of an intellectual soul" like Pascal and like Eliot himself.

But if it is true that both Pascal and Eliot explore, in their respective works, essentially the same phenomenon, then we are directly confronted with certain questions that can only be dealt with by examining Eliot's poetry still more closely. The most obvious question is how Pascal's purpose in writing the *Pensées* is related to Eliot's purpose in writing *Four Quartets*. Although Eliot is surely correct in considering the *Pensées* to be literary and autobiographical, even he recognizes that Pascal's literary meditations include certain definite assertions and arguments. These assertions and arguments are to a large extent genuinely theological, despite their lack of systematic organization. One might even say that everything in the *Pensées* has, in the final analysis, the purpose of defending the Christian faith and of illuminating the reasons that lead one to belief in the Incarnation. If Pascal's meditations are literary, therefore, they are so in a special sense. The primary purpose of their literary and even autobiographical features is to contribute to his work's capacity to declare a truth, indeed the ultimate truth. Using Wheelwright's terminology, we may say that Pascal's writing is "light" in one sense but "heavy" in another. His assertions are "light" in that they frequently transgress against the norms of steno-language, being neither strictly empirical nor strictly logical, neither univocal nor completely unambiguous. They are thus not ordinary propositions, nor do they make for strictly rational or scientific argumentation. Pascal's reasoning is often of the heart; it uses what Eliot elsewhere calls a "logic of imagination" as much as a "logic of concepts."[32] But if Pascal's work is not highly steno-linguistic in this way, in another way it is just that. For, however literary it may be, Pascal's writing is almost completely declarative. Its purpose is to make known a truth, to express thoughts (*pensées*). Almost every "expressive" trait within his language is, in the end, didactic, and as heavily assertorial as any unit of steno-language.

Now a similar statement could be made, I think, concerning Eliot's "Choruses from *The Rock*," written shortly before "Burnt Norton." And given the parallels we have discovered between the *Pensées* and the *Quartets*, the possibility certainly exists that each of the quartets is likewise exclusively concerned with disclosing a truth of some kind, even if that truth could not be stated in nonpoetic terms. Furthermore, it is possible that this truth would be of importance to theology. Thus, as we move further into our analysis of the structure of representation found in each of the quartets, we are pressed to raise questions as to the final purpose immanent within this representation: Is *Four Quartets* as a whole concerned with truth as such? If so, is it truth that is felt, truth that can be thought, or truth that must be both felt and thought? For that matter, is it a truth that the theologian also seeks to express? Does the work exist, then, solely for the sake of this truth, this ontological disclosure? These questions are certainly pertinent to any inquiry into the relation of the *Quartets* to theological and metaphysical discourse, and they will reappear in different forms in the remaining chapters. But they are questions for which I as yet have provided only partial answers. What I have said so far has mostly to do with poetic structure and representation. I have succeeded in determining *whether* each quartet represents something, since it now is apparent that it does. And I have determined *what* it is in general that each quartet represents, this being an exploration that culminates in faith. As yet, however, I have not determined exactly *how* it represents this action, and until this is done there is no telling exactly *for what purpose* the action is represented. Thus it is at least theoretically possible that *Four Quartets* may indeed have essentially the same purpose as Pascal's *Pensées*.

My next task, therefore, is to try to specify more precisely how one of the quartets in its entirety metaphorically represents the development of thought, feeling, and action that leads to a faithful mode of being. This will indicate whether Eliot's metaphoric representation is in any sense also an argument and, if so, whether that argument is in any sense theological. Once this is ascertained it should be possible to tell in what way *Four Quartets* purposefully goes beyond theological argument so as to reach into the silence.

Chapter Five Poetic Metaphor and Poetic Purpose

Four Quartets (III)

And so each venture
Is a new beginning, a raid on the inarticulate.
—"East Coker": V

The discovery of parallels between the structure and purpose of Pascal's *Pensées* (as conceived by Eliot) and the structure and purpose of Eliot's own *Four Quartets* has raised questions as to how or whether the two works differ in their fundamental aims and means. Having rejected Wheelwright's usual supposition that poems are entities that merely result from—rather than determine—the semantic traits of their parts, we have looked for what it is that distinguishes the *Quartets* as a poetic whole from the *Pensées* as a theological work.

The answer, as we have seen, cannot be simply that the poem is metaphoric or "literary," because the same can be said of the *Pensées*; nor, as I will further show, can the answer be Moynihan's neo-Aristotelian claim that, whereas a work like the *Pensées* is sheerly didactic and theological in nature, poetry like *Four Quartets* is sheerly mimetic and affective. Instead, I will argue, the essential difference between the two kinds of works has to do with the *way* in which the *Quartets* is metaphoric, and more precisely with the way in which it unites metaphoric representation (or mimesis) with metaphoric assertion (or "didactic" argument). Although the differences between this poem and other modes of discourse are never absolute, the various semantic traits and stylistic conventions of the *Quartets*, when united with its dual metaphoric capacity to represent and assert, give it a uniquely poetic capacity to address and engage whatever it is that makes us whole selves and fully human beings. In this way poetry—and specifically the *Quartets*—serves purposes that, however similar to those of other modes of discourse, are most fully characteristic of metaphoric art.

The limited scope of this study dictates that I confine my analysis to one quartet only. This analysis will itself necessarily be restricted primarily to a discussion of the main aspects of the reader's direct encounter with the work, only occasionally looking at facts ferreted out by scholarship. Furthermore, a greater proportion of the analysis will focus on the very first section of the poem chosen for examination, in the belief that a relatively thorough understanding of the semantic and structural principles at work in this one poetic passage will greatly facilitate the remainder of the discussion. In general, my procedure will be to see how what is represented in a given section of the poem is related to a particular stage in what Eliot's Pascal essay describes as "the sequence which culminates in faith." I will then determine how the poetic representation is specifically metaphoric and how it is related to a process of metaphoric argumentation. This will permit me to show more precisely how semantic metamorphosis is incorporated into the poetic structure.

If we must study but a single quartet, "East Coker" will serve our purposes better than any other.[1] "Burnt Norton" has already been discussed in some detail; and that poem, in any case, has some peculiarities due to its having been written first and with no thought of companion pieces. "Little Gidding" is also somewhat atypical, for it comes last and is therefore concerned to an exceptional extent with drawing together the themes found in the other poems in the cycle. "The Dry Salvages" might do, but it is generally acknowledged to be the weakest of the four poems. That leaves us, then, with "East Coker." This is more than merely acceptable, however, since "East Coker" is a poem that might well have recommended itself on the basis of quality alone.

The End in the Beginning: Representation, Argumentation, and Poetic Metaphor

I think it should be evident to anyone who has read "East Coker" that the opening section of the poem represents the speaker, the poetic "I," beginning in the way Eliot says Pascal begins his reflections. That is, he is pondering certain basic features of the world as he experiences it. In meditating on the village of East Coker and its surroundings, the speaker contemplates a microcosm: nature, society, history, the self. He also glimpses a higher order of things that is alluded to by way of Sir Thomas Elyot's words concerning the "concorde" of the sacrament of marriage and that is likewise implicit in the images of the circle dance and of the cosmic rhythm of the "living seasons." But that ultimate, and ultimately sacred, order is seen only in a fleeting and illusory way, appearing in what is, after all, but a brief vision of a past era that has now come to "dung and death." Consequently the speaker is deeply disturbed by the realities of his actual, present world—as will become even more evident in the next section of the poem.

But if the one who meditates here is disturbed by the realities of the world about him, he is at least as deeply disturbed by his own situation in that world, for he is facing not only the death of a cultural era but also his own mortality. Indeed, the point of departure for his whole meditation is his realization that the order of things that he would humanly desire is seemingly incompatible with the natural order, an order in which there is no life without death: "In my beginning is my end." And because the speaker is like Pascal in having a rigorous intellect as well as a passionate nature, his realizations create in him a "passionate dissatisfaction with human life unless a spiritual explanation . . . be found." It is from this incipient spiritual dissatisfaction with himself and his world that the speaker's exploration will take its impetus as it moves toward its "end" and a new beginning.

In paraphrasing in conceptual terms what the poem represents in the first section, however, we have only begun to touch on the full poetic meaning. This is because the representation is not steno-linguistic but metaphoric. In fact, our ability to obtain even a minimal conceptual grasp of what the poem depicts, to say nothing of what it fundamentally means, is contingent on our attending to "expressive" and "musical" meanings; it depends on our responding not only to what the poem and the speaker literally say but also to the way of saying. Consider, for example, the lines with which the speaker's meditation starts:

> In my beginning is my end. In succession
> Houses rise and fall, crumble, are extended,
> Are removed, destroyed, restored, or in their place
> Is an open field, or a factory, or a by-pass.
> Old stone to new building, old timber to new fires,
> Old fires to ashes, and ashes to the earth
> Which is already flesh, fur and faeces,
> Bone of man and beast, cornstalk and leaf.

This passage looks deceptively straightforward in its meaning. It appears to be a statement of an idea and an illustration and amplification of that same idea. But one cannot in fact be altogether certain what the speaker's meaning is here, or what the poem is saying about the speaker. The opening statement is much more ambiguous than, say, "I began dying the day I was born." Is "beginning" the same as birth, we wonder, and is "end" the same as death? A more general phenomenon seems to be referred to here, but we are not entirely sure what it is. We therefore expect explication and elaboration, and perhaps even some *reasons* as to why the speaker believes as he does. This is just what the subsequent lines seem to supply. But as they amplify the original statement they seem subtly to alter its meaning. Whereas the speaker's opening statement had said only that his beginning involves his end, the examples the speaker gives imply that there is also a sense in which every end involves a beginning. The speaker not only observes that houses fall, he also notes that they rise. Old stone, he plainly realizes, is used for new building. Hence, we might be tempted to conclude that, contrary to what the first statement implies, the speaker is contemplating in an objective way a natural, harmonious rhythm wherein life follows death just as death follows life. He would then be meditating on just the kind of cyclical order and dynamic unity of opposites spoken of by Heraclitus.[2]

But if one notices more than the literal logic of the speaker's thoughts, one sees that this harmony is not what the speaker is primarily thinking of at this point. What he is contemplating is not a balance but an imbalance. This is apparent from his rhetoric. Every time he describes a process of restoration or generation, he twice—or more—describes decay and destruction. Houses rise, he admits, but he stresses that they fall, they crumble. Houses are extended, but they are removed, destroyed. They are restored, but also, in their place, one finds an open field, a factory, or a by-pass. The one line that does reflect entirely on restoration ("Old stone to new building, old timber to new fires") is followed by three lines exclusively concerned with the various kinds of remnants left by death and destruction. The same kind of pattern continues in the last five lines of the subsection, moreover, since there the two lines that mainly refer to generation are succeeded by three on degeneration:

> Houses live and die: there is a time for building
> And a time for living and for generation
> And a time for the wind to break the loosened pane
> And to shake the wainscot where the field-mouse trots
> And to shake the tattered arras woven with a silent motto.

Then, as if to say he has now shown what he meant by the opening assertion, the speaker begins a new poetic paragraph by repeating that first assertion verbatim: "In my beginning is my end."

Now if we evaluate the speaker's implicit "reasoning" here solely according to the criteria of logic, it will necessarily appear very curious. As I have indicated, the examples the speaker chooses in order to illustrate his initial point all "objectively" suggest a continuing cyclical process in which houses (and other phenomena) rise and fall and rise again, whereas the speaker's opening statement refers to an irreversible succession terminating in death or destruction. The connection between the speaker's main idea and his examples thus seems purely rhetorical. Clearly the speaker's rhetoric is distorting the "facts." If we are very literal-minded we will conclude that the poem must be depicting the mental state and thought of someone who is irrationally gloomy, morose, or otherwise neurotic. That is to say, we will attribute the "defect" in the speaker's reasoning to a defect in the speaker's personality.

But if we were really to do so, it would be our own reasoning that would, in relation to the poem, be defective. For, merely in order to understand what the poem is representing, we must reason *through* the rhetoric of the poem and not against it. To be sure, the rhetoric indicates here that the speaker's emotions are involved with his thoughts. But there is another dimension of the rhetoric that strongly suggests that the feelings and thoughts expressed here are not to be interpreted as merely subjective or idiosyncratic. If we are at all attentive, we will note that the poem has the speaker's words allude to traditional authority and to wisdom beyond his own. One can hardly help hearing echoes from Ecclesiastes in the final lines of the first subsection, and in the last of these lines still another source of wisdom is referred to: a "silent motto." Furthermore, because the speaker's reference to that unspecified motto is followed by a repetition of the opening statement of the poem, we consider it likely that this statement and that motto are related, if not identical. All of which indicates—rhetorically—that the poem is representing the speaker as reaching a personal realization of an enduring truth. In view of this, one must at least entertain the possibility that the speaker's perceptions "correspond to the facts."

But we must then ask, to what facts could they possibly correspond? What in reality could support the speaker's rhetorical distortion of the nature of the processes he describes and justify his corresponding emphasis on the place of death and degeneration in the scheme of things? When one remembers the point of origin for the speaker's reflections, the answer becomes clear. The speaker's beginning point is not the observation that "in the beginning of all things is their end" but, rather, "In my beginning is my end." His thoughts in the succeeding lines, moreover, do not primarily concern purely natural phenomena but houses—human dwellings. Thus the speaker is evidently contemplating the world in the light of the realization that it is a world in which he himself must die. In this light it is profoundly reasonable for the speaker to describe the cycle of things less as one of continual renewal than as one of beginnings that emphatically end. The natural order of succession creates within the human being a great and perhaps unnatural disorder. When this is uttered the very imbalance and "irrationality" of the utterance has a certain logic, though it be of the "heart." The "facts" that support the speaker's observations are therefore real enough, being nothing other than basic realities of human experience, and the metaphoric tensions within the speaker's mode of expression correspond to real tensions within experience itself. But, again, the recognition that this is so, and that the poem is here representing reasoning of the heart, is something the reader can come to only upon using the "heart" to interpret the poem. This is the case, furthermore, even if the reader comes to feel—as the speaker himself later will—that such reasoning at this point has disclosed only a partial truth.

It would be a relatively simple matter to document other ways in which the first stage of the sequence leading to faith is represented metaphorically—that is, represented by a tensive transformation of ordinary forms of expression and thought. We could look closely at the highly sensory and concrete qualities of the second subsection, noting the feeling of waiting and repressed desire that they convey, and hence the way they qualify our understanding of the speaker and his more abstract reflections. We could also see how the speaker's subsequent vision of a scene from the English Renaissance functions as a metaphor for all the cultural, personal, physical, and indeed spiritual beginnings that the speaker feels have come to an end. But the semantic principles we would thereby highlight have already been examined in depth. Thus, having noted that these aspects of metaphor are indeed at work within the poetic representation, we turn now to the more important task of seeing how the very same semantic units employed for the purpose of metaphoric representation are likewise units within a system of assertions that is in substance a mode of argumentation. We will then see that the speaker's reasoning and exploration is a part of a larger structure of poetic reasoning and exploration that necessarily becomes the reader's own.

As we again take up the topic of poetic assertion, it will be worth recalling Philip Wheelwright's claim that the assertions in poetry are genuine and yet vary widely both in the way they assert and in the degree to which they assert. Some poetic assertions, he says, are relatively plain, some highly metaphoric; some declare seriously or weightily, some playfully or very hypothetically.

Having already confirmed this thesis, we can now go further than Wheelwright himself does toward discerning just how the varied assertions of the *Quartets* are actually integrated into some kind of unified system. We can start by making a simple observation that no one is likely to dispute: Assuming the validity of the thesis that the first section of "East Coker" constitutes in its entirety a representation of a world and does so by representing the thoughts and feelings of one of its inhabitants, it follows that every assertion in this section of the poem must, at the very least, refer to some aspect of that poetic world and of the speaker's experience and thought. In short, there is no assertion in the poem that does not say

something about a fictive reality, a "virtual" universe, within the poem itself. If this were not so, the poetic representation would lack continuity; it
could not be an integral whole.

But to say only this much would be tantamount to admitting the possibility that the statements implicit or explicit within the poem are mere
pseudo-assertions, because we would then have no way of challenging the
assumption that the world of the poem is purely hypothetical. I. A. Richards could feel that his views were vindicated, and Northrop Frye could
seem equally justified in claiming that literature "is a body of hypothetical
thought and action: it makes, as literature, no statements or assertions."[3]
The neo-Aristotelians would have no reason to question their belief that
"mimetic" literature is structured in a completely different way from didactic, and we could all be satisfied with Earl Miner's new variation on an old
tune: "A poem . . . does not propose, does not predict."[4]

If we proceed carefully in the early stages of our examination of the
structure of assertion found in "East Coker," I think it will become evident
why the above notions of poetic assertion cannot do justice to the poem
we actually read. Close scrutiny of the assertions in the first section of this
poem reveals that these assertions cannot all function on a single level of
meaning, although they do all pertain in some way to the poetic world. We
can see, moreover, that these assertions form a kind of hierarchy having
three main levels.

At the first level of this hierarchy are all those assertions that, in their
immediate context, are understood by the reader to be referring primarily
to the world of the poem and thus to be disclosing "truths" that concern,
above all, intrapoetic realities. The second subsection of the poem is predominantly made up of such assertions.

> . . . Now the light falls
> Across the open field, leaving the deep lane
> Shuttered with branches, dark in the afternoon,
> Where you lean against a bank while a van passes,
> And the deep lane insists on the direction
> Into the village, in the electric heat
> Hypnotised. In a warm haze the sultry light
> Is absorbed, not refracted, by grey stone.
> The dahlias sleep in the empty silence.
> Wait for the early owl.

In this passage assertions like those concerning the deep lane, the passing
van, the sleeping dahlias, and the early owl are all of the kind we are pres-
ently considering. One is interested in them because of what they tell one
about the world of the poem. This does not mean that such assertions have

no basis in actual experience,[5] and certainly it must not be forgotten that the reader's understanding of the nature of real lanes and dahlias is an essential ingredient in the poetic meaning and function even of assertions like these.[6] For the world of the poem is not created *ex nihilo*; it is largely an extrapolation from our experience of actuality. But the fact remains that the actual world provides little more than the raw ingredients out of which assertions of this first kind establish the fictive particulars and basic parameters (or "laws") of the poetic world. It does not matter much to the reader whether the road and the owl and the dahlias exist in "real life." It only matters that this poetic world can, and does, include such "virtual" realities.

My final observation concerning the first kind of assertion has to do with the kind of assent this form of assertion invites. Because statements of this first kind are devoid of any immediate ontological implications and thus ask us to assent to them only within the context of the poem, they can easily persuade us to "suspend" any disbelief we may feel. Their "truths" are the givens of the poem. Consequently, when we understand the intent of such assertions, our assent is nearly automatic.

At a second level we find assertions that, like those of the first kind, establish "truths" or "facts" pertaining primarily to the world of the poem. But these particular assertions do so by offering interpretations of poetic "facts" described by other poetic assertions. We see this in the second subsection, for instance, when the speaker declares that the deep lane "insists" on the direction into the village of East Coker. Needless to say, lanes do not ordinarily "insist" on anything; and it is even less likely that a country lane would "insist" on a single direction. The speaker, therefore, is not merely describing a "given" of his world; he is interpreting it. More importantly, the poem itself makes use of the speaker's interpretative assertion so as to interpret for *us* the speaker's feelings and, in a vague and almost symbolist way, to relate the scene as a whole to that inner state in which the speaker waits for a sense of direction while seeming, for the moment, immobilized.[7] To reiterate, however, such interpretations are all primarily relevant to the world within the work, and so long as the world of the poem is the primary referent of a given assertion, such an assertion may constitute the third or fourth reinterpretation of some phenomenon within the poetic world and still be, fundamentally, an assertion of the second kind.

We have seen, then, that the first kind of assertion seems merely to describe features of the poetic world, whereas the second kind redescribes, infers, and interprets—thereby indicating what a given feature of the poetic world means in relation to other features of that same world. There is another important difference between assertions of the first and second kind, however, and this has to do with what each kind of assertion requires of the reader. If the first kind of assertion requires that the reader suspend all disbelief, the second requires that the reader evaluate the assertion's claims, and thus form some judgment as to how its interpretation of the poetic "facts" seems true, coherent, or otherwise plausible within the world of the work itself. There is no way we can read the speaker's assertion about the "insistence" of the lane without wondering why he speaks of it in this way. Is it because he is bordering on a state of psychosis? Or is it because the poem itself is suggesting that he is vaguely aware of the need for outside direction, or perhaps unaware but being somehow directed nevertheless? To answer these questions at all, we cannot simply "suspend" all our critical judgments. Indeed, we must draw on our experience of lanes and people and of the poem itself so as to *evaluate* the implications of this assertion and to assess what kind of sense it makes within the poetic world. Although such an assessment is often almost instantaneous, and always provisional, it is nonetheless crucial and by no means perfunctory. We may in fact find that the poem has not earned our assent to a particular assertion of this kind. But if this is so, we judge the assertion to be untrue not to the actual world but only to the poetic. We will dissent, but for aesthetic rather than ontological reasons.

This last point raises one question, however. If assertions of this second kind draw on our actual experience and critical faculties, why do we not read them as assertions that are directly about actual experience and that therefore interpret in a rather immediate way the actual world? The reason we do not is that they and the poem become relatively uninteresting, or even meaningless, when read in this way. The idea of an actual lane's insisting on a direction is nonsensical. Or else, if we imagine the lane to be literally one-way, it is trivial. That Eliot himself might have thought of an actual lane in this way is scarcely more interesting. More importantly, the poem attracts us to its own interior frame of reference by creating an intrapoetic context wherein the assertion about the lane is more significant.

Things are very different with regard to the third kind of assertion. At this level in our hierarchy, assertions are to a large extent poetically interesting precisely because they in some way interpret the extrapoetic world even as they are interpreting the poetic world itself. Indeed, unless we are sensitive to their intention of disclosing larger meanings—in other words, to their ontological import and assertorial weight—these particular assertions will seem relatively empty and the structure of the poem incoherent or weak.

As might be anticipated, I believe that a prime example of this third kind of assertion is the statement "In my beginning is my end." To be sure, we know at once that this statement is about the poetic speaker and therefore about an aspect of the world represented in the poem. But it can hardly strike us as being *primarily* about the speaker (or even about Eliot himself). It has practically no rhetorical color or personal or narrative interest. It is, in a word, philosophical, and though it is somewhat paradoxical, it is hardly more so than the sayings of Heraclitus. Thus, in its immediate context in the opening line of the poem, this assertion invites us to consider the possibility that it is significant beyond the purely poetic world. When the same assertion recurs at the beginning of the second subsection, the invitation becomes still more definite. Even if we were to assume with Moynihan that we are to take this assertion seriously only for the purpose of taking the speaker seriously, it is hard to imagine how the assertion's effect would in the end be purely emotional. The seriousness with which we take the speaker is due in part to the seriousness and cogency of his thoughts, many of which are expressed in assertions that are as "weighty" as the one we are considering.

Assertions of this third kind do not in themselves elicit the assent they seem to invite. Indeed, they cannot fully be understood apart from the two "lighter" kinds of assertions, because much of their essential meaning is not strictly conceptual. But the meaning of the lighter assertions is itself altered by the larger context of meaning established by the heavier. Within that larger context the lighter assertions indirectly and implicitly support whatever ontological import the heavier assertions ultimately possess. That is to say, once assertions of the third kind (explicit or otherwise) alert the reader to the potential ontological import of the poem, the reader will see that even the lighter and more hypothetical assertions function indirectly to interpret some aspect of extrapoetic reality, thereby corroborating the more explicit statements and truth-claims of the work. Thus the relatively light assertions that describe the "virtual" reality of the dahlias, the lane, and the owl are actually read in a larger context that removes them, ever so slightly, from a purely intrapoetic frame of reference. When they are read together, and in context, these assertions are recognized as describing a scene that the poem as a whole leads us to interpret as pertaining to the speaker's thoughts and feelings. Since the heavier assertions of the poem interpret the speaker himself as a concrete embodiment of more universal human experiences, and his exploration as having a certain validity beyond its purely poetic context, we as readers naturally feel that the experiential qualities presented by the poetic scene as a whole help to interpret the actual experience of waiting for an "end" of one mode of existence. Indeed, one feels that this scene and others in the first section of the poem permit one not only further to understand the opening assertion but also to understand its experiential basis and, hence, its validity. By the end even of the first section, one finds that all the assertions—and in this view every utterance in the poem functions in part as *some* kind of assertion—not only test and complicate the opening "thesis" but also tend to confirm it. One therefore considers the opening assertion as at least a plausible judgment concerning not only the poetic speaker but the human condition. Although it may well seem less declarative and more exploratory than it did at first, it will also seem somehow more significant.

This suggests, however, that the three kinds of assertion are intimately related, each contributing not only to a poetic representation but also to a kind of poetic argument. To see more clearly how this can be, let us look again at our hierarchy of assertions. Regarded now as an argument, this hierarchy would seem to include the necessary ingredients of data or evidence, premises and generalizations based on the data, and conclusions that, unlike those of pure logic, seem both hypothetically valid and freighted with a real but indeterminate quantity of existential import. Assertions of the first kind describe the basic "facts" or givens of a possible world, or of some portion of such a world. They supply the essential evidence. Assertions of the second kind interpret, reason about, and "generalize" from, what has been described. They depict certain phenomena within the poetic world as more important or more fundamental than others. Then, on the basis of these interpretations and generalizations, assertions of the third kind reach conclusions about both the possible and actual (extrapoetic) significance of such a world—of such thoughts, sensations, feelings, actions, and the conditions of their possibility. The significance that the poem itself thereby assigns to its world is not ultimately a significance for anyone *in* the work but for those who apprehend the work. It is not a meaning imposed on the whole but a meaning drawn out of it.[8] Hamlet's play now catches the king's conscience, or, less dramatically, *we* now begin to sense the significance of the poetic representation and its relation to ourselves as participants in the work and not only as observers. Should this not happen, the work will simply not have registered on us.

Having said this, I must now stress that the "argument" found in the first section of "East Coker," and in the rest of the poem as well, is to be distinguished from syllogistic reasoning. Just as a poetic assertion differs from an ordinary proposition, so poetic argument differs from ordinary dialectic. This difference is something we can now explain in fairly precise terms. I have called attention to the fact that Wheelwright describes the "lightness" of poetic assertions both in terms of the *extent to which* they are declarative and in terms of the *way in which* they are declarative. According to Wheelwright, poetic assertions are "lighter" than propositions both because they are less declarative than propositions are and because they are less plain or univocal. Thus poetic assertions are actually semantic "compounds," and they are compounded in two ways: they are always somewhat conjectural even as they are declarative, and they are always somewhat polysemous and tensive even as they convey a discernible meaning. I think we can now see that something similar can be said concerning poetic arguments. For the argument begun in the first section of "East Coker" is neither entirely hypothetical nor entirely thetical;[9] it is neither completely illogical nor completely logical. (What it concludes both is and is not, or is not merely, its literal import.) The poetic argument is thus a compound, a synthesis between rhetoric and dialectic. It is "tensive," "lighter" than conceptual argumentation, and genuinely metaphoric.[10]

It should now be evident that the semantic structure of the first section of "East Coker" embodies both metaphoric representation and metaphoric argumentation.[11] Just as even the heaviest ontological assertion in the poem contributes to the poetic representation, so even the most purely descriptive or mimetic passage contributes to the poetic argument. Clearly, therefore, representation and argumentation work together in the overall poetic metaphor to transform in a significant way our ordinary patterns of thought and feeling. Indeed, we can now justifiably claim that representation and argumentation form *central* structural components of the poetic metaphor, in various ways incorporating what Wheelwright terms diaphor and epiphor. In point of fact, it is only by extending Wheelwright's theories to take into account both the representational and argumentative aspects of the poetic metaphor that we have been able to begin to discern how "East Coker" takes shape as a whole and engages and addresses us as whole human beings.

Having examined in some depth the manner in which the first section of "East Coker" does just this, and therefore the particular way in which it is related to the first stage of "the sequence which culminates in faith," we have succeeded in determining the basic elements within the poem's semantic structure. But obviously we have yet to see how that structure develops as a representation, argument, and metaphor. We also have yet to see with any clarity the complex way in which the development of the poem serves a function that is not altogether unlike that of the *Pensées* and yet is ultimately more poetic than theological.

"The Progress of the Intellectual Soul"

In his essay on the *Pensées*, and indeed in the same paragraph in which he describes the sequence culminating in faith, Eliot explains briefly what he thinks an "intellectual soul" like Pascal discovers upon examining the world within and about himself. The first thing Eliot mentions is that such a person will find the world distressingly "disordered." Second, however, Eliot notes that he will find that "certain emotional states, certain developments of character, and what in the highest sense can be called 'saintliness' are inherently and by inspection known to be good" (*Selected Essays* [1951], p. 408). As we will see, the second section of "East Coker" represents both kinds of discoveries.

The first section of "East Coker" represents the speaker's awareness of the disorder of the world, and especially of the world within himself as he confronts his own mortality. In the second section of the poem that awareness of disorder is, if anything, intensified, but it focuses more explicitly than before on the disorder of the external world. The speaker's distress is now represented as perhaps even more acute than in the previous stage of his spiritual progress. And well it might be, since what he describes in the lyrical opening of this second section is nothing less disruptive than cosmic combat and the dissolution of the order of the universe: a vast dissonance within the *harmonia mundi* accompanying the total disintegration of the order of the cosmos that had been envisioned by the Renaissance and reflected in its social, moral, and religious ideals. Thus, whereas the poetry at this point is using astrological, meteorological, and mythological imagery with which the Renaissance would have been familiar, it expresses the speaker's perception of a kind of disorder that the earlier era had believed impossible, and certainly impossible in the future "Golden Age" in which the speaker should now be living. A major aspect of the nature of that disorder becomes obvious, moreover, when one recalls the cataclysmic events of the time in which the poem is being written, this being the period of the outbreak of the Second World War.

In retrospect we see more clearly why the speaker had stressed, in the first section of the poem, that the circle dance of Tudor England and the harmonious "concorde" celebrated by Sir Thomas Elyot had come but to "dung and death." As the remainder of the second section makes clear, that former age's confidence in progress and its trust in human achievement constitute part of the deceitful inheritance of "knowledge" that has brought the present age to "destructive fire." Such pseudo knowledge imposes a false pattern on experience, with every moment now constituting a "new and shocking / Valuation of all we have been."

It is thus apparent that, if the speaker is to find values by which to live in the face of death and in a time of destruction, they cannot be those past values that modern culture has most cherished and on which it has largely been founded. One's first impression might, in fact, be that the speaker's world of experience offers *no* values and *no* knowledge that could now be of use to him—in which case he has found only disorder in his world and nothing he clearly knows "inherently and by inspection" to be good. But if this were true the speaker would certainly be moving toward the skepticism of Voltaire rather than sharing the qualified skepticism of Pascal; and the last lines of this section of the poem indicate that, to the contrary, the speaker's awareness of values is vivid. In the very act of recognizing human bondage the speaker acknowledges the reality of certain values. When he criticizes the "fear of possession, / Of belonging to another, or to others, or to God," he implicitly affirms the value of loving self-surrender to others and to God. When he speaks of losing his way in a dark wood, he is alluding to Dante—a poet who, in the middle of his life journey, so lost his way that, paradoxically, he found it. Moreover, in declaring humility to be "endless"—a very special quality, given the speaker's profound concern with "ends"—he is undoubtedly expressing a conviction that "certain developments of character" are inherently known to be good, and in a transcendent sense; and this faintly suggests the possibility of an end that might be a beginning. Indeed, almost everything the speaker sees and knows in this second stage of his journey is merely the negative form of a positive value or reality that will later be revealed. The cosmic disorder has its positive correlative in the cosmic order moved by Love; the destructive fire of the end has its counterpart in the constructive fire of purgation, the end that is the beginning; words that resist meaning are but the negative counterparts of the Word that creates Meaning; the ignorance and darkness of finite knowledge is correlated with a kind of ignorance and darkness that prepares for genuine enlightenment; the imposed pattern that falsifies is but the negative image of the true pattern of timeless moments; and the way of insecurity along which there is no secure foothold exists in relation to the Way, the Purpose, that the speaker will approach as the one final security. The speaker's knowledge is therefore negative knowledge, just as his subsequent course of action will be a *via negativa*. But it is scarcely worthless. Its worth simply is yet to be revealed to him.

The metaphoric qualities of the poetic representation of this second stage of the speaker's "progress" are so similar to those of the first that they hardly call for special comment. An entire historical, cultural, and spiritual moment is here condensed into a polysemous description of a meditative act and presented in fifty lines. Just to comprehend what is so concisely represented, to unravel the main threads of the speaker's reasoning, and to understand the feelings expressed here requires attending to symbols, allusions, puns, and clusters of images that reshape our typical patterns of thought and feeling. This is no duplication of actual experience but a transformation of it. It is a transformation in which concept and expressive rhetoric both are vital.

That the metaphoric representation is simultaneously an argument seems likewise obvious. If we do not take certain of these poetic assertions to be conclusions proposing truths that extend beyond the purely poetic world, the poem becomes utterly trivial and uninteresting. The virtual feelings and thoughts of the poem engage our actual feelings and thoughts. When the speaker declares, for example, that humility is both needful and "endless," he is making an assertion we as readers can feel is supported by the whole structure of assertion up to that point and possibly supported by the structure of actual life experience. Far from distracting us from the poem itself, the ontological implications of this claim attract us and involve us as whole human beings.

When we turn to consider in what respect the poetic argument per se is metaphoric, we come upon a feature of this section of the poem that is unique, demonstrating perhaps better than any other moment in the poem how intimate the relation between aesthetic significance and ontological reasoning can be. I am referring to the use this section makes of the opening lyric, a passage that constitutes a veritable poem-within-a-poem.

Rhymes   *Rhyme Substitutes*

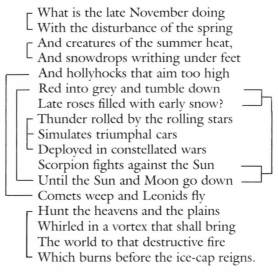

What is the late November doing
With the disturbance of the spring
And creatures of the summer heat,
And snowdrops writhing under feet
And hollyhocks that aim too high
Red into grey and tumble down
Late roses filled with early snow?
Thunder rolled by the rolling stars
Simulates triumphal cars
Deployed in constellated wars
Scorpion fights against the Sun
Until the Sun and Moon go down
Comets weep and Leonids fly
Hunt the heavens and the plains
Whirled in a vortex that shall bring
The world to that destructive fire
Which burns before the ice-cap reigns.

One of the more remarkable things about this lyric is that it is no sooner ended than judged by the poetic speaker to be a failure, a study in versification that, inspired by the past, is plainly inadequate to present needs:

That was a way of putting it—not very satisfactory:
A periphrastic study in a worn-out poetical fashion,
Leaving one still with the intolerable wrestle
With words and meanings. The poetry does not matter
It was not (to start again) what one had expected.

Then, without any sort of transition, the speaker immediately goes on to speak of the deceptiveness of the Renaissance hope for calm and serenity in the autumn of the world and to question the supposed "wisdom" of that earlier time's notion of the order of things. Such "knowledge," he says, "imposes a pattern, and falsifies," for the patterns of experience change in every moment and constitute a new valuation of all we have been.

Given the sequence of these reflections, it is obvious that the speaker is reasoning about several phenomena simultaneously, and in fact about several very different phenomena: poetic style, human history, and his personal situation as he searches for values with which to begin a meaningful mode of existence. Of these lines of reasoning, the least serious might seem to be that by which the speaker criticizes the poem he has just offered us. But this is not in fact the case. When we are attentive to this level of reflection and assertion, our own experience in reading the poem becomes a kind of metaphor for the deeper experiences on which the poem and the speaker meditate. As we encounter first the lyric itself and then the speaker's criticism of the lyric, we ourselves experience the structure of discovery that informs the speaker's own exploration at this juncture of his pilgrimage. We recognize the dynamics of deception and we become aware of an imposed pattern that falsifies; in both ways we confront what it means to need a new point of beginning.

The element of deception becomes evident, I think, when we consider our experience of moving from the lyric to the speaker's highly colloquial dismissal of the value of that lyric. Although commentators usually write as though the reader realizes all along that this lyrical passage is inferior poetry, I am convinced that the speaker's criticism actually strikes us initially as a rather "shocking valuation" of the poetry that has come before. The poetry may not have been "what one had expected," but neither are its inadequacies expected or even, at first, clearly perceived. We as readers have been deceived, and intentionally deceived, into thinking (and feeling) that this lyric is at least satisfactory. That we are so deceived is nearly inevitable, furthermore, for two very good reasons. First, one naturally trusts a poet like Eliot to know what he is doing. Second, one does not at once notice anything terribly incongruous about the writing. Although one cannot be oblivious of the embellished and somewhat archaic diction that the poet uses, the old-fashioned imagery and slightly inflated style do not seem altogether inappropriate; after all, the previous section of the poem has just envisioned a scene from sixteenth-century England and, in so doing, has used some distinctly archaic Tudor English. It is thus only when we are prodded by the speaker that we turn back to the lyric and see that it is indeed not very satisfactory. We realize now, but not before, that the very terminology used—"Scorpion fights against the Sun," "rolling stars," "constellated wars"—is antiquated and stiff. One would not be surprised to find such language in a poem by Milton or Pope, but in this context it seems artificially elevated and poetic in a negative sense.[12] It suggests, moreover, the reality of an order of things (an astral metaphysical order, to be precise) in which the speaker and most other moderns no longer believe, thereby falsifying the nature of the very experience it seeks to describe.

But there is another way in which the lyric falsifies, and that is by imposing a particular pattern of meter and rhyme onto a semantic structure that, in its ostensible meaning, is antithetical to all that such a pattern implies. Thus the artifice of the poetry is divorced from the meaning. The "poetry" ceases to matter.

The incongruity of the meter is not immediately apparent, because the iambic and trochaic tetrameter predominant here is also found in the corresponding cosmological lyric that opens the second section of "Burnt Norton." But whereas the cosmic order envisioned in the lyric in "Burnt Norton" is seen there as a pattern encompassing a final reconciliation and harmony among the elements of the cosmos, the order envisioned in the present lyric is, as I have pointed out, a great disorder and, indeed, a whirling warfare in which all will be destroyed. This difference, however, is not in the least reflected in the meter. Although the poem generates some slight sense of instability and movement, due in part to the minimal punctuation, the sensation created is very little different from that produced by the earlier lyric, similarly punctuated but with contrary import.[13] Further, the rhythmical pulse is altogether too steady and "grand" to express at all adequately the feeling of the heavens' being "whirled in a vortex" and headed toward ultimate disaster. Again, the poetry becomes "Poetry" and exhibits a certain artificiality derived from a dishonest treatment of its subject.

The relation between the rhyme scheme and the intended poetic meaning is even more problematic and intriguing than that between the meter and the meaning. It is well known that the second sections of "The Dry Salvages" and "Little Gidding" both contain novel and elaborate experiments in versification, the former including a modified sestina with an intricate and extensive pattern of rhymes and partial rhymes, and the latter incorporating a metrical adaptation of terza rima. It is interesting, therefore, that no critic seems to have noticed the unusual and highly symmetrical organization of rhymes employed in the lyrical opening of the second section of "East Coker." It is true that the passage in which these rhymes occur is immediately followed by the poetic speaker's criticism of the lyric. But this can hardly be meant to discourage the reader from carefully scrutinizing the passage in question. On the contrary; Eliot surely intends for the unexpected outburst of criticism to send us back for a closer look, in the hope of seeing why the verse is to be deemed unsatisfactory.

Be that as it may, few readers and commentators have in any way challenged or refined Helen Gardner's early (and, I think, premature) conclusion that the lyric in this second section of "East Coker" is very much like the lyric that begins "Burnt Norton" II, and that both consist merely of "irregularly rhyming octosyllabics."[14] Of the more recent critics who have bothered to note the rhyme scheme at all, Derek Traversi is in no way exceptional when he says simply that the lines of the lyric are (as Gardner had stated) "irregularly rhymed."[15]

"Regular" means, of course, ordered or formed according to some rule or principle, which is precisely why the consensus has been that the rhymes to be found in this passage are "irregular." For when one reads the poem as one ordinarily would—that is, from first to last—one's impression is that the rhymes following the opening pair of couplets reflect no clear pattern or plan. As the diagram on page 104 shows, however, appearances here are deceiving. If we look first at the three lines at the precise center of the lyric, we discover that these lines rhyme exactly. Presuming it cannot be by sheer accident that the three lines at the very center of a seventeen-line poem all rhyme, we are prompted to look for other evidence of a pattern of rhymes. Keeping in mind Eliot's penchant for assonance, consonance, visual rhyme, and similar devices, we are not disappointed. In point of fact, we discover that the three lines immediately following the center three "rhyme" (loosely speaking) in mirror-image order with the three lines immediately preceding the three at the center. ("Down" and "snow" are perhaps linked more by shared letters than by shared sounds, leaving it to the eye to make the connection, but in the very British English of Eliot's own recording of the poem, the "ow" diphthongs are actually rather closely matched, making for genuine assonance.)[16] One sees, too, that these middle three groups of verses, consisting of three lines each, are themselves framed on either side by a quatrain—the opening four lines rhyming in couplets, the closing four rhyming in the first and last lines.[17]

It therefore seems reasonable to conclude that the rhymes in this passage are to a significant extent "regular"—that there is, after all, some principle according to which they are ordered. The whole scheme exhibits a high degree of symmetry, and symmetry of a special kind. Viewed as a pattern of rhyme, the poetry turns, as it were, on a precise center. It then radiates outward from this center or "still point," so that its overall design could be said to approximate to a surprising degree a balanced and harmonious order of concentric "circles" of sound. In short, one finds in this lyric the poetic equivalent of radial symmetry, or at least the suggestion thereof.[18]

All of this would, of course, make the lyric in "East Coker" II nothing less than a marvelous (if rather curious) achievement, were it not for three considerations. First of all, we cannot ignore the fact that rhyme usually exists for the sake of sound. But here the pattern of sound is one that the ear can hardly detect and that the intellect alone can really appreciate. Second, to the degree to which one *can* attend to the sound of the rhymes, that sound seems divorced from the sense of the poem, because one will never fully perceive the larger pattern of the sound when one is reading the poem in the only order in which the poem makes sense. And third, setting aside the question of sound per se, one is struck by a certain incongruity between the sense of the lyric and the fact that the poem employs a highly symmetrical pattern of rhymes. Regardless of what this structure may *symbolize*—and in a poem so concerned with circles, centers, and vortices the possible interpretations are many—it *exemplifies* an attempt to contain within a highly ordered, intellectual form the meaning of utterances that describe a disorder of the highest magnitude. What the poetry *says* is that seasons have been thrown out of sequence and that whole constellations are in collision. The rhyme scheme, by contrast, is an orderly, balanced artifice. This is not to say that disorder cannot be expressed within the conventions of an orderly, artificial form. Haydn effectively depicts primordial chaos at the beginning of *The Creation* even while remaining within the orbit of the classical style. But, given the conventions of modern poetry and the features of Eliot's own free verse in "East Coker," the use of an elaborate and balanced rhyme scheme in conjunction with talk of final destruction is incongruous. The pattern seems imposed; it does indeed seem to falsify. As a result the "poetry" does not matter, being inadequate to convey the meaning that would now be meaningful.

Yet within the larger context of the poem, of course, this poetry *is* meaningful, and precisely because of its peculiar inadequacies. For its aesthetic ideals, and its consequent attempt to make harmonious and perfect what is chaotic and imperfect, correspond to the Renaissance ideals and to the attempt of that era to perfect knowledge, history, and humanity. The reasons for the "shocking valuation" of the lyric poem are thus analogous to the reasons for an equally shocking valuation of the dominant part of our cultural heritage.

But if this is true, we have found that "East Coker" uses our thoughts and feelings about an aesthetic object—namely, the lyric that opens its second section—to probe a deeper truth. It takes our experience of rhythm and rhyme, sound and sense, and—by using it as a metaphor for a larger phenomenon—transforms that experience into something that is, both aesthetically and ontologically, more significant. It is on the basis of this transformation that the poetic argument of the second section proceeds, searching for what is "endless" in the midst of all that has ended.

As we look now at the last three sections of "East Coker" there will be no need to belabor the points already made in the preceding pages. Nevertheless, it is important to see something of how the poetic metaphor continues to develop as a representation of a person's progress toward faith and as a kind of argument concerning the validity or invalidity of certain thoughts and feelings intrinsic to that progress.

Judging solely from the single paragraph in which Eliot concisely describes the sequence that culminates in faith, the reader of Eliot's essay on the *Pensées* might suppose that the transition from the perception of certain moral and religious values to an adoption of those values in one's life and belief would be a straightforward matter. Perhaps this impression is created because Eliot is specifically describing in that paragraph the rational component of such a sequence—the part subject to direct "explanation." But the essay as a whole shows that the actual sequence is by no means a matter of purely intellectual assent. Eliot's descriptions of Pascal's own spiritual progress indicate, moreover, that there are certain essential moments in the movement toward faith that in fact appear to be movements away from faith. For Eliot makes it clear that Pascal despairs of himself and, in his desperate realization that the vanity and emptiness of human striving extends to the very core of the human being, is tempted to despair of salvation itself. Consequently, Pascal enters a stage of waiting and preparation corresponding to the mystic's dark night of the soul. In this stage he does not yet try to possess the thought and the way of being that is fully Christian. Rather, he practices humility. Instead of moving steadily higher in his knowledge of what is true, he comes to the knowledge that he does not yet know the truth. Pascal's road to faith leads down before it leads up. His beginning must come to an end before there can be a new beginning.

This last thought is not, of course, expressed in these very words in the essay on Pascal. These particular words are derived from the third section of "East Coker." Yet they are clearly appropriate, because this third section of the poem represents the very moments of despair described above and depicts exactly the same downward turning—the turning away from the half-light of ordinary life and toward the "darkness of God."

As we might expect, however, the poem's account of these moments is anything but literal.[19] Instead of simply telling us that the speaker believes human beings are vain and empty and that he feels that the very meaning of his life is being extinguished, the poem has the speaker begin by delivering a sort of dramatic speech in which the qualities of the language itself reveal both his own condition and his perceptions of the human condition in general. Contrary to what some readers have supposed, this speech is hardly an outpouring of deeply felt grief. The whole passage is filled with the irony with which it opens: "O dark dark dark. They all go into the dark, / The vacant interstellar spaces, the vacant into the vacant." Although the speaker's first words allude to Milton's *Samson Agonistes*, he makes it quite clear that those whom he describes here have nothing like the substance of Milton's Samson, even though they too have certainly been deceived. The speaker's lament for their—and his—passing is one that sounds distinctly hollow, consisting of a litany of titles and abstract functions deemed important by an unimportant society, a society with no sense of what is ultimately important. The truth seems to be that the speaker can at this point feel no genuine grief; his own life has been emptied of the substance of which grief is made. Because the same is true for all the others participating in this funeral, it is "nobody's funeral, for there is no one to bury." To say the least, then, the speaker's lament carries a complex message. It is a metaphoric utterance holding in tension our awareness of the nature of funerals with our awareness of the tenor of the rhetoric with which this funeral is described.

Similarly, when the poem later depicts the dark night of the soul, it does so not by using ideas in themselves but by means of three analogies. The experience of letting the "darkness of God" come upon one is said, first, to be like the experience of sitting in a darkened theater as the scenery is changed "with a hollow rumble of wings, with a movement of darkness on darkness." Second, it is like being in an underground train when it stops too long between stations and a "mental emptiness" deepens behind the faces of the passengers. Last, it is as when the mind, under the influence of ether, is "conscious but conscious of nothing." These analogies seem so different from one another, and so evocative, that their affective and diaphoric components can scarcely be ignored; one cannot say, "I know just what this means," any more than one can say this of some of the parables of Jesus. Yet these metaphoric analogies have an epiphoric and logical basis as well. Random as they seem at first, one discovers that all three analogies have to do with experiences and places in which all previous modes of action and movement have ceased. All three, as Eliot describes them, depict conditions not only of expectation but also of vague apprehension. In all three the subject is waiting for an action that is, or will be, initiated by an outside agent. Thus the overall metaphoric import suggests that the speaker is, so to speak, in the anteroom of death itself, where he is also vaguely aware of something beyond this death, yet to be revealed. Again, therefore, the manifold meanings that coexist in this one passage give evidence of the essentially metaphoric quality of the poetic representation.

Finally, I have two observations concerning the poetic argument advanced in this section. First, I think it is noteworthy that the argument is building on that of previous sections, making it possible for even the smallest semantic alterations to have considerable import. This is true, for instance, at the end of the first subsection within the third section, when we come for the first time upon hints of Incarnation:

> Whisper of running streams, and winter lightning,
> The wild thyme unseen and the wild strawberry,
> The laughter in the garden, echoed ecstasy
> Not lost, but requiring, pointing to the agony
> Of death and birth.[20]

These hints are, in this context, so disguised as to be clearly discernible for what they are only by those who have read "Burnt Norton" and "East Coker" together. But the careful reader who has come this far without reference to the earlier poem will at least be able to see that here, for the first time in "East Coker," birth—rather than death—has the last word. This "minor" reversal of the prior order of things is of major significance, pointing to the possibility of a new mode of being in which the end is the beginning.

My second observation is that, in this third section of the poem, the poetic "you" has suddenly become significant beyond the world of the work, and in an immediate way:

> You say I am repeating
> Something I have said before. I shall say it again.
> Shall I say it again? In order to arrive there,
> To arrive where you are, to get from where you are not,
> You must go by a way wherein there is no ecstasy.

Because all of these lines, and the nine that follow, address a "you," we obviously should determine who is being addressed and what that means.

I would suggest that the "you" addressed here is not only the speaker himself, although it is true that the speaker has earlier addressed his own soul. This "you" is similar to the "you" addressed with less emphasis in the first section of "East Coker," where the speaker invites an unidentified "you" to share his vision of the summer midnight dancing. That is to say, the "you" seems to be a fictive representation of human beings in general and of us readers in particular. But when one considers that Eliot is here addressing the "you" with words quoted almost verbatim from St. John of the Cross, it is evident that he intends these words to carry more assertorial weight and more immediate ontological significance than did the earlier words addressed to the "you." At least initially, the earlier assertions seemed to concern something imaginary; these, by contrast, purport to concern reality itself.

The poem does not presume, however, that the truth of the sayings from St. John of the Cross will be either obvious or appealing. On the contrary; it is precisely because these sayings are difficult to accept that the tone with which the speaker introduces them is one of urging and insistence. It is as though the speaker knows that we (and he) will need persuasion if we are ever to surrender the pretense of happiness, knowledge, and self-possession. The speaker plainly presumes, furthermore, that it is not the mind only that must be persuaded but also the will, for the will always requires discipline and repeated admonishment. As for the intellect, it must now be made to yield. The truth at this juncture can be heard only as paradox.

I do not wish to imply that the effect of this poetry depends on the reader's complete assent to what is being said and urged or that we whose wills and minds are stubborn cannot continue profitably with our reading of the poem. But it does seem plain that the reader must be prepared somehow to *weigh* what is said, and not only in relation to the world of the poem but also in relation to the world of actual experience. Unless we recognize that the poem itself is proposing something and intending to disclose a truth that will be valid beyond the world of the poem, then we will not be engaged by that with which the poem intends to engage us, and for us the work will carry less than its maximum meaning. In fact, we will misunderstand one basic dimension of the purpose inherent in the structure of the work.

But why is it that the tone of the poem becomes so urgent here? Why does the poem begin at this particular point to address us so directly? The reason is that both we and the speaker are now approaching what Eliot himself once said was "in a way the heart of the matter": [21] namely, a meditation on the mystery of the Incarnation in its most scandalous dimension—the passion of the God who "became flesh and dwelt among us."

It seems fitting, both aesthetically and theologically, that a meditation on the Passion and on the work of Atonement would lie at the heart of a poem fundamentally about the process of discovering an end that will be a true beginning. The Atonement is, for the Christian tradition, the supreme instance of just such an end—both for the one whose passion it consummates and for those who try to imitate that one. Thus Atonement is the revelation and enactment of those meanings both inherent in Incarnation and appropriate to the speaker's particular mode of understanding his situation. As represented in "East Coker," however, the Atonement event is not something confined to a single moment in history but it is rather—like Incarnation in the other quartets—a principle forever at work in the structure of things.[22] The poem draws theological support for this view through its use of Eucharistic imagery in the final lines, for in the Eucharist the Sacrifice is perpetually reenacted.

Considering that Eliot's essay on the *Pensées* depicts the sequence culminating in faith as one finally and inevitably leading toward a realization of the truth of the dogma of the Incarnation, it is easy to see that this fourth section of "East Coker" is related to the last phase of that sequence. The destination has not yet been reached, however. Although the speaker recognizes the possibility of redemption, he has not yet attained the new mode of being made possible through faith. He is just now in the process of submitting to the operation of grace. Incarnation at this stage of the journey holds forth a promise but requires a kind of death before it can have efficacy.

The metaphoric and allegorical character of the poetic representation in this Good Friday lyric is well known. Christ, the "wounded surgeon," works with the aid of his "nurse," the Church, to heal the patients within the hospital of the earth—a hospital unfortunately endowed by Adam, the "ruined millionaire." He does not, however, accomplish his work of healing by following the procedure of an ordinary physician. Instead of helping the patients return directly to health, he reverses the normal practice and causes their sicknesses to grow worse. As the speaker confesses, we must be made to "die of the absolute paternal care / That will not leave us, but prevents us everywhere." Only by the prevenient grace that comes to obstruct our own perverted desires can we die to our self-possession and thus begin, after purgation, to live through the Incarnate Christ who is made present again and forever in the Eucharist:

> The dripping blood our only drink,
> The bloody flesh our only food:
> In spite of which we like to think
> That we are sound, substantial flesh and blood—
> Again, in spite of that, we call this Friday good.

The theology implicit in this lyric certainly cannot be accused of overemphasizing human merit. Indeed, as Eliot notes in a letter to Anne Ridler, Brother George Every called it "Jansenist"[23]—by which Brother George must have meant that Eliot stresses the worthlessness of human effort and the seemingly arbitrary character of grace. This is, of course, a very interesting observation in view of the fact that it was the Jansenist cause that Pascal himself took up some time prior to writing his *Pensées*.[24] But it is not only the theology that seems forbidding. The very literal representation of the Real Presence is in itself enough to jolt even the most devout believer. One notices, moreover, that the didactic thrust of this poem is scarcely at all tempered by the kind of personal tone characteristic of much of "East Coker." Because the first person singular pronoun is used only in the fifth stanza, we are very much aware that the truth asserted here is being represented as objectively valid. But the poem does not so much woo us to the truth as simply declare it.[25] Thus, all in all, the kerygma proclaimed in this poem is hardly more inviting to the "natural" mind and self than it would be if proclaimed in the manner of Karl Barth himself, whose commentary *The Epistle to the Romans* (1919) was extremely influential at the time the poem was written.[26]

What this means is that, right at the heart of the poem, where the assertions are in some ways the heaviest of all, the poetic argument reaches its most diaphoric and irrational stage. It is true that we can still understand in some fashion the basic claims of the poem and the speaker, and we certainly have some idea of the Christian dogmas related to those claims. In fact, given the transparency of the allegory, this is the most explicitly Christian moment in the whole of "East Coker." But the reasoning used here is almost sheerly paradoxical, or at least it is paradoxical insofar as it deals with the source and medium of salvation. If the poem supposes that explanations of Atonement or Incarnation might be useful or relevant, it leaves those explanations to formal theology; what it gives us instead are metaphoric *allusions* to, and *images* of, the doctrines of grace, the fall, the sacraments, and so forth—topics that theological interpretation might elucidate, thereby making the "leap" of faith more comprehensible—but they are doctrines that the poem seeks only to invoke as signs of something as yet incomprehensible. Although the poem points to the realities of faith, it suggests that those realities can in fact be comprehended only from within the context of faith and that the "leap" itself can make sense only from the perspective of one who has already taken the leap.[27] This is something that the speaker is only now doing; furthermore, it is something that (as the poem presumes) the reader may never do.

To reiterate, then, the poetic reasoning in this passage is diaphoric. It juxtaposes signs and metaphors of the realities of faith alongside a much fuller representation and more reasonable interpretation of certain basic realities the reader can acknowledge from outside the circle of faith: the realities of death and of the chaos of contemporary life, for instance; of the split between that which one feels ought to be and that which actually is; of the loss of trust in former values; of the social and personal emptiness attendant upon that loss; and, in general, the reality of the basic desire for that which will satisfy the whole being. Yet, by using allegorical symbols more appropriate to Pascal's time than our own, the poem acknowledges that the realities perceived through faith may seem quite alien to the reader, who is likely to be more familiar with their negative counterparts.

The fifth and final section of "East Coker" opens with a confession not so much of sin as of finitude. It represents the speaker's frustrated recognition of the inherent limitations of language and of poetic art in particular, in which every attempt is "a wholly new start," a new kind of failure, and hence a more or less feeble "raid on the inarticulate." The last time the speaker pondered the limitations of his language was at a point following the lyric that opened the second section of the poem, and there, of course, he was overtly criticizing his preceding effort. Here he makes no such overt criticism, but clearly the speaker's implication is that the Good Friday lyric itself was "a different kind of failure." Even this lyric was a "raid" and not a repossession or colonization: it invaded the territory of silence without inhabiting it and without thereby making it fully articulate.

If we take into account all of section V, however, we can see that there is a subtle but profound difference between what the two kinds of failure signify. The first lyric imposed a false pattern on the experience of "ending" and thus led to the speaker's realization that his effort was inadequate. It epitomized the whole idea that dominated the first part of "East Coker": namely, "In my beginning is my end." The second lyric, by contrast, comprised an integral pattern of meaning that, despite its inadequacy, pointed to a reality that was the condition of possibility for the realization that a certain kind of end could be a beginning. This is evident from the fact that section V represents the speaker as having crossed over to an essentially affirmative approach to existence. The affirmations here are tentative, to be sure. Apparently the speaker will not have arrived at the full meaning of Incarnation—of the "communion" between time and eternity—until he sees that the "here and now" of history does matter eternally, the historical pattern being simultaneously a "pattern of timeless moments" (LG:V). In the meantime, however, the speaker's fundamental orientation has shifted. Instead of seeing only that houses rise and fall (with the focus being on the fall), he sees them as places of real beginning: "Home is where one starts from." Instead of describing the succession of things as always a movement from life to death, he now describes it as a more complicated pattern "of dead and living." (The last word is again one of vitality.) Finally, when the true order of the opening motto is restored in the last line of the poem, this is an unmistakable sign that the speaker's mode of being has undergone a life-giving reversal: "In my end is my beginning." The speaker's lingering doubt is, like Pascal's, at last "somehow integrated into the faith which transcends it."

It would be possible to comment specifically—as in our discussions of the other sections—on the metaphoric qualities of the representation and argumentation found in this last section of the poem. But I think it would be more useful at this point to conclude this portion of our analysis with some observations concerning what we have found in our examination of the poem as a whole.

First of all, it is worth noting that the progression from the very first statement of "East Coker" to the last statement (and all that it signifies) is, in essence, the subject of the entire poetic representation. It is likewise the substance of the poetic argumentation. Nothing represented or asserted in the poem is unrelated to this progression. It is apparent, furthermore, that this progression contains the essential moments in what Eliot's essay on the *Pensées* describes as "the sequence which culminates in faith": it represents, metaphorically, the thoughts and feelings intrinsic to the "progress of an intellectual soul" like Pascal or like Eliot himself, and it presents a kind of metaphoric argument as to the basic validity of those thoughts and feelings, and hence—ultimately—of faith in the Incarnation.

Now, however, we are in a position to see more clearly than ever just how metaphoric that argument is. For, after examining the progression of the poem, we can see that not only does the argument use semantic units that are in some measure "expressive" in themselves; and not only does it combine the hypothetical with the thetical, the illogical with the logical; but, specifically, it incorporates a progression of thought and feeling that is dynamic rather than merely additive or cumulative; and thus it transforms logic in a particular way. This is one reason why the essence of the poem tends to elude the act of criticism and conceptual reformulation. When we are thinking back on "East Coker," we know that the statement with which the poem begins will, at the end of the poem, be inverted and thereby converted into the English equivalent of Mary Stuart's motto, "*En ma fin est mon commencement.*" We know, too, that the beginning and end referred to here are spiritual phenomena as well as physical, social as well as private, historical as well as timeless, artistic as well as linguistic, and perhaps cosmic as well as global. But if we are sensitive to the nature of our experience of actually reading the poem, we will also know that our reflection alone, however wise, cannot do complete justice to the poetic meaning. Abstract reflection tends to collapse the dynamic progression of the poem into a static simultaneity of purely "synchronic" significance, as though we were looking at time from the perspective of eternity. But the poem itself essentially exists in time. The temporal process of thinking and feeling by which the reader begins where the poetic speaker begins, and with him comes to discover the various meanings of beginning and ending, finally coming upon the original and "right" order of the motto at the very end of the poem—this process brings about a significant transformation of our ordinary patterns of experience, and a transformation somehow analogous to the speaker's more profoundly transforming discovery of the end that is a genuine beginning.

That this is the case is certainly not due, however, merely to the poem's function as an argument per se. As we have seen, the poem has the dual function of both arguing and representing. Just as the representation would not be what it is without the argument, neither would the argument be what it is without the representation. In unifying both functions, the poem unifies the two most basic metaphoric dimensions of its structure and, therefore, naturally transforms as it forms and informs. It presents and creates something new while *re*presenting and *re*creating essential qualities of prior forms of experience. While reasoning, it also imagines.

We can justifiably conclude that our responses to this work are responses to a specially ordered structure of experience that, by engaging and yet reinterpreting and reshaping our ordinary language and experience, provides a kind of experience significantly different from that provided by most other forms of language or by life in general. When our experience of the poem is *radically* different from what we ordinarily experience (or think we experience) in language and life, then the poetic metaphor is, for us, largely diaphoric; when our experience of the work seems mainly to reinforce or heighten our awareness of what is common in language and life, or of what we can readily identify as "actual" even though uncommon, then the metaphor is largely epiphoric. But in either case the element of transformation is essential—and not merely transformation, but *significant* transformation, or transfiguration, engaging and addressing us as human beings.

In speaking of "East Coker" as a medium of transfiguration, however, we have moved beyond merely the question of the work's semantic properties and structure and have implicitly raised the question of the nature of its purpose. As we now consider this question, we will see how the purpose of the *Quartets* is at once like and unlike the purpose of works of theology, of which the *Pensées* is an exceptionally "literary" example.

Poetic Purpose and the Purposes of Theology

In his extensive and often admirable study of Eliot's longer poems, Derek Traversi cautions us against supposing that the *Quartets* is "in any usual sense" a work of devotional poetry or of theological apologetics. For, as Traversi reminds us, "the *Quartets* is essentially *exploratory* and, at least initially, *tentative* in its nature." [28] In other words, the work is not dogmatic or completely didactic; it carries, as Wheelwright would say, less assertorial weight than a theological argument does. Traversi's remark that the poem is not theological "in any usual sense" seems to leave open the possibility, however, that there is at least *some* sense in which the work's purpose and structure resembles that of theological discourse. But this possibility turns out to have been raised only rhetorically. Once Traversi shows that the *Quartets* is not primarily concerned with philosophical ideas or theological dogmas in themselves, he presumes it safe to conclude that the work is "essentially non-moral, non-assertive in its final nature."[29] The poetic ideas, Traversi goes on to say, "are *not* put forward in the poem as *true*—whatever that may mean—or with a view to establishing any objective validity that they may conceivably have."[30] Indeed, he maintains, the question of truth is one that "is not raised, may even—from the standpoint assumed in these quartets—be irrelevant or incomprehensible. All that is required of the reader is that he should be willing to 'suspend' such disbelief as he may feel for the purpose of responding to the poetry as poetry. . . . In other words, the poetry of the *Quartets* requires to be read as what it is: as poetry, not as a substitute for 'philosophy' or theology."[31]

I should hope it would be clear that, far from wanting to claim that *Four Quartets* is a "substitute" for philosophy or theology, I have wanted to establish more precisely what it is as *poetry*. But, in the process of doing just that, I have shown that we cannot reasonably leap from the premise that the *Quartets* is "essentially exploratory" to the conclusion that it is "essentially non-moral, non-assertive"; for what this assumes is that a genuine assertion cannot be exploratory or tentative. The present study, however, has invalidated this assumption by confirming the theory that poetic assertions vary widely in declarative weight without being less genuine on that account. Indeed, we have shown that every semantic unit in "East Coker" belongs to a hierarchical system of assertions that can be described as an exploratory and tentative argument. This poetic argument, furthermore, either states or alludes to the essential stages of the particular argument by means of which Pascal—in Eliot's words—"explains to himself the sequence which culminates in faith." Though the poem cannot be reduced simply to the status of an argument, that dimension of the poetic structure which goes beyond argument is itself one that seems in some way and to some extent concerned with truth. This latter dimension of the poem constitutes a metaphoric representation of the essence of certain thoughts and feelings and actions intrinsic to the discovery of a faithful mode of being in time.

Unlike Traversi, therefore, I think there is a sense in which the purpose of *Four Quartets*, like that of the *Pensées*, is truly theological. I think we are able to say of *Four Quartets* what the Protestant theologian Langdon Gilkey says of theology itself when he writes that the theological enterprise seeks "to understand the dimension of ultimacy and sacrality, as it is apprehended in ordinary life, *through* the symbols of the Christian tradition," thereby serving as a "symbolic structure making . . . secular experience intelligible, bearable, and hopeful."[32] Like theology, *Four Quartets* is at once a language of religious belief—"speech in response to an involved apprehension of the sacred within the finite"[33]—and a particular form of religious language that uses Christian symbols to interpret the sacred as related to the realm of the finite. In this way it too tries "to articulate, to clarify, and to bring to stronger . . . expression the dimension of sacrality . . . dimly experienced in ordinary life."[34]

Furthermore, I think it would not be farfetched to describe *Four Quartets* as having, in some measure, the specifically apologetic function underlying a work like the *Pensées*. For, according to the Catholic theologian Johannes-Baptist Metz, apologetics is a "re-affirmation of the understanding of faith in the face of a given situation"; it is "a basic effort of theological responsibility in which the 'spirit,' the full intelligibility of Christian faith itself, and its immanent power to form and transform the mind are mobilized."[35] It is true that the *Quartets* is meaningful even when it does not succeed in fully transforming the mind and thus in persuading the reader to move into a new way of life and belief. Its primary requirement is only that the reader engage in an exploration of the meaning and possibility of such a transformation. But the same is true of most theological writings. The rest is grace.

To claim that *Four Quartets* is in some sense theological is not to claim, however, that it *is* theology. In fact, *Four Quartets* has much more in common with other works of literature than with works of theology per se. We can begin to see why this is the case by returning to the question of the nature of theology.

The truth of the matter is that the impression of theology given by the above definitions is distorted. This is not due to any fault of the theologians themselves but to the fact that I carefully edited the definitions in such a way as to minimize one whole side of theology. What was thereby suppressed is the important fact that theology is usually thought of as an essentially conceptual enterprise. Thus, as all the above theologians would insist, it is primarily systematic and rational (that is, steno-linguistic) in the way it seeks to express truth—although the truth it seeks to express is seldom regarded as conclusively verifiable or falsifiable. Even mystical and "literary" theologians like St. John of the Cross and Pascal, who advance arguments using "expressive" semantic units like paradox and symbol, are relatively rigorous and intellectual in their reasoning. The premises of their arguments may be metaphoric, being rooted in "reasons of the heart," and certainly they may be analogical. But the arguments themselves are not wedded to extended metaphoric representation, and they generally strive for logical, conceptual integrity and validity. Hence, an acceptable definition of Christian theology in general might be that it is the endeavor to articulate, evaluate, and elucidate at a conceptual level what is fundamentally affirmed in the symbols, myths, rites, and creeds of the Christian faith. In short, theology is faith in search of understanding (*fides quaerens intellectum*), where "understanding" is taken to mean "rational comprehension" and "reasonable explication."

But if this is true, *Four Quartets* is obviously not fundamentally a work of theology. Insofar as it aims at what Gilkey calls "clarifying," "expressing," and "interpreting" the realities of faith, it does so through a medium that is far from steno-linguistic. Insofar as it sets in motion what Metz terms the "spirit" of Christian faith and its power to "form and transform the mind," the *Quartets* (even more than the *Pensées*) does so as a metaphor that transforms more than the "mind," narrowly conceived, and thus "confuses" thoughts and feelings. Consequently, it fails to give expression to what many a theologian would consider to be the "full intelligibility" of faith.

It must be said, in fact, that Christian belief is more *presumed* than *explained* by the *Quartets*. Although the work as a whole alludes to theological understandings of such truths as the reality of God, the Incarnation, the Atonement, the descent of the Holy Spirit, and the community of the Church, anyone attempting to reconstruct the essence of Christian belief on the basis of *Four Quartets* alone would be in need of divine inspiration. Indeed, the work seems intentionally *uninformative* and ambiguous in its treatment of orthodox beliefs, speaking merely of "Incarnation" instead of "*the* Incarnation," and often leaving some doubt as to what "Incarnation" really means for those living in time, whose situation of emptiness and of anxiety Eliot so vividly portrays. Thus, like "East Coker" itself, the *Quartets* as a whole conveys, even in the end, something less than a confident faith in either the "life eternal" or the earthly prospect of the "life abundant."[36] As theology, therefore, it leaves much to be desired.

As poetry, however, the work fulfills a purpose that is both different from that of theology and yet also of potential significance to theology. If the poem does not primarily aim at embodying the mode of being, or the insight, given in faith itself, it does aim at exploring in a significant way the dynamics of the experience of coming-to-faith. It explores dimensions of experience apart from which faith would be unapproachable, unintelligible, and in fact unwanted. Although the poem is exceptionally reflective and exceptionally theological, it is also highly attentive to levels of experience at which the realities conceptualized in theology are first glimpsed and half understood. In *Four Quartets* the basic human perceptions related to faith are not pure concepts—"clear and distinct ideas"—but more fundamental and equally vivid perceptions that are at least partly preconceptual, even as they are in a sense postconceptual (having been shaped to some extent by prior concepts and systems of concepts). Thus, specifically in relation to religious belief, the crucial perceptions in this poetry are apprehensions of certain values mediated by experience as a whole, of the desires of the self, of special moments in time, and of fugitive signs of transcendence; or they are perceptions of private and cultural anxiety, emptiness, and frustration—no more than negative analogs of a condition of wholeness. If the poem gradually reasons and feels its way toward religious and eventually Christian insights into the meaning of such experiences, it nevertheless stays (even in the end) with what perplexes and with what impresses itself upon the senses and the imagination before and after being "baptized."

The world of *Four Quartets* is therefore less the world of distinct ideas or beliefs in themselves than it is one of patterns of experience shaped by, and giving shape to, ideas and beliefs. The work interrelates not only thoughts and feelings but also belief and unbelief. In this dialogical relationship, moreover, each side interprets the other. Just as the Christian symbols and concepts operate in the poem in such a way as to interpret experience as a whole, so the many layers and nuances of experience not identified as Christian reinterpret those symbols and concepts, complicating the Christian understanding of things and lending it new significance. Hence the work will be of value even to one who feels that the poetry is in some sense "mistaken" in what it takes to be either the ultimate human goal or the nature of the reality at the center and circumference of time. For the poem will not seem merely mistaken; it will seem *profoundly* mistaken, and it will have earned the right to be taken seriously. In point of fact, whether or not one finds *Four Quartets* to be a work to which one can finally and basically assent, it will necessarily be the case that the images, thoughts, and life experiences one brings to the poem will be reexperienced, reunderstood, and therefore significantly transformed in one's encounter with the work. In this way the words of the poem reach into the language and silence of one's overall experience rather than remaining mute on the page.

How, then, should we characterize the purpose fulfilled by such a work? The fundamental purpose of the poem, it seems to me, is not simply to create an emotion or feeling as such, nor a concept or vision, nor even (as in the *Pensées*) some form of cognition dependent on the unification of feeling and thought. I would say, rather, that the purpose of *Four Quartets* is to offer a significant transformation of experience that will cause one to become, in a very particular way, alive to one's whole being—including one's being in relation to a whole larger than oneself. Thus it engages and addresses the vital *unity* of oneself—the self that has purposes in living and that seeks (consciously or not) to have a significant purpose within the

Whole. Although the poetic argument primarily addresses that in us which reflects, analyzes, and synthesizes, the poetic representation primarily engages that in us which values and fantasizes, senses and emotes, associates and remembers, wills and hopes. The metaphoric whole thereby speaks to, and involves, what is essential to who we are.

The *Quartets*, of course, fulfills its purpose in a specifically religious and even theological way because it interprets the essential dynamics of the process of coming-to-faith. Consequently, its status in relation to religious language of all kinds, including theology itself, is special and, as we will continue to see, of special interest to a study of poetry's relation to the formal languages of religious and metaphysical belief. But the principle of transfiguration—that is, of significant transformation—is of even more basic interest from a religious point of view, and this aspect of literature is by no means peculiar to the *Quartets*. What makes a poetic transformation significant, and therefore transfigurative, is simply that the metaphoric process it involves does in some way alter one's ordinary experience in such a way as to engage and address what is essentially one's whole self. Without exaggerating the degree to which this occurs (or is intended to occur) in literature in general, I think we can safely say that literary metaphor—wherever it is found—tends to bring about transformations of this very kind. In this way, as Eliot himself states, "The author of a work of imagination is trying to affect us wholly, as human beings, whether he knows it or not; and we are affected by it, as human beings, whether we intend to be or not."[37]

Having seen some of the ways in which one major work of imagination affects us wholly, as human beings, we can now turn to an examination of how poetic metaphor relates in a distinctive manner to the task of articulating in theological and metaphysical terms the beliefs of fundamental importance to us as whole human beings.

Chapter Six Poetry and Religious Reflection

Alfred North Whitehead on Metaphysical Thinking

I mean that intuition must have its place in a world of discourse; that there may be room for intuitions both at the top and the bottom, or at the beginning and the end; but that intuition must always be tested, and capable of test, in a whole of experience in which intellect plays a large part.
— T. S. Eliot

My point is that understanding is never a completed static state of mind. It always bears the character of a process of penetration, incomplete and partial. . . . Philosophy begins in wonder. And, at the end, when philosophic thought has done its best, the wonder remains.
—Alfred North Whitehead

To say with Eliot that poetic art "affects us wholly, as human beings" is to speak in terms that are admittedly vague and therefore less than ideal from a philosophical point of view. The same is doubtless true of my related claim that metaphoric art addresses and engages our whole selves by transfiguring ordinary language and experience. For that matter, the near cliché that poetry generates new levels of awareness by uniting thought and feeling—an idea Eliot, Wheelwright, Whitehead, and I all hold dear—fares no better under the analytic microscope. But I trust that my analysis of metaphor and of the dynamics of poetic art has given considerable content to these initially ambiguous expressions. In any case, until we have a truly adequate and comprehensive philosophy of mind, self, and imagination, such relatively imprecise ways of describing the means, purposes, and effects of poetry will continue to have important uses. At the least they point to realities our current philosophical and critical "steno-languages" are hard pressed to describe with any exactitude.

Among those realities is what I take to be metaphoric insight—creative, "tensive" perception essential to the cognitive process yet elusive of exhaustive conceptual formulation and clear-cut methods of falsification or verification. A second reality is the pragmatic dimension of metaphor—the tendency of metaphor to change not only how we understand but also how we orient ourselves. Postponing further consideration of the pragmatics of metaphor, I intend to begin now to explore the importance of the cognitive function of poetic metaphor to formal religious and philosophical reflection, especially as undertaken in metaphysics and metaphysical theology. Unlike Wheelwright, of course, I will not be claiming that poetic meaning and truth is entirely sui generis, particular, and completely beyond conceptual criticism or systematic expression. (Poetry's relation to conceptual discourse is both more complex and more intimate than Wheelwright leads one to believe.) Though I will argue that the philosophical and theological interpretation or criticism of poetic meanings is always a *transformation* of those meanings, I will nonetheless continue to hold that such a transformation is invited by the very kind of listening, reading, and attending that poetry itself demands.

From this it will follow that an adequate account of the dynamics of poetry is consonant only with a truly dialogical conception of language and thought that gives neither the poetic nor the steno-linguistic the final word. It will also follow that many prevalent philosophical notions about cognitive and reasonable discourse must be revised. More to the point of my particular inquiry, I will want to question whether it is any longer defensible to maintain that formal theology, as an essentially conceptual or "steno-linguistic" discipline, can in itself be expected to make manifest what Johannes-Baptist Metz calls the "full intelligibility" of faith.[1] Perhaps surprisingly, much of the groundwork for the kind of philosophical and theological reconstruction that is called for is provided by the writings of Alfred North Whitehead.

Important as Whitehead has been to much contemporary theology,[2] few students of theology (and still fewer of philosophy) have given careful consideration to various aspects of his thought lying outside his metaphysical system per se. Even scholars like Bernard Meland[3] and Lyman Lundeen,[4] despite emphasizing that there is more to Whitehead than a metaphysical scheme, have discussed such matters as his theory of language without ever giving a truly satisfactory account of the specific topic that concerns us here—namely, Whitehead's views of the connections between "empirical" metaphysics, theology, and poetic art.

Whitehead, of course, was no theologian—at least not in the usual sense of the word.[5] His approach to literature, moreover, was that of a dedicated, sophisticated amateur. Yet, as we will see, Whitehead's ideas concerning poetry's relation to metaphysics and metaphysical theology are by no means peripheral to his thought or lacking in theological import. In point of fact, Whitehead argues in a distinctive way that a thorough grounding of religious truth-claims rests not only on a defense of some kind of metaphysics (as the "process theologians" emphasize) but also—given the nature of metaphysics itself—on a defense of poetry as that kind of discourse which is closest to "integral experience." What is perhaps more interesting,

Whitehead's particular argument suggests, if only implicitly, a model of religious and metaphysical understanding that could be called "dipolar." For it assigns the language of poetry an ongoing role complementary to, and in dialogue with, the contrasting language of the theologian and philosopher. In doing so it identifies these two modes of language with two rather different modes of thought and cognition.

I am not trying here to present even a synopsis of Whitehead's actual metaphysical system. The issues with which I am concerned have less to do with any particular metaphysical theory than with a particular theory of metaphysics, that is, with what is sometimes rather humorously called "meta-metaphysics." I readily grant that we cannot understand precisely what Whitehead means by any of his theories without fully understanding the metaphysics that is intended to be their exemplification. Even such terms as "feeling," "concept," and "proposition" take on a highly technical meaning within Whitehead's system proper. But since Whitehead himself makes every effort to explicate his theory of metaphysics in ways that are intelligible outside the context of his speculative system, I see no reason why we cannot do likewise.

Finally, it seems necessary to preface this phase of my inquiry with the observation that the theologian reflecting at present on the task of justifying and rendering more intelligible the ontological or metaphysical implications of religious beliefs cannot take the validity of such an enterprise for granted. Theologians and philosophers of the modern era in particular have often argued, for a variety of reasons, that religious claims are of a kind that cannot be supported—much less convincingly justified—on the basis of human experience or philosophical reflection. Given the nature of many of the most philosophically respectable notions of experience—notions that the theologian has often accepted uncritically—it is no wonder that many thinkers question whether any religious claim could ever "philosophically" be warranted or defended. But, as we will now see, these influential notions are far from indisputable. Although we cannot speak of conclusively "proving" the truth or value of our fundamental religious beliefs, we may well find that much of our difficulty in defending them at all has been simply that we have been suffering from inadequate conceptions of what it means to experience, think, know, and articulate. This, at least, is the conclusion Whitehead's philosophy suggests.

In examining the basic elements of Whitehead's position, we will first look at his critique of classical empiricist doctrines concerning experience and knowledge. Second, we will examine his conception of the aims and limits of metaphysics in general. In the third section we will consider his view of the special experiential sources of metaphysical insight and of the consequent viability and necessity for a theological metaphysics. Then, finally, we will analyze his ideas as to the importance of poetic language in relation to metaphysical and theological reflection. This will, I think, provide a basis for a clearer and broader perspective on poetry's relation to languages of religious belief.

Experience and Knowledge: Whitehead the Empiricist

Generally speaking, those philosophers whom we call empiricists have held that knowledge is either factual and experiential or else logical, mathematical, or otherwise "analytic." They have maintained, further, that all knowledge of the world is necessarily *derived from* experience or perhaps even *restricted to* its immediate contents. Thus, to the extent that empiricists have been consistent, they have rejected the notion of innate ideas and of a priori truths concerning reality. To this general description of empiricism we may add the observation that the rationalist Kant was himself sufficiently influenced by empiricism (and by David Hume in particular) to insist that, although there is indeed a "synthetic a priori" knowledge—due to the structure of the mind itself—such knowledge is always in part based on experience; that is, on sensible intuition. Though it is not totally derived from such intuition, knowledge is genuine only when it comprehends that which can be experienced and not when it claims to know some supernatural or purely ideal realm.

In view of the rather broad idea of empiricism outlined above, we can see why Whitehead considered himself to be an empiricist, albeit of an unusual kind. "Our datum is the actual world, including ourselves," he writes. "And this actual world spreads itself for observation in the guise of the topic of our immediate experience. The elucidation of immediate experience is the sole justification for any thought; and the starting-point for thought is the analytic observation of components of this experience."[6]

As to what "experience" consists of, however, there has been endless debate, even among the most ardent empiricists.[7] Furthermore, insofar as modern philosophy of language has held to the classical empiricist judgment that language is of cognitive value only when its claims are experientially verifiable or falsifiable, the ambiguities concerning the nature of experience have naturally confused and complicated discussions of what the essential features of cognitive discourse might be. Obviously, then, the concept of "experience" requires careful scrutiny by any philosopher who wishes to claim, as Whitehead does, that his metaphysical statements and beliefs have experiential backing.

Being well aware of this fact and of the peculiarity of the very idea that a metaphysic such as his own could conceivably claim to be "empirical,"

Whitehead sets out to challenge certain commonly accepted theories of experience and knowledge. The main object of his attack is "sensationalism"—a doctrine embraced not only by the empiricists but by many rationalists and other philosophers as well. In essence, "sensationalism" is the belief that immediate experience is "sense experience," narrowly defined—experience "given" by the five senses and capable of being analyzed by means of clear and distinct ideas. Although this doctrine is not always directly espoused or consistently maintained by the philosophers with whom it is associated, Whitehead argues that it is indeed presumed by the founders of modern epistemology. As he points out, "When Descartes, Locke, and Hume undertake the analysis of experience, they utilize those elements in their own experience which lie clear and distinct, fit for the exactitude of intellectual discourse. It is tacitly assumed . . . that the more fundamental factors will ever lend themselves for discrimination with peculiar clarity."[8]

Whitehead's whole philosophy aims at challenging this assumption. Analyzing it into four related theses, he criticizes each one. In summary form, these theses are the following:

> (1) that all perception is by mediation of our bodily sense-organs, such as eyes, palates, noses, ears, and the diffused bodily organization furnishing touches, aches, and other bodily sensations; (2) that all percepta are bare sensa, in patterned connections, given in the immediate present; (3) that our experience of a social world is an interpretative reaction wholly derivative from this perception; (4) that our emotional and purposive experience is a reflective reaction derived from the original perception, and intertwined with the interpretative reaction and partly shaping it.[9]

It would be impossible here to trace all of Whitehead's arguments against these closely interrelated claims, because almost every one of his works attempts to refute such notions, and in a wide variety of ways. Yet the basic elements of Whitehead's critique can easily be set forth and in such a way as to seem at least suggestive if not immediately convincing.

First of all, let us consider Whitehead's answer to the claim that all perception is mediated by our five senses. Given the prominence of sense perceptions related to specific organs like eyes and ears, this notion seems reasonable enough. But it is also surely reasonable to ask whether we should assume that the most basic way in which we experience is necessarily through any media so vivid as eyesight and hearing, or indeed through anything that would make our experience a composite of various distinctive modes of perception rather than an integral whole. Upon asking this question, we might find some "sense" in Whitehead's claim that, when we experience and perceive, we do so—in the most immediate way imaginable—as embodied selves rather than as bundles of separate sense organs. That is, it may seem sensible to say, as Whitehead does, that "the living organ of experience is the living body as a whole"[10] and that "the unity 'body and mind' is the obvious complex that constitutes the one human being. Our bodily experience is the basis of experience."[11] Whitehead's point is not, of course, that the sense organs are somehow inessential to our distinctly human experience, but that they are *specialized* ways of perceiving that are integral to one's experience as a unified self consisting of body-mind. This is why no one says, "Here am I and I have brought my body with me."[12] The experiencing whole is more than the sum of its parts.[13]

To anyone accustomed to thinking in a traditional empiricist fashion this point of view will seem strange and perhaps not even comprehensible. But the rest of Whitehead's critique of the "sense-data" view of experience makes his position more intelligible and more credible.

We turn, therefore, to consider Whitehead's objections to the thesis that, whatever our organs of perception may be, all we really perceive are bare sensa that are somehow connected and yet experienced only as existing in the immediate present. David Hume was, of course, the philosopher who most forcefully and consistently articulated this concept. He did so most memorably in his rejection of the idea that there is actually any such thing as causality. It will be recalled that Hume's reason for rejecting this idea was one thoroughly consistent with the very epistemology that Whitehead is calling into question: the theory that the objects of knowledge are either matters of fact capable of being observed directly through the "impressions" of the five senses or else the necessary truths of mathematics and logic, which merely connect the ideas derived from "impressions." Hume's reasoning was that, because causal connections are not logical necessities and because they cannot themselves be directly observed (our "knowledge" of them being strictly inductive), causality cannot really be something we *know* of at all. Induction itself cannot, therefore, be rationally justified. Why, then, do we believe there are causes? Because we grow accustomed to associating certain successive events. "Causality" is a notion derived from mental habit and not from sensory impressions. As such, it is imaginary.[14]

Almost every philosopher has recognized that Hume's conclusion is counter-intuitive. But it has also generally been recognized that if our knowledge of the world is experiential, and if our primary experience consists of sense-data, then his conclusion is the logical one. Naturally, therefore, many philosophers have questioned the premises on which it is based. Some have felt compelled to reconsider the possibility of a totally nonempirical dimension of knowledge; others have chosen to think of phenomena like causes as "subjective" and yet no more so than sense-data themselves. Whitehead is one of the few to accept the empiricist premise but to challenge in a fundamental way the sensationalist notion of experience that Hume's version of empiricism entails. His response is to point out that what we *feel* intuitively about causes may in fact be what we most basically perceive in our immediate experience. According to Whitehead, the problem with Hume's argument has nothing to do with Hume's reasoning itself, nor with his empiricism per se, but only with his idea that experience basically consists of distinctly analyzable sense impressions.

One of Whitehead's own illustrations will perhaps clarify this point. Suppose, for example, that a light is suddenly turned on in the darkness, and one's eyes then blink. The distinct sense-data involved are a perception of a flash of light, the feeling of eye-closure, and an instant of darkness while the eyes are closed. Using Hume's theory one could never justifiably conclude that the flash caused one to blink, for one has had no distinct sense perception of a cause. But Whitehead argues that Hume's theory is untrue to what we really experience. If one's experience can verify anything at all, it can verify that the flash did indeed cause the blinking of one's eyes. To be sure, one could not see the cause itself, nor touch, smell, hear, or taste it. But this simply indicates that these five media of perception are in some ways superficial.[15] Indeed, Whitehead argues, in the fullness of life experience we always perceive, in a dim but persistent way, that each present occasion has a real relation to the past and is qualified by that past, even as it qualifies the future. This is something we know immediately and intuitively rather than something we infer and imagine derivatively. Thus, according to Whitehead, we all are deeply acquainted with a mode of perception that is in a way "non-sensuous" (though felt) and that is nevertheless highly informative because it tells us of, among other things, our relations to the past and future.[16]

As for the third thesis of sensationalism—that our social world is derived from "sense experience," narrowly defined—Whitehead considers the direct converse to be true. We know ourselves essentially and primarily as subjects-in-relation, not simply as subjects who happen to perceive sensory objects and to respond to them. Because we are essentially related to what we experience, we are not, as Descartes thought, participants in a strictly dualistic universe of subjects versus objects. All objective experience is indeed comprehended and shaped by our subjectivity, but we in turn know ourselves as intimately related to that which we comprehend and hence to the subjectivity of others. "There is the feeling of the ego, the others, the totality," Whitehead writes. "We are, each of us, one among others; and all of us are embraced in the unity of the whole."[17] Accordingly, our basic and primordial act of comprehension constitutes a "vague grasp of reality, dissecting it into a threefold scheme, namely, 'The Whole,' 'That Other,' and 'This-My-Self.'"[18] Were this not the case, solipsism would be unavoidable. But, again, this perception of the fundamental "togetherness of things" cannot reasonably be derived from one's cognizance of mere sense-data.[19] Sense-data, therefore, can hardly be the core of experience.

Finally, we must consider Whitehead's unequivocal rejection of the thesis that the emotional and purposive dimension of experience is merely derivative. It is this critique that he regards as the sine qua non for any metaphysical thinking that hopes to interpret experience in such a way as to do justice to religious beliefs. What Whitehead maintains in his criticism of this final thesis of sensationalism is that there is nothing self-evidently more derivative about certain emotions than about any other aspect of our experience. Emotion is not basically *added to* experience. In the very act of experiencing we feel enjoyment, suffer loss, take interest, feel valued.[20] We do not in fact know our actual experience at all apart from its "emotional tone":[21] "It is never bare thought or bare existence that we are aware of. I find myself as essentially a unity of emotions, enjoyments, hopes, fears, regrets, valuations of alternatives, decisions."[22] Thus, for all of us, there exists a primary level of experience that "lies below and gives its meaning to our conscious analysis of qualitative detail."[23] At this level of experience, Whitehead writes, "Our enjoyment of actuality is a realization of worth, good or bad. It is a value experience. Its basic expression is—Have a care, here is something that matters! Yes—that is the best phrase—the primary glimmering of consciousness reveals, something that matters."[24] Indeed, as Whitehead says, this experience of value, essential to our existence as selves, already entails an incipient awareness of transcendent worth beyond ourselves, a sense of what we may rightly call God.[25] "This," he says, "is the intuition of holiness, the intuition of the sacred, which is at the foundation of all religion."[26] No such intuition is presented by sense-data in and of themselves, of course, but there are no sense-data in and of themselves. There is only experience in which sensory impressions participate, and this experience is always characterized by value.

Even in this brief examination of Whitehead's critique of the sensationalist doctrines underlying much modern philosophy, we have seen the basic outlines of Whitehead's views on the nature of the experiential foundations of thought and cognition. Stating these in summary form, we can say that Whitehead believes there are two basic modes of perception,[27] both of which in actuality constantly intersect in our experience and thus provide the basis for cognition. The first mode is one in which we are aware of clear, distinct, and variable sense-data, vivid in their immediacy, and ever experienced as existing in the present moment.[28] The second mode is more fundamental, being more intimate, emotional, and complex.[29] This latter mode of perception is characterized, however, by much less clarity than the first because its content is so persistent in our experience as to call little attention to itself. Through this mode of perception we become aware of our past, of our relatedness, of selfhood, of others, of purpose, and of our worth within the Whole. Hence, while perceptions in the second mode are imprecise and elusive, they are the more important. This is why Whitehead concludes:

> The prominent facts are the superficial facts. They vary because they are superficial; and they enter into conscious discrimination because they vary. There are other elements in our experience, on the fringe of consciousness, and yet massively qualifying our experience. In regard to these other facts, it is our consciousness that flickers, and not the facts themselves. They are always securely there, barely discriminated, and yet inescapable.[30]

Those familiar with Whitehead's thought will presumably recognize that what I have given above is a nontechnical exposition of ideas that Whitehead's system expounds under the rubrics of "presentational immediacy," "causal efficacy," "symbolic reference," "the reformed subjectivist principle," and so forth. I have intentionally restricted my analysis of these ideas to their application to human experience rather than exploring their metaphysical implications. We are not concerned here with whether Whitehead's own metaphysical system is equal to the task of interpreting the general features of experience. Rather, we are interested in his theory concerning the nature of the experiential evidence to which a satisfactory empirical metaphysic must attend. Yet we are also interested in what Whitehead conceives to be the aims and limitations of any such metaphysic, theological or otherwise. This, then, is our next topic.

Metaphysics: Its Aims and Limitations

In considering Whitehead's views concerning the nature of metaphysics, it is important to note that what Whitehead means by "metaphysics" cannot sharply be distinguished from what he means by "cosmology," "speculative philosophy," or even simply "philosophy." One quickly realizes in reading Whitehead, furthermore, that his definitions of any one of these terms subtly alter from context to context.

We can say with confidence, however, that Whitehead does not conceive of metaphysics in ways it is sometimes conceived. He does not, for instance, conceive of it as the elaboration of a purely deductive system of thought grounded in axiomatic and indubitable truths.[31] To be sure, he sometimes sounds as though he wished metaphysics could be like logic and mathematics, where definite conclusions are deduced from premises as public and general as any conceivable. In remarks made several years after the publication of *Process and Reality*, Whitehead goes so far as to express a fond hope for a future epoch, analogous to that of St. Thomas Aquinas, when symbolic logic would somehow be expanded to become the foundation of aesthetics, ethics, and even theology.[32] But this logician's dream can easily be misunderstood.[33] Even if Whitehead does think of the *ideal* metaphysical scheme as a sort of axiomatic system—and even though, as R. M. Martin has noted, his own metaphysics may be viewed as "a kind of logico-mathematical system in disguise"[34]—one must realize that Whitehead regards the basic "axioms" of metaphysics not as self-evident truths but as imaginative hypotheses accountable to life experience. We must take seriously his warning that philosophy in the past has been misled by the example of mathematics and has therefore been "haunted by the unfortunate notion that its method is dogmatically to indicate premises which are severally clear, distinct, and certain; and to erect upon these premises a deductive system of thought."[35]

Certainly Whitehead never regards metaphysics as giving an "explanation" that will ever be complete or entirely adequate. Thus, in introducing *Process and Reality*—his most complete exposition of his own metaphysics—Whitehead writes: "There remains the final reflection, how shallow, puny, and imperfect are efforts to sound the depths in the nature of things. In philosophical discussion, the merest hint of dogmatic certainty as to finality of statement is an exhibition of folly."[36] Yet neither is metaphysics, for Whitehead, simply a flight of fancy: it is not, that is to say, what Anders Nygren has called "conceptual poetry."[37] Nor is it a narrowly circumscribed exploration of some area of truth not yet covered by the special sciences.[38]

What, then, does Whitehead consider metaphysics to be? I think we can probably best answer this question by looking at three different definitions he has given. In the first chapter of *Process and Reality* Whitehead states: "Speculative Philosophy is the endeavor to frame a coherent, logical, necessary system of general ideas in terms of which every element of our experience can be interpreted."[39] Elsewhere he says: "Philosophy is the attempt to make manifest the fundamental evidence as to the nature of things."[40] Or, putting it still another way: "Metaphysics [is] the science which seeks to discover the general ideas which are indispensably relevant to the analysis of everything that happens."[41] Taking all three of these definitions into account, we can see that metaphysics, as Whitehead describes it, has four basic traits: it is concerned with the fundamental nature of things; it is rational; it is empirical; and it is somehow both "necessary" and speculative. We need to determine more precisely, however, what Whitehead means when he says this.

First of all, in what sense does metaphysics try to make manifest the fundamental evidence as to the nature of things? Whitehead is claiming here that metaphysics is a kind of "total description," but this does not mean that it describes everything. What it attempts to do is to discern and describe the generic features common to all experience—the basic realities that make possible the distinctive features studied by the social and natural sciences. In its more cosmological dimension, it attempts to coordinate and evaluate the discoveries of such sciences in relation to an overall view of reality.[42] Thus, in Whitehead's understanding, a metaphysical system could never show whether a single act in history was an act of God or a manifestation of God's love, nor could it, in itself, determine whether some historical figure was God's prophet. But a metaphysical theology could suggest what the general conditions of the possibility of Divine action, abiding love, and human prophecy might be. In contemporary terminology we might say that a metaphysical system adequate to religious belief and experience could, theoretically, provide a conceptual model of reality in terms of which it would be meaningful and truthful to assert that God acts, or that God loves, or that life has everlasting significance. If that model also took into account the essential elements of experience as a whole, it would be credible, even if still imperfect. Whitehead would argue, in short, that such a model would merit qualified assent.[43]

One major way in which metaphysics invites that assent is by being not only general but also rational. If a metaphysical system were only a general or "total" description, it would be hardly more than a comprehensive mythology in which abstract notions had replaced vivid images.[44] But in fact, Whitehead says, metaphysics tries to meet two distinctly rational criteria. First, it is committed to logical reasoning and to avoiding logical inconsistencies.[45] Second, it is committed to coherence, for every fundamental idea within the system must necessarily be related to, and in some way presupposed by, every other fundamental idea used in the system. Thus, if one's system postulates the existence of two kinds of substances—corporeal and mental, or physical and spiritual—there must be some reason, internal to the system, as to why this is required. Otherwise the system will suffer from incoherence, as Descartes's does.[46]

Even more important than the internal logic and systematic coherence of a general metaphysical description, however, is its empirical character, or its claim to be able to elucidate experience. In this connection the first thing to note is that metaphysics cannot claim to be empirical merely on the basis of reasoning from one or two "self-evident" axioms but must show itself to be applicable to experience in its myriad forms. As Whitehead says in one famous passage:

> Nothing can be omitted, experience drunk and experience sober, experience sleeping and experience waking, experience drowsy and experience wide-awake, experience self-conscious and experience self-forgetful, experience intellectual and experience physical, experience religious and experience sceptical, experience anxious and experience care-free, experience anticipatory and experience retrospective, experience happy and experience grieving, experience dominated by emotion and experience under self-restraint, experience in the light and experience in the dark, experience normal and experience abnormal.[47]

It is plain that, in Whitehead's view, metaphysics is not concerned with specifying the a priori conditions of the possibility of there being any world at all, but rather with setting forth a theory as to how it is possible for this very world to be fundamentally as it is.[48] Whitehead believes a metaphysical system needs to be "necessary" not in a logical or "eternal" sense but in an empirical sense: it should be the theory required in order to account for the nature of experience as we find it.[49]

As an essentially empirical mode of understanding, a metaphysical system must meet two criteria. It must, on the one hand, be applicable to *some* actual experience, perhaps of a kind mentioned in Whitehead's delightful catalog. On the other hand, it must be, in principle, adequate to describe the basic features of all experience.[50] Apart from such applicability and relative adequacy, even the most internally coherent and logical system has extremely limited value.[51] This is not to say that there is, or even should be, a one-to-one correspondence between the elements of a metaphysical description and observable phenomena. (Few would claim this is true even of the theories of natural science.) It is merely to say that the method by which metaphysics proceeds is one that begins and ends with the observation of actual experience: "The true method of discovery is like the flight of an aeroplane. It starts from the ground of particular observation; it makes a flight in the thin air of imaginative generalization; and it again lands for renewed observation rendered acute by rational interpretation."[52]

Yet, in emphasizing the experiential basis of metaphysics, Whitehead would not have us forget that metaphysical understanding is speculative to the core and always incomplete.[53] Taking his cue from Aristotle, but making a more radical claim, Whitehead declares that philosophy both begins and ends in "wonder," using constructs that require imaginative leaps rather than simple deductions or inferences.[54]

Now to say that an empirical system of thought begins and ends in "wonder" is totally mystifying if one has a narrowly empiricist notion of experience. One ordinarily thinks of empirical reflection as starting from "hard data," or at least from clear statements concerning such data. Furthermore, Whitehead's description of the philosophical "method of discovery" may leave one with the impression that he himself believes that the only imaginative and speculative stage in metaphysical thinking is the "flight" of descriptive generalization—a flight wherein clearly analyzable factors discerned in particular areas of human interest like physics or social thought are extended into "generic notions which apply to all facts."[55] At the start and finish of this flight, it might appear, one stands on the terra firma of immediate observation.

The obvious problem with this line of interpretation is that it ignores Whitehead's theories as to the nature of experience and the consequent limits of direct observation. In point of fact, it is Whitehead's view that the imaginative flight of speculation is necessary at all only because "our primary insight is a mixture of clarity and vagueness" rather than "hard data."[56] What we can see clearly and describe plainly are "superficial facts" not to be confused with the full content of immediate experience. As Whitehead rather bluntly states: "The equating of experience with clarity of knowledge is against evidence. In our own lives, and at any one moment, there is a focus of attention, a few items in clarity of awareness, but interconnected vaguely and yet insistently with other items in dim apprehension, and this dimness shading off imperceptibly into undiscriminated feeling."[57] Thus nothing whatever in our immediate experience—or at least nothing of what is more important for metaphysical reflection—is susceptible of "clear-cut complete analysis."[58]

At best, then, the first principles guiding the "flight" of descriptive generalization are hypotheses based on a very partial understanding of some sphere (or spheres) of experience. Derived from "flashes of insight"[59] rather than from precise observation, they are expressed in words and phrases that "remain metaphors mutely appealing for an imaginative leap."[60] This in no way negates the value of rational speculation itself. Although no understanding derived from such thought can hope to be completely adequate, the advantage of speculation is precisely that it transcends what is obvious,[61] permitting one to think analytically about what otherwise tends to be almost imperceptible, being obscured by more variable and vivid elements of experience.[62] Without this sort of act of intellectual distancing and abstraction one would have great difficulty in discerning the most concrete aspects of the world, in evaluating and coordinating insights, and in judging between the accidental and the essential.

Still, one does not look to metaphysics for proofs. When one returns to the realm of observation after the speculative flight, one hopes for more acute observation. But there are no "neat and tidy" facts to be uncovered and verified through metaphysics.[63] At any rate, metaphysics is not concerned with such facts. Its whole effort is to illumine and elucidate what Philip Wheelwright calls a "sense of reality." Theories about "facts" can be proved or disproved, but an overall theory of the fundamental nature of things can only strive for an effect of "sheer disclosure" in which one's basic understanding of one's self and world is amplified and made manifest.[64] This is hardly a matter for ordinary argument. Like every system of thought, metaphysics rests on presuppositions that must be taken for granted within the system itself.[65] But a metaphysical system differs from others in that it seeks to be the most fundamental explanation possible. Consequently, it cannot appeal to any other area of inquiry for confirmation of its basic hypotheses. These must be tested by one's overall experience and in relationship to the whole of thought. That is why metaphysics is a speculative "adventure" and why Whitehead believes so strongly that philosophy must end, as well as begin, in wonder.

Finally it must be said that, in Whitehead's opinion, the value of speculation ultimately consists more in its various penetrating insights than in its systematic character. "The art of speculative Reason consists quite as much in the transcendence of schemes as in their utilization."[66] This alone explains Whitehead's judgment—astonishing, I am sure, to many of his disciples—that Plato was "the greatest metaphysician, the poorest systematic thinker."[67] For Plato's greatness, Whitehead says, consists in the fact that, in spite of his failures in creating a system, he "always succeeded in displaying depth of metaphysical intuition."[68]

In view of the great value Whitehead attributes to penetrating insights, it should not be surprising that he believes an adequate metaphysic derives not only from an analysis of ordinary experience but also from an appreciation of the moments and areas of special insight and intuition that make manifest those important regions of human experience we but dimly discern in our everyday awareness. It is because of this that the metaphysician—in an effort to frame a general, rational, empirical, and speculative system—must take into account the sphere of religion and "revelation."

Religion, Theology, and Metaphysics

In his analysis of how philosophy begins to develop its fundamental insights into the nature of things, and so to formulate its "first principles," Whitehead (as we have seen) insists that the philosopher must consider the features of experience in a variety of contexts. But it is clear that he would not have us expect all experience to be equally revealing. In his opinion philosophy can hardly content itself with generalizing strictly from commonplace observations or from nothing but the "hard facts" provided by clear and distinct sense-data.

Accordingly, Whitehead designates certain areas of experience as resources of particular value for metaphysical reflection. The experiential resources he most frequently singles out are language (especially literary), secular social institutions, the special sciences (natural and social), aesthetics, practical experience, and religion.[69] It is thus evident that metaphysics, as Whitehead understands it, reflects less on "raw experience" than on experience already interpreted at some level through "civilized intercommunication."[70] For this reason Whitehead calls metaphysics a "secondary activity."[71]

Now there is doubtless some sense in which each of the resources named above is also "secondary," because each at some point interprets other interpretations of experience. But none of them tries to interpret the essential features of experience common to *all* spheres of inquiry and expression—none, that is, except religion. Whitehead, therefore, considers religion to be distinctive. In point of fact he describes it as being at least a nascent form of metaphysics, especially when it tries, in its maturity, rationally to elucidate and justify its beliefs.[72] For this reason, as we will see when we examine his basic ideas concerning the nature of language, Whitehead considers the linguistic issues faced by the philosophical theologian to be essentially the same as those faced by the metaphysician. Indeed, all of the tasks of the philosophical theologian and the metaphysician are, in Whitehead's eyes, much the same.

Yet even Whitehead admits that there are some important differences between religion and metaphysics in general, so that the relationship between these two phenomena merits special comment, particularly with respect to two questions: In what way does metaphysics need religion? And in what way does religion need metaphysics?

Reading certain of Whitehead's statements, one could easily think that he believes metaphysics has no need whatever for religion. In *Adventures of Ideas*, for example, Whitehead asserts: "The essence of Christianity is the appeal to the life of Christ as a revelation of the nature of God and of his agency in the world."[73] This at first sounds as though the life of Christ would merit considerable attention on the part of the metaphysician. But then Whitehead asks, rhetorically, "Can there be any doubt that the power of Christianity lies in its revelation in act, of that which Plato divined in theory?"[74] Given Whitehead's love of Plato, this is probably meant as a compliment to Christianity. But, obviously, if the philosopher already knows through Plato what the believer in Christ knows through the Christian religion, then there is no reason for the philosopher to look to Christian revelation for any additional insight. Whatever its value, the Christian *mythos* would seem to be of no special cognitive significance.

Whitehead's thinking on this matter is not so simple as it sometimes seems, however, as is apparent from another observation he makes in this very same context. In the next paragraph Whitehead goes on to say that the theologians who developed the doctrine of the third person of the Trinity were "the only thinkers who in a fundamental metaphysical doctrine have improved upon Plato."[75] There is a certain amount of unintentional irony in this remark, for it is plain that any theologian who assumed, with Whitehead, that the truth of the Christian revelation had already been exhaustively expressed by Plato would never meditate on the Christian fact in such a way as to improve on Plato's own metaphysics. Be that as it may, Whitehead is consciously pointing out that it is by no means impossible for the person reflecting theologically on the meaning of a religious tradition and dogma to advance the cause of metaphysics in general.

That this is the case is not due to any theological or metaphysical sophistication inherent in religion, however. Few religions begin as a developed metaphysical system, Whitehead notes. Historically they involve at least four factors: ritual, emotion, belief, and rationalization.[76] Although Whitehead reaches the rather odd conclusion that rationalization is the factor of deepest religious importance,[77] he acknowledges that religion is impossible without emotion and perhaps ritual as well. Thus the story of the life of Christ, together with the rituals of the church and the nucleus of beliefs central to the worshiping community, presents a quite different phenomenon from a metaphysical system. Far from exhibiting the structure of thought alone, it and the expressions of religions as a whole provide what Whitehead terms a "supreme fusion" between emotion and conceptual thought or belief.[78]

The ordinary empiricist, of course, would hardly cherish a form of language, ritual, and experience that fused emotion with thought, bringing to consciousness the realm of values. Such a fusion would be seen as mere confusion in which the subjective is mistaken for the objective and by which one is deluded as to the real "nature of things." But, in Whitehead's view, it is in just this "fusion" that the genius and metaphysical importance of religion resides. Mere emotion or mere conceptualization produces "life tedium."[79] But such tedium is untrue to the essence of our experience— experience that metaphysics exists solely in order to elucidate; for, as we have already seen, Whitehead claims that at the heart of our experience is our sense of value, of relatedness, of transcendence, and of the sacred.[80] Thus, he writes, our "deeper experiences" are religious and mystic.[81] Religion is of special interest and value to metaphysics because it makes manifest this depth of experience: "The peculiar character of religious truth is that it explicitly deals with values. It brings into our consciousness that permanent side of the universe which we can care for. It thereby provides a meaning, in terms of value, for our own existence, a meaning which flows from the nature of things."[82] The task of metaphysics—whether theological or philosophical—is, consequently, not to transcend religion but to elucidate and justify in general terms the sense of reality that is intrinsic to religious belief and practice and dimly apprehended in all of life.

But to say this is inevitably to raise the question of whether theological and metaphysical interpretation does not do violence to the very beliefs it seeks to elucidate. Is it not the case that religious truth can and must always appear foolish according to philosophical standards? (One can cite, of course, Paul's statements in First Corinthians.) Instead of requiring metaphysical explication, does not religious belief reject the very possibility of metaphysics? Whitehead, so far as I know, never responds directly to this question. Indirectly, however, he gives two different answers to it, both intended to be valid from within the perspective of religion itself. First of all, he argues that the religion that claims its dogmas to be infallible, and so refuses to subject them to rational reflection and possible criticism, is engaging in a form of idolatry that is false to the very mystery of things to which it claims to be true. It is precisely because "we know more than can be formulated in one finite systematized scheme of abstraction" and because we do dimly discern that "which stretches far beyond anything which has been expressed systematically in words" that we cannot claim any one expression of truth to be ultimate.[83]

Second, Whitehead claims that religion itself seeks a metaphysic simply because religion holds that its truth is not private or purely emotive but universal and ultimately real. It is, to be sure, indisputable that religions spring from special events and special people and thus begin with moments of "revelation."[84] But it is only when the incipient rationality of religious doctrines is developed through philosophical reflection that religion can show what it most desires to show, namely, that "its concepts, though derived primarily from special experiences, are yet of universal validity, to be applied by faith to the ordering of all experience."[85] In sum, Whitehead says: "Rational religion appeals to the direct intuition of special occasions, and to the elucidatory power of its concepts for all occasions. It arises from that which is special, but extends to what is general. The doctrines of rational religion aim at being that metaphysics which can be derived from the supernormal experience of mankind in its moments of finest insight."[86] Thus, while metaphysics requires religion in order to achieve genuine profundity of insight into the most important dimensions of experience, religion requires metaphysics in order to attain greater self-understanding and to justify its claim to express truths concerning what is of ultimate significance to humanity.

Neither religion nor metaphysics exists without language, however. Accordingly, Whitehead's analysis of both religion and metaphysics leads to the conclusion that the theologian or philosopher can be true to neither one without attending specifically to the nature of the linguistic medium and its different means of expressing our deepest insights.

Metaphysical Theology and the Importance of Language

In *Adventures of Ideas*, Whitehead makes a statement that contemporary philosophical theology has since reexpressed many times. There he ventures to say: "I suggest that the development of systematic theology should be accompanied by a critical understanding of the relation of linguistic expression to our deepest and most persistent intuitions."[87] My aim here is to see just what kind of critical understanding of language Whitehead himself proposes.

Whitehead makes no secret of his belief that most ordinary language, as well as much of the special language of philosophy and theology, is by no means ideal as a medium for "evolving notions which strike more deeply into the root of reality."[88] Though Whitehead's critique of language differs in some very important ways from Wheelwright's, many of his judgments should sound familiar to anyone who knows Wheelwright's semantic theories. In Whitehead's view, the greatest problem we face in trying to use language to reflect on matters of depth is that much of our language has been reduced to the status of a mere tool for managing practical affairs and for thinking about superficial facts—facts that are neat, tidy, and ontologically trivial.[89] Thus most of our language is both abstract and reductive; it is, to use Wheelwright's terminology, a "steno-language," treating all phenomena whatever as plain, matter-of-fact data.[90] For this reason it properly expresses neither the general but probing ideas crucial to metaphysics nor the vivid apprehensions of life experience fundamental to religious insight. Instead, our language commonly "halts behind intuition," or else obstructs intuition entirely because of faulty and uncriticized presuppositions.[91]

Whitehead maintains, however, that there are forms of language that can permit us to attend to the depths of experience and can also genuinely elucidate those apprehensions of reality present in a dim and primordial way prior to adequate verbalization.[92] In his opinion the two forms of language that possess this potential most fully are poetry and philosophical discourse, especially metaphysical discourse. This he states forthrightly in a little-noticed passage in *Process and Reality*: "After the initial basis of a rational life, with a civilized language, has been laid, all productive thought has proceeded either by the poetic insight of artists, or by the imaginative elaboration of schemes of thought capable of utilization as logical premises. In some measure or other, progress is always a transcendence of what is obvious."[93] It is important for us to see, therefore, what Whitehead says about both the poetic and the metaphysical modes of imaginatively transcending the obvious and to determine what he understands their relationship to be.

Even a cursory reading of Whitehead turns up many passages in which he speaks of the "penetration of literature and art at their height."[94] It is, he claims, "one function of great literature to evoke a feeling of what lies beyond words" and to suggest meanings "beyond its mere statements."[95] In his view these "meanings miraculously revealed in great literature"[96] refer to "depths beyond anything which we can grasp with a clear apprehension."[97] Although Whitehead does not believe literature is strictly cognitive in purpose, he does believe it to be of real cognitive significance. He is convinced, for example, that the Romantic poets, who shunned "dry philosophical statements," succeeded in expressing in vivid, imaginative form six notions essential to an adequate philosophy of nature—namely, "change, value, eternal objects, endurance, organism, interfusion."[98] Although this claim may elicit a smile, because these notions just happen to be central to process philosophy, it is nevertheless significant. For Whitehead is here arguing that, at one point in history, the primary sources for these notions were the poets rather than the contemporary scientists and philosophers. Elsewhere, moreover, Whitehead asserts that the fundamental insights of literature—like those of other major modes of knowing—are unlikely to be surpassed: "The world will not repeat Dante, Shakespeare, Socrates, and the Greek tragedians . . . . We develop in connection with them, but not beyond them in respect to those definite intuitions which they flashed upon the world."[99]

We may well ask, however, whether Whitehead believes there is anything truly distinctive about the way in which literature probes the mystery of things. Again Whitehead's answer (confined to a few, scattered passages) will sound familiar to the student of Wheelwright. Whitehead's basic explanation for literature's special place in language is that most works of poetic art—like most religious rituals and symbols—express the "transitions in emotion" pertinent to our actual thought and life.[100] In other words, they convey the "*inward* thoughts" and "concrete outlook" of human beings.[101] In particular, "the poetic rendering of our concrete experience" lets us "see at once that the element of value, of being valuable" is an essential part of our experience of ourselves and of our world.[102] Because literature combines universal truths with an imaginative treatment of particulars,[103] and because it expresses emotion together with thought, this form of language has the capacity to give utterance to our most intimate life experience, which is known in a way scientific and philosophic abstractions may easily disregard or simplify. In short, Whitehead would agree with Wheelwright's observation that literature serves the "phenomenological" object—as this quotation from *Science and the Modern World* attests: "I hold that the ultimate appeal is to naive experience and that is why I lay such stress on the evidence of poetry."[104]

Any overt resemblance between Wheelwright's views and Whitehead's ends at this point. Whereas Wheelwright contends that poetry is the only form of language capable of depth and thus able to escape the shallowness of steno-discourse, Whitehead believes that the language of philosophy and of metaphysical theology is no less deep and is (to say the least) as valuable in the long run. Philosophy, he declares, "reverses the slow descent of accepted thought towards the commonplace. If you like to phrase it so, philosophy is mystical. For mysticism is direct insight into depths as yet unspoken. But the purpose of philosophy is to rationalize mysticism: not by explaining it away, but by the introduction of novel verbal characterizations, rationally coordinated."[105]

Wheelwright, of course, would argue that such philosophy is nothing more than a specialized form of steno-language that stipulates in a precise way the meanings of its terms. He would conclude that it is for this very reason doomed to failure, because the mystical insight it hopes to "rationalize" can never precisely be articulated nor systematized. Wheelwright's position therefore seems diametrically opposed to Whitehead's. Whereas Whitehead is persuaded that "there is no first principle which is in itself unknowable, not to be captured by a flash of insight,"[106] Wheelwright would insist that no fundamental insight can be "captured," and least of all in steno-language. Perhaps this simply confirms what we knew all along: Whitehead trusts reason, Wheelwright does not.

It should by now be obvious, however, that Whitehead's rationalism is at least as unusual as his empiricism. I would contend that it consists largely in his faith that the pursuit of rational schemes can continue gradually and indefinitely to increase our quite limited understanding. Whitehead maintains, to be sure, that human language and knowledge have an infinite potential. But he considers this to be true only in principle. In actuality the limitations, as he sees them, are not only real but also so great as to leave no room for "the merest hint of dogmatic certainty."[107]

This sense of the actual limitations of rational thought and conceptualization is directly reflected in Whitehead's theory of the nature of metaphysical language itself. In the first place, a metaphysical system—as

Whitehead envisions it—is always an *imaginative* construct that starts from a *metaphoric* base: "Words and phrases must be stretched towards a generality foreign to their ordinary usage; and however such elements of language be stabilized as technicalities, they remain metaphors mutely appealing for an imaginative leap."[108] Hence, such a system of concepts is "steno-language" of a kind Wheelwright never contemplates. It is, admittedly, an "adventure in the clarification of thought"[109] that necessarily depends on one's willingness to argue "boldly and with rigid logic."[110] This in turn means that, within the system itself, the meaning of the metaphors it uses must be "stabilized" and the metaphors themselves conceptualized, thereby being deprived of most of their peculiarly metaphoric vitality. But all this is done in the context of an experiment, an adventure in ideas, for which no absolute validity is being claimed nor any direct correlation with the phenomena of reality itself. Indeed, one misunderstands Whitehead's whole concept of metaphysics if one supposes that any metaphysical concepts or inferences refer immediately to the world outside the metaphysical system. Whitehead's view is plainly that the argument found in a metaphysic is a hypothetical and speculative exploration of the implications of certain premises or "first principles" that, for the sake of philosophical inquiry, must of course be defined in such a way as to become clear and distinct. But we have already seen that there is no way experientially to verify whether these clear and distinct ideas themselves adequately represent anything in actuality. They in themselves can have no unambiguous meaning *outside* the system because the only unambiguous "facts" of any importance are those found *within* the system. Clarity is a function of the whole hypothesis, not of any particular thesis that can be abstracted from it and applied directly to experience. This is apparent not only from Whitehead's account of experience and perception but also from his assertion that, "apart from a complete metaphysical understanding of the universe, it is very difficult to understand any proposition clearly and distinctly, so far as regards the analysis of its component elements."[111] If one could attain a complete and perfect metaphysical understanding of everything, then one could claim a complete and clear understanding of something. But, as Whitehead repeatedly insists, our metaphysical understanding is always very incomplete.[112] It follows, therefore, that we can have no perfectly distinct concept of any fundamental element of actual experience—not even of the ideal entities of mathematics and logic.[113] Or at least we can claim for none of our concepts any ontological precision corresponding to their apparent linguistic exactitude. To believe otherwise is merely to be deluded by the "fallacy of misplaced concreteness"[114] and so to succumb to a subtle but insidious form of dogmatism.

In summary, then, Whitehead argues that the language of metaphysics, although highly rational, fundamentally derives from an act of imagination. Its concepts are always to some extent ontologically imprecise even as they reach further toward the truth, slowly clarifying our dim understanding. This is what makes metaphysical discourse an adventure. Metaphysics itself—whether philosophical or theological—constitutes a significant transformation of our ordinary modes of thought. Contributing no certain knowledge, it nonetheless gives insight into the ideas and faith by which we live. It is for this reason that Whitehead says: "Our metaphysical knowledge is slight, superficial, incomplete. . . . But, such as it is, metaphysical understanding guides imagination and justifies purpose."[115]

With this in mind, we cannot be too surprised to find that, different as poetry and speculative thought are from each other, Whitehead sees them as in some ways parallel enterprises. "Philosophy is akin to poetry," he observes;[116] or, more generally, it is "analogous to imaginative art."[117] Again, in *The Function of Reason*, he suggests that the truth of "the utmost flight of speculative thought . . . may be the truth of art."[118] For both poetry and metaphysics transcend ordinary ways of interpreting and understanding experience, pursuing depths of meaning in such a way as to involve "imagination far outrunning . . . direct observations."[119]

Whitehead, however, is not saying that philosophy and poetry are identical in substance and function. On the contrary, he argues that philosophy strives to be conceptual, analytical, rational, and critical whereas poetry tends to be concrete, synthetic, emotional, and "naive." Philosophy, and theology as well, further differ from poetry in that, whereas the former enterprises both have a central concern for truth, it is often the case that the whole of a poem is concerned with truth only indirectly, if at all.[120]

Now, precisely because there *are* major differences between the language of poetry and the language of theology and philosophy, Whitehead believes these languages are in the end not entirely parallel but also intersecting and in some ways interdependent. Although he seldom seems to consider the possibility that poetry might at times be deepened as a result of its contact (however indirect) with metaphysical reflection, Whitehead does indicate that metaphysics is in various ways indebted to the language of poetry, broadly conceived. In point of fact he claims that, because many elements of experience on which metaphysics and theology seek to reflect enter our consciousness first as flashes of insight rather than as definite concepts, the philosopher or theologian must rely on the "intermediate imaginative representations" of poetry, art, and ritual if he or she is to glimpse what is essential in such moments of illumination.[121] He recognizes, in other words, that if the philosopher and theologian are to reflect rationally on "the supernormal experience of mankind in its moments of finest insight,"[122] they can hardly do so adequately without attending to the kind of language in which such insight is embodied most fully, although not yet raised to the level of critical understanding. Consequently, Whitehead states, "Philosophy is the endeavour to find a conventional phraseology for the vivid suggestiveness of the poet . . . and thereby to produce a verbal symbolism manageable for use in other connections of thought."[123] Applied to theology, this would mean that the philosophical theologian has as a central task the conceptual interpretation and critical understanding of the primary language of parable, symbol, story, myth, and so forth, because it is such basically metaphoric language that often provides the "best rendering of integral experience."[124]

Whitehead thus holds that the theological and philosophical enterprises would hardly be possible, let alone adequate, apart from a foundation constituted by the language of integral experience, of which poetic art is in some respects the epitome. This conviction becomes apparent in *Process and Reality* when Whitehead attributes the "thinness of so much modern metaphysics" to its neglect of the poetic and artistic utterance of ultimate religious feeling.[125] One likewise discovers a similar point of view implicit within many passages of *Modes of Thought*, one of the most interesting being that in which Whitehead states: "The father of European philosophy [Plato, of course], in one of his many moods of thought, laid down the axiom that the deeper truths must be adumbrated by myths. Surely, the subsequent history of Western thought has amply justified his fleeting intuition."[126]

Certainly there can be no doubt that a metaphysics like Whitehead's own does indeed seek to interpret the kind of integral experience he says is often best "rendered" by the "vivid" languages of poetry and myth. For, as we have seen, the experiential evidence to which Whitehead appeals is known only through "felt" awareness. Apart from reflection on the actual experience of love, of creativity, of temporal passage, of relatedness, of value, and of transcendence—phenomena scarcely susceptible of purely logical and scientific analysis—there could be no Whiteheadian metaphysics nor, in his view, any other metaphysics that could claim to be adequate to religious experience. It might be true that—as Whitehead's metaphysics tries to show, and as the Christian tradition and *Four Quartets* perhaps testify—"the world lives by its incarnation of God in itself."[127] But this insight cannot metaphysically be justified merely on the basis of rational reflection on the bare "fact" that something exists, or that we are able to know, or that there are causes. What matters both metaphysically and religiously is the *significance* of existing, knowing, and having purposes; and it is this significance, known through one's whole being and becoming as an embodied self, that is the core even of the *cognitive* meaning within the concept of incarnation. Consequently, a metaphysical theology cannot begin to be adequate if it does not take into account the felt quality of the experience of being a valued self related in time to an eternal purpose.

But if the poetic rendering of experience is plainly seen by Whitehead as something vital to philosophy and theology, we may nonetheless want to ask at this juncture whether Whitehead conceives of poetry (or myth or symbol) as a kind of ladder that one can cast aside once one has made the ascent to rational reflection and conceptualization. This, after all, could be taken to be Plato's own view as well as the view of numerous other Western philosophers. Even though Whitehead never offers any sustained discussion of this question, his answer can reasonably be deduced both from his practice and from his theories of perception, thought, and language. Looking at Whitehead's interpretations of Romantic poetry in *Science and the Modern World*, for instance, one can easily discern a confidence that the sensitive and patient thinker can indeed articulate in conceptual terms the essential insights to be found in this or that particular work of literary art. But Whitehead's frequent insistence on the tentativeness of schemes of thought, when combined with his assertions concerning the almost miraculous power of literature to evoke a feeling of what lies at "the edge of consciousness,"[128] allows of no interpretation but that the philosopher or theologian reflecting on some major topic can hardly expect to incorporate into his or her formulations all the relevant wisdom embodied in the primary language of art, poetry, and scripture. So elusive are our depth perceptions, and so subtle their poetic and artistic expression, that the effort to elucidate and criticize them through a "conventional phraseology" can never entirely be finished. This is why, in Whitehead's words, "the transitions to new fruitfulness of understanding are achieved by recurrence to the utmost depths of intuition for the refreshment of imagination."[129]

That some measure of inadequacy is inevitable is certainly not taken by Whitehead to mean that our more reflective enterprises, whether metaphysical or otherwise, cannot intellectually be justified. The idea that one cannot responsibly claim cognitive worth for any system of assertions sure to retain at crucial points some hidden margin of ambiguity or some as yet incalculable degree of inadequacy is simply alien to Whitehead. In this connection one need only recall his emphasis that "understanding is never a completed static state of mind. It always bears the character of a process of penetration, incomplete and partial."[130]

Nevertheless, if the primary sources for theology and philosophy are deemed virtually inexhaustible, the clear implication is that there will always need to be not only what Whitehead terms an "interplay of thought and practice"[131] but also an ongoing dialogue between the more poetic and the more conceptual modes of discourse. As Whitehead describes the matter, such understanding as we do possess appears to emerge from a process that is fundamentally dipolar. At one pole we find the kind of experientially rich understanding embodied in poetic, artistic language and arising from the awareness generated by our whole selves and minds acting as a unity. At the opposite pole we find the understanding derived from critical, logical reflection. Although Whitehead considers the latter a higher—and definitely clearer—form of knowledge, he nonetheless never leads us to believe that we can expect, at any given time, an exact fit between these two modes of discourse and understanding. Hence it becomes obvious that, just as a viable theology needs metaphysics for its most reasonable expression, so both metaphysics and theology continually require what Whitehead calls the "evidence of poetry." [132]

But in the end, it must be observed, Whitehead himself is somewhat vague as to just how the poetic and theological or metaphysical modes of discourse might interact while at the same time remaining distinct. His "hermeneutics" and theory of poetry, moreover, may now seem at points relatively unsophisticated, although his observations on the indeterminacy of meaning in discourse anticipate certain claims of the current deconstructionists (whose antimetaphysical bent he would obviously reject). Then, too, Whitehead's notion of the theological task could with some justification be criticized as overly influenced by his preoccupation with metaphysics. Yet Whitehead's analysis of poetry's connection with theology and metaphysics remains provocative. Especially when it is correlated with his theories of experience and understanding, it is also distinctive, giving ample testimony to his conviction that "the development of systematic theology should be accompanied by a critical understanding of the relation of linguistic expression to our deepest and most persistent intuitions." [133] I now intend, therefore, to build on the foundation Whitehead has provided, as well as on the theory of poetic metaphor already put forward, by outlining a more comprehensive theory of the relation of poetry not only to the formal theological interpretation of religious beliefs but also to the modes of existence correlated with those beliefs. In so doing, I will be examining both the linguistic and the religious patterns of transfiguration.

Chapter Seven Transfiguration
Metaphor, Theology, and the Languages of Religious Belief

The transitions to new fruitfulness of understanding are achieved by recurrence to the utmost depths of intuition for the refreshment of imagination.
— Alfred North Whitehead

We must recognize and make room for whatever fresh, unexpected, and unpredictably diverse modes of synthesis may find expression when the mind operates at levels and at moments of highest poetic intensity.
—Philip Wheelwright

Near the beginning of this study I noted how Philip Wheelwright's ideas and those of many other students of language and literature constitute, in part, a response to certain theses first advanced by modern philosophical movements such as critical philosophy, empiricism, and especially logical and "semantic" positivism. What has proven to be especially provocative in these philosophies and their current descendants is their tendency to divide statements into two separate classes, one consisting of meaningful and/or cognitively valuable assertions, the other consisting of utterances deemed meaningless and/or cognitively worthless—the latter class containing most metaphysical, religious, ethical, and poetic assertions.[1]

In reaction to this way of viewing language and cognition, a great many literary critics have taken one of two tacks. They have either argued that a poem is indeed meaningful and truthful but have qualified this claim by maintaining that poetic meaning and truth is strictly "contextual"; or they have conceded that poetry is nonassertorial and noncognitive but have gone on to contend that poetry is nonetheless meaningful as an emotive language satisfying some distinctly human needs. Whereas the theories of certain New Critics typify the former response, those of I. A. Richards and certain later psychological or philosophical critics typify the latter.

These literary-critical responses to modern philosophical criteria of meaning and truth have almost exact parallels in theological responses to the same philosophical ideas, the primary difference being merely that the theologian's concern has, of course, been with religious language instead of with the language of poetry proper. Just as one group of literary critics has insisted that poetry's truth is, as it were, transcendent and hence beyond criticism or comparison—revealed to us in a medium fundamentally different from ordinary discourse and thought—so a great many theologians, adopting a linguistic form of Kierkegaardian fideism or neo-orthodox supernaturalism, have maintained that Christian beliefs and assertions are both meaningful and true and yet have also maintained that they are specially revealed and self-authenticating. Other theologians (especially those influenced by recent philosophy) have taken a position analogous to that of I. A. Richards and his contemporary counterparts. These theologians have conceded that religious language proposes no truths and yet have argued that such language has important noncognitive functions. When they have taken the later Wittgenstein to be the most fruitful resource for a contemporary understanding of language, they have often claimed specifically that religious language is meaningful as a kind of autonomous "language game"—one among many, to be sure, but nevertheless legitimate and played according to rules unique to itself.[2]

This latter approach to language and meaning anticipates the latest strategy of all, which is to deconstruct all such ideas as truth, knowledge, and reality. If the deconstructionists are right, these weighty concepts can be jettisoned (or at least "de-centered") along with the whole baggage of Western "logocentric" metaphysics—a prospect many successors to the death-of-God theologies readily welcome.[3] Similar results would follow, moreover, from Richard Rorty's recent proposal that philosophy become an "edifying" discipline cured of the pretensions of epistemology and engaged in "conversation" rather than "inquiry." It is hard to imagine a deconstructionist dissenting from Rorty's claim that "we have to understand speech not only as not externalizing inner representations, but as not a representation at all. We have to . . . see sentences as connected with other sentences rather than with the world."[4] Or, if one cannot go this far, there is Stanley Cavell's less confining invocation of the "moral of skepticism," which is that "the human creature's basis in the world as a whole, its relation to the world as such, is not that of knowing, anyway not what we think of as knowing."[5] This suggests, at least, that we might still profitably think of there being a world or worlds beyond sentences and of there being some kind of knowledge beyond sheerly arbitrary constructs, however different it may be from anything absolute. But the skeptical side of the "moral" is what Cavell often chooses to emphasize.

My aim is not to deny the potential fruitfulness of some of this recent thought but to remark on the degree to which, in the areas of literature, philosophy, and religious thought, we have witnessed increasing emphasis either on the independence of languages and ways of knowing or on the plurality and ubiquity of kinds of meanings not strictly related to the "mere" expression of truth. No doubt these developments have already had many positive effects, not the least of which is the disclosure of how diverse and complex human language and culture is. But at least two possible effects are, I think, deleterious. On the one hand, if every major locus of meaning and/or truth is felt to be entirely independent of every other such locus, we are seemingly forced to dwell in multiple, unconnected worlds and thus to suffer from what I earlier termed a sort of ontological (and perhaps social) schizophrenia. Under these circumstances the notion of truth itself loses much of its force and meanings lose much of their significance.[6] Even if the Tertullians of the world may be able to believe something because it is absurd from every other point of view, most of us begin to feel it is absurd, in a situation of purely relative or separate truths, to believe at all. On the other hand, if all languages are seen to be so interconnected as to be parasitical on each other without ever affording access to actualities beyond language itself, then one pays the price of removing the "other" from discourse and thought. When this happens, one witnesses the disappearance of any self, neighbor, world, or God that might warrant love or care. Either way, the cost is high. The firmest of convictions begins to appear unfounded or naive, as is perhaps indicated by the disintegration in our century of even the confident "metaphysics" of scientific naturalism and its reduction to various forms of conventionalism or functionalism. At the same time, life begins to be focused not on the good and the true, nor even on the beautiful, but rather on the practical, the arbitrary, and the merely pleasing.

Within the sphere of religion per se the consequences of this development are obviously not minor. For those who cannot simply surrender themselves to belief systems that seem strictly unbelievable, one major alternative seems to have been to embrace religion strictly as a way of being—a mode of living—that is unrelated to any genuine way of knowing.[7] But this is far from satisfactory from a truly religious point of view. It is indeed salutary to realize that the question of knowledge as such is not the sole or even the foremost concern of religion. Religion has to do with praise, confession, celebration, ritual, promises, decisions, and acts of love and justice—all of which transcend simply the question of truth or knowledge. But if it is the case that even a work of poetic imagination can be meaningful to us as persons only so long as it is felt somehow to relate to realities beyond the special world of the work (and our study certainly suggests that this is so), then the same is true a fortiori of the language of religion. However self-referential or noncognitive some functions of religious language may be, the "game" played by such language as a whole becomes trivial and even incomprehensible unless it is understood as concerned, ultimately, with more than itself. In fact, the language game played when we use religious language is precisely that of interpreting the ultimate significance and purpose of playing any "games" at all, linguistic or otherwise.[8] This must be so if religion is really concerned, as Whitehead says, with our "intuitions into the ultimate mystery of the universe,"[9] and thus with making manifest "a meaning . . . for our own existence, a meaning which flows from the nature of things."[10]

It would seem, therefore, that the question of what we can justifiably believe and reasonably claim to know is not one that can well be forgotten, although neither should it be allowed to crowd out all other questions. For the Christian tradition itself, at any rate, it is imperative to try to comprehend more fully how human beings can justifiably believe themselves to be addressed not only by multiple languages of their own making but also by a Word that is more than merely a human construct and is yet "incarnate" in human experience and language.

My basic assumption in this whole inquiry has been that our comprehension of this crucial relation between experience, words, and a higher or deeper Word can be made more penetrating if we realize not only that our sense of reality is intimately related to the languages we use, but also that the languages we use in articulating and shaping our sense of reality are themselves intimately related to one another and to something beyond themselves. Thus I have claimed that metaphoric and conceptual discourse—which Wheelwright regards as the two most basic kinds of language—should be seen as interdependent even while irreducible one to the other and as mediating a sense of what lies beyond language as such even while coloring and shaping all awareness of the not yet spoken.[11] Because the two subspecies of language that have seemed to me to epitomize the "deeper" forms of metaphoric and conceptual discourse are poetry (or literary art) and metaphysics (or metaphysical theology), I have wanted in this study to show in what way specifically poetic and metaphysical interpretations of experience are interrelated, both directly and indirectly.

Much of what I have wished to say in this regard is already implicit in what Whitehead says, especially when his ideas are considered in the light of the semantics of poetry I have been developing on the basis of Wheelwright's work. Few thinkers, it seems to me, have been at once so committed as Whitehead is to a rational, theistic metaphysics and so sensitive to the actual limitations of metaphysical systems, reckoning with the ontological significance of poetic and even nonverbal insight. What Whitehead does not provide, I think, is a truly adequate understanding of how the concepts of metaphysics are related to the requirements of a Christian theology (he was not, of course, a theologian). Nor does he provide a very satisfactory notion of the dynamics of metaphoric discourse itself. As a result, he partly misrepresents the connection between theological and metaphoric expression, and he does so primarily by placing too much confidence in conceptual language as such.

In what follows, therefore, I make selective use of Whitehead's ideas and correlate them with the semantic theories I have been exploring so as to see more clearly poetry's relation to the theological task of understanding the meaning and truth of religious (and, in this case, Christian) beliefs. To facilitate my exposition, I rely on what David Tracy calls a "revisionist" model of theology, because I believe that this model is probably the most viable one for contemporary theology.[12] But the issues addressed here are by no means the exclusive province of any one theological method. And though I am obviously in sympathy with certain tenets of specifically Whiteheadian or "process" revisionist theology, I look with a critical (if also appreciative) eye at how one process theologian—Schubert Ogden— views the role of conceptual discourse in relation to the language of metaphor. This done, I offer a more constructive statement of what I understand to be the relation of the language of poetry to the language and task of theology and, further, to nonverbal dimensions of religious belief. In this connection I return to the idea of transfiguration, placing it within a religious context of meaning. This last phase of my study, like those preceding it, is naturally not intended to exhaust its subject but merely to contribute to an ongoing inquiry—or "conversation"—and to introduce several ideas that must necessarily await further development.

Experience, Concepts, and the Task of Theology

In the course of examining how Whitehead understands metaphysics to be possible as an empirical enterprise, we saw that, in his view, any metaphysics that hopes to provide an adequate interpretation of the essential content of human experience must abandon the common assumption that experience is reducible to sensation, narrowly conceived. Whitehead's critique of sensationalism—which I find basically convincing—is by no means without parallel in twentieth-century thought. In fact, as process and "empirical" theologians have been quick to point out, his conclusions are in many ways similar not only to those reached by continental phenomenologists like Husserl, Merleau-Ponty, and Heidegger but also to ideas found in the American pragmatist and "radical empiricist" tradition represented by figures like William James, Charles Peirce, and John Dewey.[13] In this area Philip Wheelwright too seems to share many of Whitehead's views.[14] Thus Whitehead's concept of experience, quite apart from its application to a general metaphysics, certainly cannot be dismissed as a mere oddity. It belongs to a vital and continuing philosophical tradition that today provides a genuine alternative to the classical empiricist and rationalist ways of thinking. It is therefore pertinent to contemporary linguistic philosophy as well, whenever such philosophy again examines the relation of language to experience.

The question of how and whether metaphysics can actually be done on the basis of experience so understood is more problematic, however, as is quite evident from the fact that few of the philosophers mentioned above consider a full-blown metaphysics to be viable. Even more problematic is the question of whether theology has use for any such metaphysics, should it be possible. Can the God of philosophy—even Christian philosophy—ever be the God of religion and, specifically, of Christian faith? How legitimate is Whitehead's insistence on the importance of metaphysics for religion itself? Or, to put the question still more broadly, and in the form most relevant to our present inquiry, of what value to religious understanding can *any* highly conceptual system be, whether "anthropological" (for example, existentialist) or metaphysical? (We should again recall that Whitehead's metaphysics ventures into cosmology and the special sciences, so that an absolute distinction between the understanding of human nature and the nature of human understanding is not applicable to his philosophy.) These questions have been raised time after time within the field of theology, but each fresh theological development adds nuances to the questions themselves and lifts up new possibilities for answering them.[15] I now intend to place these questions within the context of contemporary revisionist (or postliberal) theology and to show how the revisionist sense of the importance of theological and metaphysical conceptualization can perhaps best be defended by tempering, rather than intensifying, Whitehead's enthusiasm for conceptual discourse per se. In so doing, I call into question the inclination of some revisionists simply to equate the "fullest possible understanding of faith" with the conceptual elucidation and explication of faith.

It has widely been acknowledged in theology since Tillich that the theologian has a dual obligation. On the one hand, the theologian must try to articulate the meaning and truth of Christian faith in a way that is appropriate to the Christian tradition and especially to Christian scriptures. On the other hand, the theologian must try to explicate the meaning and truth of that faith in a way that is adequate to contemporary experience and is thus genuinely understandable and meaningful in the present historical moment.[16] In other words, the Christian "message" and the cultural "situation" must in some way be correlated, and correlated understandably.[17] Thus the task of philosophical theology necessarily involves, in David Tracy's words, "reflection upon the meanings present in common human experience and language, and upon the meanings present in the Christian fact."[18] It is perhaps the chief hallmark of what Tracy calls "revisionist" theology, moreover, that it takes both spheres of meaning and truth with full seriousness. That is, such theology feels responsible to criteria derived from both spheres while realizing that the critical correlation between them can be no simple matter, because "common human experience" will always, to some extent, be in tension with the "Christian fact."[19]

Given the revisionist theologian's dual commitment, it is not difficult to see why such a theologian has often been attracted to Whitehead's metaphysics, perhaps as a complement to an existential phenomenology like Heidegger's. Whitehead, although not a theologian, does consider the "evidence" of religious belief and language, arguing that religion as such makes manifest a fundamental religious dimension of human experience—namely, our primordial trust, our sense that life somehow matters, and our awareness (however obscure) that we exist at all only in relation to a context of ultimate value, and finally in relation to God.[20] Furthermore, Whitehead's metaphysics seems especially responsive to the interpretation of existence and reality expressed in Christianity's belief in both the transcendence and immanence of God, in the centrality of love and grace, and in the meaning and purpose of history.[21]

But precisely by assuming that the revisionist model for doing theology is in many ways more viable than the orthodox, neo-orthodox, liberal, or radical models, one necessarily acknowledges that the theologian cannot afford uncritically to adopt any metaphysical system. Every system of thought whatsoever must be considered in relation both to the scriptural understanding of humanity and God and to the various understandings that arise out of our present situation and common human experience. We are therefore pressed to ask: In view of the nature of the scriptural texts, and thus of the normative discourse of Christian belief, in what way and to what extent can any conceptual (steno-linguistic) system hope to be appropriate to the "Christian fact"? And how, and in what measure, can any conceptual system alone really be adequate to our common human experience?

Ironically, the responses that certain process theologians and philosophers have given to these questions are much less equivocal than Whitehead's own. But they are also, I believe, less satisfactory than his, being unduly influenced by certain of the narrower forms of modern linguistic philosophy. Of these responses, the clearest is probably that of Schubert Ogden, whose incisive and provocative thinking on this subject deserves careful scrutiny at this point because of the direct challenge it presents to the position I am wanting to advance.

Ogden first gained widespread theological recognition for his book *Christ without Myth*, a study that carried Rudolf Bultmann's program of demythologizing beyond Bultmann's own self-imposed limits and thus applied it to issues of Christology and revelation in a manner that was (many theologians believe) fully consistent with Bultmann's premises, even if not with Bultmann's conclusions.[22] Later, and especially in *The Reality of God*,

Ogden wedded demythologizing to metaphysics, synthesizing a Heideg-gerian-Bultmannian anthropology with a "neoclassical" or "process" meta-physics that is closer to Charles Hartshorne's than to Whitehead's and yet is still indebted to Whitehead.[23] Most recently, he has sought to develop a theology of liberation and to point the way toward a liberating Christol-ogy that would be both appropriate to the earliest New Testament "wit-ness" and credible in the present moment.[24] What is pertinent to this dis-cussion, however, is not Ogden's proposal for liberation theology, his claim as to the point of Christology, his overall view of demythologizing as such, or even his overall view of metaphysics, but specifically his view of the value and place of conceptual, propositional language in faith's en-deavor to understand itself.

In his essay "The Task of Philosophical Theology," Ogden sets forth his ideas on this topic with great clarity.[25] There he writes: "Because of its own inner nature and dynamic, faith seeks the fullest possible understanding of itself and its claim, and this means, finally, that it seeks a theological under-standing."[26] Elsewhere in this same essay Ogden explains that by "theo-logical understanding" he means "reflective understanding" and "critical interpretation."[27] Clarifying this point still further, he states: "Theology is possible at all only in terms of concepts. Reflective understanding in the full sense applicable to theology means precisely conceptual understand-ing."[28] And ultimately the kind of conceptuality required by theology, he says, is nothing less than "a complete theistic metaphysics."[29]

It is therefore evident that, for Ogden, the "fullest possible understand-ing" of faith is at once reflective, critical, conceptual, and in the end meta-physical. But the crucial term here is "conceptual," because Ogden sees re-flection, criticism, metaphysics, and indeed theology itself as possible at all only in the language of precise conceptualization.

Yet Ogden is a good revisionist, insisting that the conceptual interpreta-tions provided by theology must simultaneously be appropriate to the meaning and truth of Christian scripture and adequate to human experi-ence as we actually find it. And it is at just this point that Ogden and all theologians confront a significant difficulty. At least in theory the concep-tual language of theology might easily be made both appropriate and ade-quate if the normative texts of Christianity were already conceptual in es-sence and if our human experience basically comprised clear and distinct ideas. But, as Ogden himself avers, such is not the case. On the one hand, analysis of the scriptures reveals that their language is, in large part, the language of myth, parable, and symbol. In short, it is what I would call the language of metaphor.[30] On the other hand, the basis of human experience in general is itself hardly intellectual. Ogden would be the first to admit that our fundamental awareness of ourselves and our environment is existential and prereflective. Thus, in Ogden's view, the clearest of our deeper ideas about ourselves and the world do not derive from correspondingly clear dimensions of experience.[31]

Ogden is quite undaunted, however, by the realization that the phenomena on which theology is required to reflect, and which it is supposed to try fully to understand, are of a different semantic and experiential order from the intellectual and conceptual one exemplified by theology itself. With regard to scripture, Ogden readily grants that some of the meanings its mythic, metaphoric language expresses cannot be captured in conceptual discourse.[32] But insofar as mythic and symbolic meanings are genuinely cognitive in nature, he argues, they can and must be conceptually interpreted. Otherwise they cannot fully be understood, nor their truth defended. "It is all well and good to insist that there is a truth in myths and that they therefore must always be taken seriously," he writes. Nevertheless, he says: "The claim of a mythical utterance to be true is simply unsupportable unless one has some conceptuality in which its meaning can be literally and properly stated. . . . If theological thinking and speaking have to do properly and primarily with the God who discloses himself in Jesus Christ, then they involve claims to truth which can be conceptually stated and justified."[33]

In a similar way, Ogden freely admits that there is an aspect of human experience and knowledge that is inaccessible to precise conceptual understanding and expression. This is—as Heidegger and Bultmann claim—the realm of one's purely personal encounter with reality, the realm of that which is known in the moment of existential decisions and private meaning.[34] But Ogden contends that this existential (*existenziell*) understanding must clearly be distinguished from the existentialist (*existenzial*) understanding we articulate when we describe the basic structure of existence in general. The latter, which can (and must) be expressed conceptually, in fact comprises everything we can claim to know *about* even our own existence. It alone is what we can really know objectively—although this knowledge is still not "objective" in a scientific sense, because its objects are not ones that empirical science can fully analyze.[35] Thus Ogden agrees with Bultmann's contention that in finding a friend and experiencing friendship one learns nothing more *about* friendship but simply discovers it as an *event*, a reality *for oneself*.[36] This, then, becomes another way of his stating that everything that can be known or said *about* existence can be put into concepts, and that it is this conceptual understanding, and only this, that constitutes communicable knowledge concerning existential phenomena.

Finally, as we should expect, Ogden apparently believes that everything we can justifiably claim to know and articulate even about the sphere of dim and intuitive perception that Whitehead calls "causal efficacy" can and must be expressed conceptually, literally, and "properly." Thus he declares, as a matter of principle: "I fully accept the argument . . . of virtually all contemporary analytic philosophers, that cognitive status may be claimed for statements only if one is prepared to support the claim by clearly specifying the principle in accordance with which the truth of the statement can be rationally determined." [37] Needless to say, "rationally determined" means, in Ogden's terminology, nothing less than "conceptually stated and justified" and eventually explicated by means of a system that is "frankly and fully metaphysical." [38]

All of which goes to show that Ogden, at least, is one revisionist theologian who has little doubt that conceptual discourse in itself is capable of providing a fully appropriate and adequate understanding of the meaning and truth of the Christian "witness" (to use Ogden's term) and of our human experience in the cultural and historical situation in which we find ourselves. For this reason Ogden believes that theology, precisely as a conceptual mode of discourse, is the supreme medium of faith's self-understanding. In this regard he represents one major line of theological opinion since Anselm. He allies himself, moreover, with a distinguished tradition of philosophy and hermeneutics. On this traditional view, understanding begins with the symbol, the *Vorstellung*, the metaphor, or myth; but it moves on to the concept and proposition, with the aid of which it becomes both critical and positive and is enabled to reach its peak. The movement toward fuller understanding is thereby seen as a difficult but epistemologically straightforward movement toward adequate conceptualization. And the task of justifying belief is seen as identical with that of justifying theological concepts.

The virtues of Ogden's position are considerable, and they are especially worth heeding at a time when many theological and religious scholars seem (again) in danger of sheer irrationalism. Especially welcome is Ogden's view that faith entails claims to truth and understanding and that these claims deserve rational support and/or criticism. As should be evident by now, moreover, I can also endorse his related judgment that a rigorous philosophical—and even metaphysical—theology can play an important role in understanding the realities to which faith testifies. Indeed, I would go so far as to agree with Ogden's stronger claim that theology is not only desirable but also necessary if we are to attain the fullest possible understanding of faith. But to take the final step of concluding that theology in and of itself can provide the fullest measure of all understanding that is more than purely existential—this is, I think, to make a serious mistake. First, such a conclusion relies on far too sharp a distinction between "understanding" as a strictly conceptual or steno-linguistic function and "understanding" as the act of apprehending or grasping through metaphoric outreach. Second, Ogden's conclusion overlooks the limitations of primarily conceptual discourse vis-à-vis the modes of experience and language it is called on to criticize and interpret. Third, his position ignores some unique features of metaphor and metaphoric understanding. In making a start toward remedying these oversights, we will see that the route toward faith's fullest self-understanding cannot be as Ogden describes it.

In calling into question the validity of Ogden's argument, I would first of all call attention to the little noticed fact that, with regard to our present topic, Ogden's views—like the views of his mentor Charles Hartshorne—are very different from those of Whitehead. This may mean that Ogden has improved on Whitehead, but I will contend there are good reasons to doubt that this is in fact the case.

In certain respects, of course, Ogden's position and Whitehead's are similar. Whitehead would certainly accept Ogden's premise that the normative Christian texts are by no means abstract and conceptual. This is apparent when Whitehead declares: "The reported sayings of Jesus are not formularized thought. . . . The ideas are in his mind as immediate pictures, and not as analyzed in terms of abstract concepts. . . . He speaks in the lowest abstractions that language is capable of, if it is to be language at all and not the fact itself."[39] Like Ogden, Whitehead nevertheless insists that the special insights revealed in the "supernormal" visions and highly concrete sayings and events of religious history must be "rationalized" and conceptualized if they are to be widely recognized as the universal truths they claim to be.[40] Furthermore, Ogden and Whitehead are agreed that, although human experience is not basically susceptible of narrow empirical and scientific analysis, neither is it completely beyond the powers of "objective" expression. It is evident, finally, that both thinkers share a trust that the structure of reality in all its forms is somehow itself rational and best elucidated conceptually and metaphysically.

There is little indication, however, that Ogden either shares Whitehead's keen awareness of the limits of clear conceptualization or fully appreciates Whitehead's deep concern for what lies beyond those limits. This important difference is perhaps most immediately seen in Ogden's theory of the relation between language and cognitive claims. Ogden, as we have observed, equates our capacity responsibly to claim that we have understanding with our capacity to express our understanding clearly and conceptually. Without conceptual, systematic explication of our statements of belief, Ogden argues, the claim that these statements are cognitive "cannot be responsibly *made* or *supported*."[41] This much, Ogden admits, he readily grants to the modern analytic philosophers and to "radical" theologians like Paul van Buren.[42] Where Ogden differs from these thinkers is not in his semantic and cognitive theory, therefore, but in his conviction that we can indeed achieve both conceptual clarity and adequacy to experience—and hence genuine cognition—by means of metaphysical and existentialist discourse.

Whitehead naturally shares Ogden's convictions as to the validity and cognitive value of metaphysics and also Ogden's commitment to rationality.[43] But he does so without paying the price of simply equating precise, conceptual verbalization with our capacity to claim to know something *about* a phenomenon. Whitehead sees no *direct* correlation between depth of understanding and clarity of conceptual expression, nor between one's right to claim some measure of understanding and one's ability to articulate that understanding in a way that is universally understandable. "Language halts behind intuition," he writes; "our understanding outruns the ordinary usages of words."[44] And all the words we use retain an indeterminate measure of ambiguity.[45] The only really direct correlation Whitehead sees, therefore, is between one's ability conceptually and systematically to formulate one's limited understanding and one's ability to make publicly evident and thoroughly reasonable the truth of what one can already grasp in some less rational form, such as through the "vivid suggestiveness of the poet."[46] Moreover, even our clear "understanding," so clearly expressed, never contains all that we genuinely know *about* the world. This is plainly implied in Whitehead's contention that "we know more of the characters of those who are dear to us than we can express accurately in words"[47] and in his slightly sentimental statement that "mothers can ponder many things in their hearts which their lips cannot express."[48] Ogden might reply that, although these claims are in some sense true, they refer only to purely existential understanding—that is, to personal "knowledge-as-event." But Whitehead never says this. He knows of no such absolute distinction between existential knowledge *of* and objective knowledge *about*. Thus, contrary to the views of Ogden and Bultmann, Whitehead evidently holds that even what one knows *about* relationships cannot be expressed with complete conceptual "accuracy"; and yet this sort of knowledge constitutes "the ultimate religious evidence, beyond which there is no appeal."[49]

When seen from Whitehead's perspective, therefore, the issue of what one can responsibly claim to know, and of the linguistic implications of such a claim, looks very different from the way it looks when Ogden describes it. If Whitehead is correct, it could be argued that it is only reasonable to claim that we do know more than we say and that we can and do adumbrate in myths what we cannot yet articulate with clarity.[50] For we always are somehow in possession of insight and even wisdom that lies beyond exact conceptual formulation and systematic expression. This is why Whitehead believes that rationality consists as much in being able to transcend tidy systems of thought as it does in composing such systems.[51] It is true, of course, that Whitehead's own ideal of knowledge would be a perfect, conceptual, metaphysical system; and he maintains that even the limited metaphysical knowledge that is ours is distinctive in value, permitting us to make judgments and coordinate insights in a valid—though still provisional—way. But until the *eschaton* of perfect knowledge has come, it would seem that, as Whitehead sees the matter, the fullest possible understanding available to us at any given historical moment must necessarily include both that which we can formulate with relatively adequate conceptual clarity and that which we must discover in the relatively less conceptual forms of language such as the poetic and symbolic. "The defect of a metaphysical system," Whitehead writes, "is the very fact that it is a neat little system of thought which thereby over-simplifies its expression of the world."[52] This being the case, "the transitions to new fruitfulness of understanding are achieved by recurrence to the utmost depths of intuition for the refreshment of imagination."[53] This in turn means that "understanding is never a completed static state of mind."[54] Certainly it encompasses more than clear conceptualization.

But if this really is so, knowledge is a very complex phenomenon, occurring at multiple levels of awareness and accompanied by varying degrees of critical judgment. Accordingly, the criteria of truth are likewise complex and may often be difficult to grasp. It is easy, then, to see why Ogden would wish to formulate (and satisfy) more decisive and clear-cut criteria of truth and to that end would distinguish so sharply between understanding or knowledge of an intuitive or existential kind and knowledge in a strict, "objective" sense.[55] Indeed, this is exactly what Ogden seems to accomplish when he argues that we have reason to claim truth for a myth, metaphor, or theological assertion only if we can state its cognitive meaning literally, conceptually, and in the end metaphysically.[56] For this indicates very plainly that we should say we know the truth only when we can say precisely what we are claiming to know, and on what basis.

Doubtless Ogden's rule as to when we have a right to claim truth for an assertion, or knowledge for ourselves, applies very well in domains in which it is commonly agreed that we *can* in fact say precisely what we claim to know and can therefore be expected to state more or less unambiguously the warrants for our claim. The paleontologist who asserts that he or she has discovered a new kind of trilobite is rightly expected to be able fully to explicate and back up the claim, or else be prepared to relinquish it. For trilobites are empirical phenomena made manifest to us through our five senses. In other words, paleontology, like many other kinds of natural science, treats realities perceived largely through the mode of what Whitehead calls "presentational immediacy." But this is not true of metaphysics in any of its more adequate forms nor of existential concepts. Consequently, metaphysical understanding, like existential phenomenology, can always be expected to have such a margin of ambiguity that we would be unreasonable to demand complete precision of meaning either in the articulation of such understanding or in any statement of the conditions that would *warrant* a particular claim to metaphysical knowledge.[57]

Ogden, of course, would deny this. Indeed, his latest book, *The Point of Christology*, shows more plainly than ever the tenacity with which he holds onto the idea that assertions, even if metaphysical, can be deemed credible only to the extent to which they can be formulated literally and "properly." Here Ogden makes the surprising move of rejecting not only classical but also neoclassical attempts to do what he terms "categorial" (or analogical) metaphysics—including theistic metaphysics of the kind one finds in much of Hartshorne and in virtually all of Whitehead.[58] Ogden's argument against such metaphysics is that it is grounded not in statements that have precisely determinate meaning and truth-value but in statements like "God is boundless love." Although thinkers such as Hartshorne and Ogden himself have long maintained that this kind of statement has a perfectly definite, rational meaning—a "properly" analogical meaning as opposed to either a purely symbolic or strictly everyday meaning—Ogden now disputes this claim. The problem, Ogden says, is that, given our lack of any prior and immediate conceptual knowledge of God, we lack any clear-cut basis for judging whether and in what measure the ordinary meaning of a term like love, for instance, is applicable to divine reality. Ultimately there is no way to distinguish this kind of talk from discourse that is overtly symbolic and metaphoric. Consequently, it is not "properly" analogical at all. In fact theistic metaphysics by its very nature excludes the possibility of "proper" analogy. And because only "proper" and conceptually precise discourse is credible, and hence useful in metaphysics, no credible metaphysics can be based on analogy any more than it can be based on explicit metaphor.[59]

In Ogden's view, however, this does not mean we must abandon metaphysics altogether. For he has come to believe in the possibility and necessity of a theistic process metaphysics that would be strictly literal in character, this being a "transcendental" metaphysics articulating truths the applicability of which necessarily extends to all experience and the denial of which would presumably lead to incoherence and logical contradictions.[60]

To be sure, Ogden would not, even now, reduce all religious language to literal metaphysical statements like "God is relative as well as absolute" or "ultimate reality is a distinct center of universal *interaction* that, being acted on by all things as well as acting on them, is their sole final end as well as their only primal source."[61] He still sees a place for metaphoric expressions like "God is the rock of our salvation." Yet he has not begun to allow for the possibility that metaphoric language could in principle have any unique cognitive worth. What he currently says, instead, is that literal religious and metaphysical discourse has one major job: to denote the structure of reality itself. Metaphoric language has a different job: to persuade and move one to adopt in life the kind of existential self-understanding and moral behavior that is consonant with the structure of reality denoted by literal language.[62] Whatever cognitive role metaphor plays, that role is purely secondary and is inherently untrustworthy apart from "proper" standards established by literal concepts and logical thinking.

Ogden, then, is consistent in wanting to tie metaphysical (and all other) cognitive claims to perfectly literal, conceptual assertions. But his consistency does not make his position more plausible. Using Ogden's criterion for meaning and truth, we could justify making truth-claims for a metaphysical system only if we could reasonably argue that the metaphysic under consideration was strictly coherent, intelligible, logically (and perhaps empirically) required or "necessary," and hence apparently secure in its validity (though Ogden never explicitly says this). For only then—in view of the nature of metaphysics itself—could we claim to be able to comprehend exactly and literally what this system meant and to comprehend just how and what it really permitted us to know. But there is good reason to doubt that this argument can ever in fact reasonably be made. One may certainly *believe* that a given metaphysic is entirely coherent, adequate, and in every way required or "necessary." But this belief cannot itself be rationally justified. This is because, as Whitehead points out, the truth of a metaphysic, or at least of any metaphysic of use to religion, cannot be purely logical or completely demonstrable, given the ambiguities inherent even in our most logical reasoning. The conceptual precision of relatively adequate metaphysical ideas is a function of a hypothetical, speculative, empirical system that cannot be expected to have any *exact* correlation with reality itself. Nor can the ways in which a given metaphysical system lacks precision be determined precisely, because such a determination would itself require a perfect metaphysical understanding. Accordingly, it is only reasonable and responsible to conclude that a metaphysical system is bound to be both true and false in ways in which those who believe in it can neither fully grasp nor fully specify, although they may possess a peripheral and important awareness of its latent possibility and limits. This, after all, can surely be said with regard to the classical theistic metaphysics that Ogden, Whitehead, and Hartshorne all respect and yet criticize as rationally incoherent and experientially inadequate. Yet classical metaphysics seemed, in its day, the very height of rationality and adequacy.[63] Indeed, it seemed perfectly "necessary."

Ogden himself acknowledges, furthermore, that the neoclassical metaphysics he embraces will itself doubtless someday be superseded.[64] Since Ogden cannot possibly state in advance in what way this metaphysics will eventually come to be considered incoherent or inadequate, and therefore unnecessary, he seems to be in the position of having to amend his earlier criterion to say something like this: We can rationally claim to have understanding of the general structure of reality if and only if we can formulate a conceptual, clear, and systematic expression of that understanding, and one that *seems* to us to be literally and necessarily true—or perhaps unavoidable—although in point of fact our conceptuality will almost certainly turn out to be incoherent and inadequate in ways we cannot foresee. This constitutes an admission, however, that one can, after all, reasonably claim some measure of truth for an assertion or system of assertions in relation to which one cannot in fact say *precisely* what one really knows or *exactly* on what basis one's supposed knowledge rests. When one admits this, one is admitting a great deal. For it seems plain that the cognitive advantages of believing what *seems* literally and necessarily true are, at least in the sphere of metaphysics, relative rather than absolute—in which case both the original and the amended criteria as to when one can reasonably or responsibly claim to have metaphysical understanding should be drastically revised.[65]

As it happens, there has been, for quite some time now, a tendency in semantics and epistemology to move away from directly correlating cognitive claims with total conceptual explication, and thus toward recognizing just how complex the criteria of both meaning and truth must be if they are to reflect the nature of human experience, thought, and language. Interestingly enough, one can observe this shift even within that analytic tradition of philosophy and theology which Ogden cites as previously insisting on the kind of criteria of meaning and truth that he himself accepts. One now finds that Paul van Buren, for example, both guardedly endorses the thesis that religious language makes "quasi-metaphysical" assertions that can be judged true (or false), and argues that it does so by way of "speaking at the borders of language."[66] Again, Max Black—whose credentials as an analytic philosopher are impeccable—long ago reached the signal conclusion, recently reiterated, that a literal paraphrase of metaphor may be at once extremely valuable and yet inadequate as a cognitive substitute, because the loss of meaning that a paraphrase entails is in such cases a loss in cognitive content.[67] Finally I would call attention to the work of Stephen Toulmin, whose critiques of positivism Odgen himself time after time leans on for support. Toulmin does not now appear to hold to Ogden's own rather narrow concept of what it means to know or to make a claim to knowledge. He argues, instead, that "there is more to knowing / believing / having reasons for our beliefs than any formal philosophy can encompass."[68] In his recent textbook on philosophy, moreover, Toulmin closes his entire discussion with the observation that, in the end, the philosopher's task is "concerned with human nature in its very largest and most comprehensive framework." In seeking to understand human nature in this way, Toulmin says, a final question arises:

> "May not the philosopher be obliged, in this respect, to take on the additional functions of the *poet* or creator of *myths*?" Certainly this was a role in which the classical Greeks were prepared to cast philosophy and philosopher. To them, the poet Homer himself appeared as a kind of philosopher, while all of Plato's geometry, logic, and dialectic went hand in hand with myth-making.[69]

Toulmin then suggests that the "integrative activities of the philosopher-as-poet" are indeed legitimate and that they must be related to the other philosophical tasks. I cannot imagine that the work of the philosophical theologian would be excluded from this suggestion.

But it is not the theologian or philosopher as poet who is our major concern here; rather, it is the relation of the highly conceptual language used by the theologian to the essentially metaphoric language used by the poet. Although Whitehead has provided us with clues that have become especially meaningful within a revisionist framework of understanding the task of theology, perhaps the last clue we need is supplied by Toulmin, who maintains that there are two basic approaches to reasoning. The chief concerns of the first are expressed in the question: "How can we achieve formal rigor in our logical connections, and absolute certainty in our fundamental grounds, so as to yield geometrical certainty?"[70] All the methods of argumentation that take this question as their point of departure would obviously be, in Wheelwright's terms, steno-linguistic and steno-logical. They would of course more than satisfy Ogden's requirements for cognitive discourse. Other methods of reasoning originate from a somewhat different question, however, which is this: "How can we establish the common standpoint and shared experience required in order to achieve general and warranted agreement?"[71] This second question, I believe, may well be the primary one for the theologian at any time, and its special relevance at present seems undeniable. What it suggests is that anyone who would reason theologically must somehow succeed in mobilizing a shared awareness of the experiential grounds to which one's theological concepts appeal for their very meaning. Otherwise one's language, no matter how conceptual, is simply not understandable. In other words, only when a common stand-point of shared "religious" *experience* is established—and continually re-established—can meaningful and sound reasoning using shared theologi-cal *concepts* be a real possibility. This in turn suggests the possibility that theological discourse will seem truly understandable and reasonable only as long as it is heard in dialogue with discourse that can—in Toulmin's words—tread "the boundary line separating logic from rhetoric."[72] For we have seen that rhetorical, expressive language has a special capacity to com-municate the character and dynamics of actual experience and of germinal thoughts and perceptions.

What we must now examine, therefore, is how the "rhetorical" language of poetic metaphor interprets, reflects, and shares the vital experiential di-mension undergirding theological concepts and reasoning. In this connec-tion, however, it will be necessary to criticize certain of the presupposi-tions of Whitehead himself.

Transfiguration: Poetry, Theology, and Religious Belief

As I begin to map more precisely the experiential and linguistic ground common to theology and poetry, I need to make several observations that were only implicit in my earlier discussion of the "revisionist" approach to theology. According to the revisionist theologian, religious assertions can be said to have meaning only if we can show that there is a dimension of our common human experience that they address, express, or elucidate. Furthermore, the specifically "empiricist" type of revisionist assumes that even meaningful religious assertions can be considered to be truthful only if they can be shown to have a basis in something more than our own sub-jectivity (narrowly conceived). Consequently, such a theologian tries to find or construct a metaphysical model of the world disclosed through ac-tual experience. This model is to be one that can at once account for the essential features of experience in general and support the validity of the religious dimension of our common experience—namely, our persistent trust in, recognition of, or at least longing for, transcendent meaning in life. Moreover, according to the revisionist, the only kind of model ade-quate to support the faith that this trust or longing is justified is one that can somehow show the relation of existence to an ultimate ground, source, or horizon of all that is: a reality to which all our fundamental experience and knowledge somehow points. Finally, the revisionist theologian takes seriously the requirement that any metaphysical system or model useful to theology per se must not only be adequate to interpret our essential and common human experience but also be appropriate to the meaning and truth expressed in the Christian tradition and especially the Christian scriptures.[73]

We have already seen that this dual requirement is none too easily met. One reason for this is that neither scriptural language nor life experience is essentially conceptual in nature, whereas theology does generally strive to be conceptual. But I think there are two other reasons for the difficulty in meeting this requirement, both of which are highlighted by a Christian understanding of human nature.

First of all there is, for the Christian, the undeniable fact of our finitude. We know only in part, as the apostle Paul testifies; we see in a mirror dimly rather than face to face (I Cor. 13:12). Or, as Whitehead says, we find ourselves "wandering dazed in the abundant universe."[74] Because of finitude, every discovery of some essential truth concerning ourselves or the realities to which we are inherently related is just that—a discovery, and not merely an act of recognition or recollection; it is not only a confirmation of what we already dimly knew, but also a transformation of our prior understanding. In short, the higher (or deeper) insights always come to us as both *more* than what we can ordinarily grasp and as *different*, and sometimes radically different, from our ordinary perceptions. This is in fact suggested by all the gospel accounts of Jesus' transfiguration. The event is invariably described as following Peter's confession that Jesus is the Messiah and Peter's subsequent denial that, as the Messiah, Jesus need suffer and die. In the moment of transfiguration the disciples perceive a transformation in the appearance of Jesus, signifying his status as Messiah and thus confirming the validity of Peter's prior confession. Yet the event is altogether extraordinary, accompanied by nothing less than the descent of a cloud of glory from which God's voice speaks, calling Jesus the "beloved Son" and filling the disciples with awe and even bewilderment. In Matthew and Mark this is immediately followed by a reminder from Jesus that he will indeed necessarily suffer and die—at which point Peter's (and their) inherited and common understanding of the nature of the Messiah is profoundly challenged. Whatever else this story may mean, I think we can take it to indicate that what Whitehead terms "the supernormal experience of mankind in its moments of finest insight" (whether it be found in Athens or in Jerusalem) is bound to be difficult to express adequately or appropriately. Furthermore, when expressed in a relatively adequate and appropriate way, it is bound to seem rather strange and perhaps wonder-ful to anyone first coming upon it, and this despite the Christian supposition that it will already have been known (or at least sought) at some level of one's prior existence.

The second major factor preventing any easy fulfillment of the twofold theological task has to do with that aspect of human nature which is biblically known as "sin"—or, in modern theological parlance, "estrangement." Although Whitehead has remarkably little to say on this subject, I think its pertinence should not be minimized. To be sure, many forms of Christian theology would maintain that we are never so totally depraved as entirely to forget the aim of human existence—the courage of authentic decisions, the love characteristic of right relationships, the goodness of a will responsive to moral demands, and the faith intrinsic to an acceptance of life as embraced and supported by God. Yet the theologian attentive to scriptural norms must also state that in actuality we are "fallen" or estranged from the realization of the essential possibilities of existence as created by God. For this reason, the Christian will say, we are always inclined to love darkness rather than light, ignorance rather than truth—and to do so precisely in order to live within an illusion of our own infinitude and godliness (John 3:19-21). Consequently, when the truth finds us—whether it be the truth of our worth in spite of our estranged state or the truth of the possibility of a new mode of being—it is not only informing but profoundly transforming. Transfiguration in this context means nothing less than a "redemptive" mystery: an outward and visible sign of an inward and spiritual grace, and thus a sacrament mediating at once the presence of God-in-Christ and the power of the renewal of all things, including the self. It is also a theophany humans both desire and fear, because they are at once made for God and judged by God.

The Christian theologian who takes seriously human finitude and sin, therefore, will recognize that every effort at understanding—including that of the theologian and philosopher—is inevitably qualified by both of these factors. What is now even more important from the standpoint of this study, however, is the obvious conclusion that, if finitude and sin are real, the concepts put forward by theology—*especially* when they are most appropriate to Christian faith and most profoundly adequate to interpret the essence of our human experience—will usually *not* be understood readily and *not* appear immediately attractive. They can and will address the human situation, but at the same time they will constitute a wonder and a threat. This is not because they will offer totally impenetrable wisdom, or truths completely alien to our being, but because our common human experience involves the hiddenness of what we most deeply know and, paradoxically or perversely, an element of willful blindness. But if this is the case, then there is no simple way in which the theologian can, in Toulmin's words, "establish the common standpoint and shared experience required in order to achieve general and warranted agreement."[75]

This observation, however, naturally leads us to wonder if there is a linguistic medium in which the challenge to understanding posed by both finitude and sin is in *any* way met more fully and adequately than it is by the resources of conceptual discourse. I think that we now have indications that there is and that this medium is the language of metaphor.

I wish to stress that I do not want to claim for metaphoric discourse the capacity completely to evade or transcend the problems of finitude and sin. This would be to succumb to an untenable romanticism. Rather I am suggesting that the Christian theologian has reason to believe that, on the whole, the language of metaphor addresses and engages finite and sinful selves in a way that necessarily complements—even as it also exists in tension with—strategies of conceptual discourse as such, metaphor being strong where conceptual language is weak, and vice versa. We can perhaps best comprehend how this could be by again reflecting on the semantics of the special, extended form of metaphor constituted by poetic art. Furthermore, the aspects of poetry most relevant at this point can probably best be seen if we once more consider the semantic properties and ontological import of the admittedly exceptional poem on which this study has already focused, namely, *Four Quartets*. For, precisely because the *Quartets* is in some respects exceptional, it brings into full view certain features of poetic language as a whole that one might otherwise overlook. Once we have determined whether any important aspects of the *Quartets'* religious significance are likely to be shared by other works of literary art, or by poetic metaphor in general, we will need again to ask whether the cognitive component of this metaphorically embodied significance is susceptible of conceptual paraphrase and theological expression. The answer to this question will lead us, in the end, to reconsider the relation between literary metaphor and the language of formal—and especially metaphysical—theology.

Turning first to what may be the most unusual characteristic of the *Quartets* as a work of religious significance, we recall that this poetry makes a kind of argument and that the argument it makes is in some sense theological. We can now add that the task of theology to which the argument of each quartet appears to relate most closely is that of establishing the common standpoint and shared experience relevant to a religious and, finally, Christian mode of being and understanding. The poetry seeks to find a standpoint from which the reader might recognize the *logos* common to all, and to illumine the relation of all to the ultimate *Logos*, the meaning and reality of which we ordinarily fail to comprehend due to our finitude and "fallen" condition. This means that each quartet acts to interpret the shared experience informing, and informed by, concepts and insights that are neither strictly scientific nor strictly logical. Consequently, the basic premises of its argument are not derived from narrowly empirical observation or from logically self-evident principles. The fundamental "facts" of the world of *Four Quartets* are neither discrete sense-data nor clear and distinct ideas. They are phenomena like values, memories, sensations, imaginings, the awareness of time, a sense of eternity, perceptions of social relatedness, love, anxiety, moral failure, and so forth. In short, the phenomena the poem treats as irreducibly real are those belonging to what is today often called "lived experience." At the same time, they are the kind of phenomena on which a theological and even metaphysical interpretation of our life and world must be based—or so a Whiteheadian would argue.

If we are to understand what is uniquely poetic about this work, however, we must take into account the specific "transfigurative" or transformative traits of its linguistic strategy. In my analysis of *Four Quartets* I have already pointed out, of course, that the work constitutes at once a metaphoric representation and metaphoric argument, transforming ordinary experience in such a way as to address and engage thought, feeling, and indeed the reader's whole self. In this way, I said, the poem provides a kind of "transfiguration," that is, a significant transformation of the ordinary. It discloses what is commonly hidden within what is known and makes a raid on the inarticulate, so that its words reach beyond mere words into the silence of nonverbal experience. This is true even of the work's mode of relating to the Christian tradition. Each quartet locates and explores tensions within Christian faith itself, moving toward a realization of its meaning precisely by moving at various points beyond, and away from, any simple notion of what the tradition represents or calls for in the present situation. There is thus nothing perfunctory or "closed" about the significance assigned in these poems to Incarnation or to God's love. It is a meaning not merely given but also discovered, a meaning uncovered as well as recovered, though still partly through the language of classical theism:

> Love is itself unmoving,
> Only the cause and end of movement,
> Timeless, and undesiring
> Except in the aspect of time.
>
> (BN:V)

What this indicates is that the work, as an expanded metaphor, embodies not merely static entities but the experiential realities, ambiguities, and tensions inherent even in belief. As each quartet complicates and reshapes the "received" answers of the Christian tradition, it deals not only with ideas but also with the form and inner dynamic of life and faith. Even where it is not specifically religious in nature, the poem works with language and experience in such a way as to be of religious significance.

Granted this, however, we still must see how *Four Quartets* is a representative literary work. Here we encounter two major obstacles: the fact that the *Quartets* is exceptionally explicit in its religiosity and the fact that it is exceptionally reflective or intellectual.

I have already suggested the route around the first obstacle. What *Four Quartets* shares with literature of almost all kinds, and what turns out to be of paramount importance from a religious perspective, is neither a theology nor an explicitly religious subject matter but a mode of address and engagement—the use of often complex metaphoric strategies that, however subtly, significantly involve the whole self that attends to them. Precisely because human selves naturally attend to the possibility of purpose in the parts of life and in the whole, they also naturally make and use things like poems to discover, explore, entertain, and take delight in both the actual and possible purposes of the parts and whole of life itself. Poetry— literary art—thereby confirms for us that we are indeed purposefully alive, and it transfigures our sense of what "being alive" means. In different ways, this is as true of *Don Quixote* or even *The Wind in the Willows* as it is of *Four Quartets*.

Yet *Four Quartets*, I have admitted, is an exceptionally intellectual poem. How can I claim its modes of addressing the whole self are in any way truly characteristic of literature in general? First of all, many major literary works are reflective indeed: *The Divine Comedy*, *Paradise Lost*, the *Duino Elegies*, *The Brothers Karamazov*, *Gilgamesh*, the *Oresteia* (to take examples quite at random). Conceptual thought of considerable sophistication is likewise important in many lesser works, including much science fiction. In all these cases, to the extent to which they are effective literature, the metaphoric process operates through, and purposively shapes, abstract levels of ideation, often by combining argument with narrative or imagistic representation. Our study of the *Quartets* clearly shows how this can be.

To be sure, other major works, like *Macbeth* or the *Iliad*, present the dynamics of certain features of human existence with such particularity and imaginative immediacy that, although thought is inevitably stimulated and even demanded, the direction of one's thoughtful response is not always controlled by cues from the work itself. Thus lovers and haters of war can (apparently) both value Homer's *Iliad*. What matters most in such works is their almost overwhelming transformation, re-creation, and intensification of life passions and conflicts—a transformation brought about by the work experienced as a metaphoric world. But this does not mean such works are altogether different from the *Quartets*. We have in fact seen a similar phenomenon in the *Quartets* where, in the pivotal fourth section of each poem, the possible "resolution" of the speaker's conflict is glimpsed apart from any genuine sense of intellectual closure. What counts at that moment is the experiential realization of what it means to relinquish ordinary sense before a reality that sense cannot encompass.

Still another kind of literature literally entertains thought. It uses thought for play. One sees this, for example, in the fiction of Donald Barthelme or Laurence Sterne. But even here it is the whole thinking and feeling person who, as reader, participates in the play—and partly through a tacit awareness of all the life and thought the playfulness omits or intentionally distorts. In any case, Eliot's own poetry is hardly free of ironic twists and parody, as the mock funeral lament of "East Coker" III illustrates. This, too, is part of what engages us as humans.

Finally we cannot discount the poem—a haiku, perhaps, or a symbolist lyric—that is almost pure musical presence. The whole of *Four Quartets* undoubtedly has more assertorial and conceptual weight than such poetry. But the *Quartets* includes moments of poetry in this vein. And the way in which it incorporates those moments into a larger, more reflective structure indicates the way in which other very "musical" poems are in fact taken up into the mind and life of the reader. Like the scents of wildflowers and shrubbery taken in as one climbs a mountain, such poems deserve and receive attention in themselves, but they also qualify, and are qualified by, a much larger range of experience and observation.

Thus, without denying the enormous variety within what we call "poetry" or "literature," I would maintain that *Four Quartets* exhibits many of the nearly endless ways in which literary art is significantly metaphoric and transfigurative. Certainly one would be hard pressed to find many "classic" literary texts to which our study of the *Quartets* would be irrelevant.[76] In one's encounter with all such works, one somehow comes to know more of what and who one is as a whole and perhaps to sense more deeply one's relationship to a larger Whole. Beyond that, moreover, the work of literary art inevitably has some effect on one's mode of being—one's attitudes and life orientations—as well as on one's mode of knowing. This inevitably is what it means for the work to address, and be heard by, the whole self.

All of which leads me now to say that such metaphoric transfiguration, wherever it is found, is intrinsically related to transfiguration in the two religious senses examined in this chapter. In transforming in a significant, if subtle, way one's mode of knowing, poetic metaphor alters and expands one's ever finite understanding of oneself and of the realities within and by which one lives.[77] In transforming one's mode of experiencing, it affects one's mode of being, causing one to imagine what one might otherwise be or do and perhaps newly to envision those authentic possibilities from which one finds oneself estranged. This latter aspect of poetry is referred to by Paul Ricoeur when he writes: "The strategy of discourse implied in metaphorical language is . . . to shatter and to increase our sense of reality by shattering and increasing our language."[78] Thus, in Ricoeur's words, "What is changed by poetic language is our way of dwelling in the world."[79] Ricoeur, I will grant, may overstate the case. Our way of dwelling in the world is seldom so dramatically transformed as he imagines— and seldom indeed by means of the average metaphor or poem. Furthermore, Ricoeur places too much emphasis on literal falsity and the negative precondition for the metaphoric transformation of meanings. Accordingly, Ricoeur's description of metaphor as that which "shatters" our prior sense of reality focuses too exclusively on what Wheelwright would call the "diaphoric" component of metaphor. But the claim that metaphor affects one's way of "dwelling in the world" is nonetheless legitimate, however hard to document.

Assuming, then, that poetry generally does address and engage us as feeling and knowing selves who choose modes of being in the world, and assuming that it does so specifically as a form of metaphor, it follows that not only the dynamics of *Four Quartets* but also the dynamics of poetic metaphor in general are somehow related to whatever religious significance our modes of understanding and being (or becoming) may manifest. This necessarily means, in terms of the theory of metaphor I have developed from Wheelwright, that the religious dimension of our common human experience is potentially addressed and engaged by both epiphor and diaphor together. And I believe we can now specify how.

First, with regard to our modes of *understanding* religious truth, it seems reasonable to conclude that the epiphoric element within metaphor discloses that which we recognize as like, or analogous to, what we already know. A highly epiphoric transfiguration derives its power scarcely at all from a sense of the falsity of the literal. Here the heart of the matter is not the copula "is / is not" or the "it was and it was not" that Ricoeur's Protestant sensibility locates as in every instance crucial.[80] Rather, one's sense is of a sacramental "is / is more" or an "it was and it was not merely." This is why, in my account though not in Ricoeur's, myth is metaphoric even when it is believed uncritically and so taken "literally."[81] The literal is metaphorically transcended, not abolished or denied. Through the interaction between semantic fields, the ordinary focus or gestalt shifts, letting us see through the glass of the literal and ordinary onto the field of the supraliteral and extraordinary. For example, one sees the reign of God in and through human acts of justice. Or one sees God's love as like, but more than, a parent's love. By contrast, the diaphoric element within religious truth and language is that which confronts us as paradoxical, turning our rational norms upside down and defying explanation in terms of our previous understanding. It points to the dimension of radical mystery within knowledge itself: the reality that the last shall be first, or that the God who is present is also hidden.

Second, in relation to our modes of *being* (living, acting) in response to religious truth, the primarily epiphoric transfiguration—because of its basis in the realm of the familiar and the understood—profoundly affirms what we already are and orients us toward living more abundantly within our established orientation in the world. On the mundane level, it is as when one's love for, and relationship with, another is confirmed and deepened by a physical act in which one's love is embodied. In specifically religious terms, it is God's pronouncing that the created order is good. The strangeness of the diaphoric element, on the other hand, calls our mode of existence into question, opening us to radically new possibilities. Insofar as it affirms our existence, it does so paradoxically—in spite of all we are—as a word of both judgment and grace.

What we have found here is not merely an analogy between the semantic elements in metaphor and the deeper elements of scriptural witness and human existence that various languages of religious belief seek to interpret. We have discovered, rather, that the dynamics of metaphor, in principle, serve to incorporate and help create the vital tensions and awarenesses fundamental to the religious dimension of human existence and to do so even though a given metaphor may have no explicitly religious significance.[82] In part, therefore, I am reiterating in a new way what has often been claimed: poetic art gives imaginative form to our basic human experience, and this experience always has to do with faith—not faith as something added to existence, but something intrinsically important (even when dormant or distorted) to our simply being human. And I would say with Tillich, Bultmann, Ogden, and others that such "covert" faith is already implicitly religious, because it is concerned with religion's ultimate concern, that is, with affirming existence in spite of all. But in speaking as I have of epiphor and diaphor, I have again stressed that poetry works in a distinctive way to *transform* the common features of our common faith so prone to misunderstand itself and to lose itself in idolatry. Poetry's linguistic transfigurations reshape the patterns of thought, feeling, and being to which we as finite and "fallen" creatures continually become captive. As a consequence, poetry is, for all its limitations and considerable demonic potential, especially equipped to engender the very kinds of experiential understandings and personal transformations that are crucial to religious life and belief— religion itself being, as Frederick Streng has shown, a means of ultimate transformation.[83] No doubt this is why "root" metaphors not only ground every major religious tradition but also nurture its ongoing reflection, liturgy, and worship.[84] It is also why poetry joins ritual, music, dance, and other "arts" to become one of the truly primary languages of religious belief.[85]

Given poetry's close ties with faith, we can hardly avoid returning to the question raised by our discussion of Schubert Ogden's views of language and cognition: To what extent is the understanding of faith that is embodied in metaphoric discourse susceptible of theological explication and analysis? Everything we have observed concerning epiphor argues that metaphoric meanings and understandings can in some measure be translated into abstract concepts, although the process of translation may be slow and unsure. But nothing we have seen suggests that the meaning and truth of poetic metaphor or of a complex of such metaphors can be translated without remainder. To suppose it could, one would have to ignore the whole dimension of diaphor and deny the cognitive role played by metaphoric tension. Because metaphoric understanding, like that conveyed by the parables of Jesus or the stories of Flannery O'Connor, derives from an engagement of the whole self, such understanding is always in process—partly emerging into concepts, partly reaching beyond them, and partly combining sheer vision with lucid thought. Perhaps the less conceptual side of such understanding is better called "insight." But even it leaves one with a sense of having grasped, as well as having been grasped by, something ineluctably real. It too invites assent.

In view of the above observations we can readily say, with Whitehead, that there are indeed "meanings miraculously revealed in great literature," that these meanings disclose and partially create the essential elements of our "integral experience" as whole selves, and that experience thus disclosed provides the basis of faith and religious belief. We can also agree with Whitehead that metaphysical and theological reflection, which necessarily must take such experience into account, adds to our understanding by analyzing and criticizing in a rigorous and systematic way insights or meanings mediated by all those "intermediate" languages closest to the concrete and vital qualities of life experience—languages of which poetic art is in some ways perhaps the epitome. Where we cannot agree with Whitehead (or Ogden) is in the contention that philosophy or theology can be counted on to find "a conventional phraseology for the vivid suggestiveness of the poet" sufficient to "rationalize" completely any central truth of or about human experience as interpreted by even one major work of literary art. This claim ignores essential features of metaphor and overlooks the dynamics of transfiguration, in the sense explored in this book. This means, of course, that we need to alter the image Whitehead and certain theologians have of the task of theology and its relation both to the language of poetry and to the other less theoretical languages of religious belief. Accordingly, I now venture an outline of how I believe this relationship might better be conceived.

Poetic Metaphor and Theological Reflection

If my argument up to this point has any real validity, it will naturally lead to the following conclusion: the fullest possible understanding of Christian faith (which is necessarily an understanding of the "witness" of scriptures and of our common human experience) is inherently dialogical and "dipolar." It does not employ a single mode of thought but, rather, moves back and forth between metaphoric and conceptual thinking, and particularly between poetry and theology. As it does so, it not only uses concepts to interpret metaphors but also uses metaphors to interpret concepts, both the metaphoric and the conceptual entering into and interpreting the common ground of life experience, action, and commitment that gives rise to all understanding whatsoever.

If my claim is not to be misunderstood, however, I must precede its further exposition with a reiteration of assumptions. Unlike Paul Ricoeur, who holds that, within a limited context, the semantic procedures of the conceptual order can be utterly free from the allegedly preconceptual dynamics of metaphor,[86] I hold that every actual semantic situation and every moment of meaning is dipolar, marked by some degree of interplay between the powers of rational conceptualization, on the one hand, and the powers of imaginative fabrication and semantic innovation, on the other. In actual discourse and thought there is no such thing as purely conceptual and determinate meaning, even in logic, and there is no such thing as purely affective meaning, even in poetry.[87] Metaphor—the union of epiphor and diaphor—can thus be seen as the strategy for maximizing in one semantic situation the dialogue or tension that is always to some extent present in thought and communication. The difference between what we term "metaphoric" and "conceptual" modes of discourse and thought is in this respect a difference only in degree.

But the difference is nonetheless highly significant, making it possible for certain kinds of language to do certain kinds of work for which other kinds of language are ill suited. Specifically within the realm of religious languages, I hold, there is a special function to be fulfilled by a language of faith that reflects on faith's realities in a way that strives to be conceptual and clear, logical and coherent. Such language is what in this context I mean by "theology."

What I want now to suggest is that our fullest understanding of faith emerges from a dialogue that takes place not only between two modes of language and thought—the metaphoric and the conceptual—but also within each of two major areas: in the historical ("diachronic") development of awareness and in the transhistorical ("synchronic") event constituted by the act of comprehension itself. We will look first at the historical dimension of this ongoing dialogue.

Over thirty years ago Karl Jaspers, echoing Kant, wrote: "The symbol is never without thought. It incites the thinking which, as in the discovery of the symbol, never reaches the end. . . . Thinking strives for the meaningful realization of the symbol's content."[88] Perhaps mindful of the words of Jaspers, whose philosophy he studied in depth, Paul Ricoeur was later to take as a kind of motto the statement: "The symbol gives rise to thought."[89] Recalling that Ricoeur, like Wheelwright, comes to regard the symbol as a form of implicit or covert metaphor, we can readily concur with this assertion—one that Ricoeur admits he finds "enchanting." With this the revisionist theologian is likely to be in full agreement, taking it to be a warrant for theology itself. For (the argument goes) the mythic, symbolic, or parabolic language of scripture incites thinking that is of a nonsymbolic, conceptual, and literal order. I want to emphasize, however, that metaphors and symbols have the capacity to give rise to thought not only at the dawn of critical thinking but again and again throughout history and at various levels of understanding. Sophoclean drama gives rise to Aristotelian concepts, early Christian hymnody to Johannine theology. Victor Lowe has written that "Wordsworth probably influenced Whitehead as much as any philosopher did, Plato excepted."[90] And no one can deny the influence of Hölderlin and Rilke on Heidegger, nor that of T. S. Eliot on Wheelwright, nor even that of Charles Wesley's hymnody on Schubert Ogden (whose citations of "pure unbounded love" are innumerable).[91] Nor, finally, can anyone easily ignore the enormous impact of Homer, Sophocles, Dante, and Milton on intellectual history in general.

But in thus calling attention to the symbolic and metaphoric foundation of all philosophical and theological reflection, we must be careful not to form too simple a notion of the relationship between that which gives rise to abstract thought and the thought itself. If the theory of metaphor I have put forward is essentially sound, then the thought to which symbol and poetry give rise can exhaust neither the meaning nor the truth of its source. In fact, abstract thought transforms even what it succeeds in expressing. Consequently, no conceptual interpretation can be regarded as having a once-and-for-all status. No anthropology or metaphysic resulting from the theologian's interpretive labors can be considered precisely and finally appropriate to the Christian texts or adequate to our experience. It will always be the case that some of what the metaphoric meanings in any given instance show forth is either not yet capable of abstract expression or else so strains our finite minds that it will forever elude full conceptual expression.

Nevertheless, it is only through conceptual explication and elucidation that certain implications and meanings of the truths embedded in metaphoric language become clear and therefore amenable to intellectual evaluation, criticism, and further elaboration in connection with other truths or other systems of thought. We can hardly afford to regard theology and metaphysics as simply superfluous or to banish them from our republic of religious discourse. We must here part company with Wheelwright, Heidegger, and others when, in their admiration for poetry, they write as though "being" could dwell or appear only in an opening cleared of rigorous, systematic, and metaphysical inquiry.[92] For when the symbol gives rise to thought, it gives rise to a level of understanding not fully encompassed by the symbol itself.

In explicating what it means to say that the symbol gives rise to thought, we have still told but half the story with regard to the historical dialogue between metaphoric and conceptual discourse. Although we may all share Ricoeur's enchantment with that saying, I believe the spell it casts by itself is not so powerful as that cast when it is complemented by another, namely, "thought, in turn, gives rise to the symbol." It is this that makes for dialogue rather than monologue. But, again, thought could not give rise to symbol and metaphor if it had not added something to the understanding it first received from symbol and metaphor. Although an adequate theology of hope or of the Kingdom of God, for example, can never exhaust the understanding opened up by the eschatological mythology of the New Testament, it may nonetheless let us understand something beyond what we have previously understood from scripture itself. By the same token, however, metaphoric understanding can itself add to—even as it alters—our prior conceptually articulated understanding. To be sure, theological understanding is uniquely clear, precise, and amenable to rational analysis and criticism. Yet we have seen that metaphoric understanding is not unreflective. Indeed, by responding to prior intellectual achievements, it can be as *post*-conceptual as it is *pre*-conceptual. Furthermore, it is uniquely full, experientially rich, and epistemologically immediate. One can easily imagine, therefore, that the understanding of love and grace embodied in Dante's *Divine Comedy* at once comprehends, builds on, and transcends in certain important respects the understanding offered by Thomas Aquinas, whose Unmoved Mover sometimes seems devoid of the very traits that would make for real love.[93] Evidently this kind of possibility is envisioned by Karl Jaspers when he writes: "In metaphysics more than anywhere else, conclusiveness would doom philosophizing. Speculation is a thing in process. . . . Philosophy leads to frontiers where its own language ceases while art seems still to speak."[94]

We should not follow Jaspers too far, because the very distinctions I have been trying to make between metaphysical or theological thinking and metaphoric thinking eventually break down in his philosophy. Yet Jaspers gives a valuable hint in suggesting that every metaphysical system (or theology) ultimately points beyond itself. And since, as Whitehead says, the two modes of language having greatest imaginative penetration are metaphysics and poetic art,[95] it is not unreasonable to suppose that literature itself may move beyond the limitations of a given way of conceiving the depths of things—whereupon it may give rise to new systems of theological and philosophical reflection.[96]

The process I have just described might be considered an example of what Ricoeur calls "the intersection and interanimation" between modes of discourse. But I have been interested in counter-balancing Ricoeur's tendency to concentrate on the movement from the poetic and metaphoric levels of discourse to the philosophical and conceptual.[97] In any case, if what I have said above is valid, it is in the very nature of metaphor and thought that the historical development of faith's self-understanding would occur in part through an ongoing dialogue between conceptual and metaphoric discourse, with each mode shaping the very presuppositions with which the other works. But this process is hardly to be thought of as a kind of Hegelian dialectic in which, necessarily, there are ever greater vistas opened up and ever higher levels of *Aufhebung*. At every stage of greater conceptualization at least some element of insight is lost or reduced, and at every stage of experiential assimilation and metaphoric interpretation something is obscured, confused. This means that the moments of fullest disclosure, or of what we come to regard as supreme revelation, are never totally surpassed, their meaning never totally exhausted. But such meaning can be reapproached and reappropriated and in certain respects extended and possibly heightened. Consequently, our continual search for a more adequate understanding of the realities of faith need not be an exercise in futility. The wonder at the end of each stage of the process is at least *potentially* deeper than the wonder at the beginning. Furthermore, because the basis of our understanding of special revelatory moments shifts from culture to culture and from era to era, we have no choice but to reinterpret faith's claims in new ways, in contrasting and complementary languages, and always in the hope of new insight. Thus faith's historical search for understanding is an adventure—not only of ideas (as Whitehead at times implies) but also of humanity's whole being and becoming.

The historical dialogue described above is not the only one, however.

There is a second kind of dialogue, and it too takes place between meta-phoric thought and theological or philosophical conceptualization. This is an inner, hidden dialogue that occurs whenever one tries to understand either mode of thought or discourse in its own right.

That such an inner dialogue takes place was implicit, of course, in what we discovered in examining *Four Quartets*. We saw that the world and meaning of the poem results from a kind of transaction rather than from passive contemplation.[98] Although the reader cannot simply import exter-nal criteria to evaluate the action, ideas, and sense of reality integral to the poetic universe of "East Coker," for example, the universe of the poem will not even take shape for the reader who is unwilling to bring ideas and ex-perience to the work. Ultimately, to be sure, one's prior understanding is interrogated, complicated, enriched, and transfigured by the major work of poetic art. Yet the meaning of that transfiguration is conditioned by the content of what is transfigured.

With regard to the way we understand poetry and metaphor, therefore, the thrust of our analysis pushes us beyond the notions of poetic auton-omy and self-referentiality. The fact is that the world and space created by a work of metaphoric art, or even by a single metaphor, is perceived as it is because it is seen against the background of other ideas, experience, and language. Because this is so—because the work of metaphoric art emerges out of a transaction with our existing ideas of order and chaos—all our concepts of self, others, world, and God help lend significance to the pecu-liar transfigurations of language and experience provided by the meta-phoric structure. In short, the realm of conceptual reflection (including theology) supplies what Michael Polanyi would call a "tacit dimension" of our understanding of the realm of poetic metaphor.[99]

At the same time, the converse is equally true when we try to understand theology's own assertions. Ogden and others have made much of the fact that, because religious claims need to be *understandable* in order to merit assent, they need theological conceptualization. This is at least partly true. But there is a danger here of confusing understandability with conceptual clarity. Adequate concepts are, of course, an important part of fully under-standable communication. Because of this, the theologian naturally makes use of concepts from a variety of sources, including philosophy, psychol-ogy, sociology, and so forth. But in some spheres even the most adequate concepts fail to insure understandability. They themselves cannot fully elicit the understanding they invite. Theology is just such a sphere.

The reason for this lies in the nature of what it is that theological con-cepts seek to understand. Few theologians would claim that the referents of such terms as "love," "faith," "God," "freedom," "evil," "grace," and the like are phenomena that are quantifiable and measurable. These realities are not "hard facts." Neither are they logical deductions (in the strict-est sense), a priori truths readily known by intuition, or only regulative ideas.[100] Even when they are explicated with the aid of phenomenology or metaphysics, their public status is more problematical than that of objects perceived with the five senses. This does not mean the theologian's con-cepts lack content and an experiential basis. But it does mean their content derives from particular ways of construing what Whitehead calls "integral experience," that is, the experience of the whole, embodied self.

In other words, theological concepts—not unlike those of philosophical metaphysics, ethics, and aesthetics—are nothing less than an attempt to interpret at an abstract level those very aspects of experience that are (as Whitehead says) most resistant to clear-cut analysis.[101] If the hearer of the theological word is not made cognizant of specific, felt qualities of such experience, then the common standpoint of shared experience will not be found; basic presuppositions will not be held in common; and the hearer will simply not understand, let alone appropriate, the truth of that word. Clearly an understanding of Whitehead's metaphysics depends on one's sense of the reality of certain primordial perceptions of freedom, value, change, and so forth—without which the system will seem simply vac-uous, confused, or irrational.[102] A theologian's interpretation of the idea of sin is similarly dependent on one's particular sense of what is involved in knowing the good and yet not doing it. Unfortunately for theology (and for metaphysics), the qualities of such integral experience and awareness are just exactly what intellectual concepts themselves are powerless to re-create. They obviously can refer to such experience, but they cannot pre-sent us with its inner dynamics. Thus, even if the concepts were handed down directly from God, they would remain somewhat ambiguous. In fact, they would remain empty apart from a context in which their expe-riential (but not merely existential) import was communicated to the whole self of the hearer. This is why the language of theology, when considered in isolation, fails to satisfy fully Ogden's own requirement of understandability.

It is also why one's understanding of theological discourse is necessarily dialogical, depending in part on one's capacity to bring to it understand-ings vividly informed and transformed by the metaphoric discourse found both in culture at large and in explicitly religious language, art, ritual, and worship.[103] For, as we have seen, it is metaphor and poetic art that does in fact convey through the medium itself the dynamic qualities of the life ex-perience and actions it shapes and interprets. The understandings it con-veys are thus rooted in existential awareness. Yet they are more than *merely* existential meanings heard only as "word-events." They tell *about*, even as they *re-create*, realities and possibilities. If metaphoric understanding is itself transfigured when placed in dialogue with theology, this is but another instance of the process we have seen pervading faith's quest for self-understanding.

Perhaps, in making this observation, we have located the nucleus of truth in the common Christian claim that theology is always a task of the church and of the church alone. If theology does not itself fully elicit or create the understanding it potentially communicates and elucidates, this means it can often most fully be understood within a community of more or less explicitly shared belief—a community whose multiple religious languages of ritual, worship, action, arts, and social interaction foster not only a way of life but also ways of understanding and ways of relating with understanding to those central realities to which the scriptures and the community testify.[104] Most "revisionist" theologians would of course argue (and rightly so, I believe) that the task of theology is not simply to speak exclusively to this community or to speak from a standpoint identified only with this community's language and practice. Indeed, part of the theological task is to illumine the common experiential and universal dimension of the truth to which the whole life of the community ideally bears "witness." This is imperative if the truth understood in a given religious community is also understood by that community as a truth in some way mediated by human experience as such, calling existence everywhere to a truly faithful mode of being in the world. Furthermore, it is imperative if the community is to engage in dialogue with other understandings of life and faith. But I would again contend that to suppose that the conceptual language of theology provides the primary basis for a genuinely *understandable* dialogue or proclamation is to succumb to an illusion based on a misconception of the nature of language and understanding.

Our inquiry has thus led once more to the hypothesis that the fullest possible understanding of faith does not belong to theology or to poetry alone, to metaphysics or to metaphor. Paraphrasing Kant, we might say that, as a mode of conceptual understanding, theology tends to be empty in its clarity of vision and in its generality, and thus to need metaphoric and experiential interpretation. As a mode of metaphoric understanding, poetry (in the broadest sense) tends to be blind in its experiential fullness, and so to need conceptual clarification, criticism, and generalization. In dialogue, however, poetry and theology play a vital role in the unending process of understanding faith and transforming life.[105] As modes of mutual transfiguration, they belong to, interpret, and together enrich the various languages of religious belief.

Notes

Chapter 1. A Prefiguration

1. For a comprehensive discussion of the resulting situation in religious studies see David Tracy, *The Analogical Imagination: Christian Theology and the Culture of Pluralism* (1981). Some taste of the ferment in English-language philosophy is provided by Richard Rorty, *Philosophy and the Mirror of Nature* (1979), and Stanley Cavell, *The Claim of Reason: Wittgenstein, Skepticism, Morality, and Tragedy* (1979).

2. For surveys of recent developments in the study of language and literature see Jonathan Culler, *Structuralist Poetics: Structuralism, Linguistics, and the Study of Literature* (1975); Culler, *On Deconstruction: Theory and Criticism after Structuralism* (1982); Gerald Graff, *Literature Against Itself: Literary Ideas in Modern Society* (1979); and Frank Lentricchia, *After the New Criticism* (1980).

3. "Metaphor," in *Language, Thought, and Culture*, ed. Paul Henle (1958), p. 173.

4. *Metaphor: An Annotated Bibliography and History* (1971).

5. "The Turns of Metaphor," in *The Pursuit of Signs: Semiotics, Literature, Deconstruction* (1981), p. 189.

6. See, especially, Sheldon Sacks, ed., "Special Issue on Metaphor," *Critical Inquiry* (1978), and Andrew Ortony, ed., *Metaphor and Thought* (1979).

7. (Editions du Seuil, 1975); trans. Robert Czerny, *The Rule of Metaphor: Multi-Disciplinary Studies of the Creation of Meaning in Language* (1976).

8. See Graff, *Literature Against Itself*, and Lentricchia, *After the New Criticism*.

9. See, for instance, Norman Perrin, *Jesus and the Language of the Kingdom: Symbol and Metaphor in New Testament Interpretation* (1976), and Mary Ann Tolbert, *Perspectives on the Parables: An Approach to Multiple Interpretations* (1979).

10. *Speaking and Meaning: The Phenomenology of Language* (1976).

11. Ricoeur, *Rule of Metaphor*.

12. This, it seems to me, is the end result of the radically different arguments advanced by the logical positivists, the New Critics, the later Wittgenstein, neo-Kantians like Cassirer, neo-Cassirerians like Nelson Goodman, and many others.

13. See Claude Lévi-Strauss, *Structural Anthropology*, trans. Claire Jacobson and Brooke Schoepf (1963), and *The Savage Mind* (1966).

14. A short but insightful analysis of structuralist ideology is given by Brian W. Kovacs, "Philosophical Foundations for Structuralism," *Semeia* (1978). For discussions of how structuralism can be used as a method rather than as an ideology see Robert Scholes, *Structuralism in Literature* (1974), and Elizabeth Struthers Malbon, "Structuralism, Hermeneutics, and Contextual Meaning," *Journal of the American Academy of Religion* (1983).

15. *The Order of Things: An Archaeology of the Human Sciences* (1973), p. 300.

16. Ludwig Wittgenstein, *Tractatus Logico-Philosophicus*, trans. D. F. Pears and B. F. McGuinness (1961), pp. 150–51.

17. *The Living Principle: 'English' as a Discipline of Thought* (1975).

18. *A Reformation of New Criticism: "Burnt Norton" Revisited* (1972).

19. *The Achievement of T. S. Eliot: An Essay on the Nature of Poetry*, 3d ed. rev. and enl. (1st ed., 1935; 1958).

20. *T. S. Eliot: Between Metaphor and Metonymy* (1979).

21. *The Burning Fountain: A Study in the Language of Symbolism*, 2d ed., rev. (1968), pp. 240–68.

22. *Experience and Being: Prolegomena to a Future Ontology* (1969), p. xii.

23. *Risk and Rhetoric in Religion: Whitehead's Theory of Language and the Discourse of Faith* (1972).

24. "Speaking from the Depth: Alfred North Whitehead's Metaphysics of Propositions, Symbolism, Perceptions, Language, and Religion" (1976).

25. Loomer's dissertation has been read widely though never published.

26. See, for example, *The Realities of Faith: The Revolution in Cultural Forms* (1962), and *Fallible Forms and Symbols: Discourses on Method in a Theology of Culture* (1976).

27. Thomas Altizer, *The Self-Embodiment of God* (1977), p. 1.

28. See Robert N. Bellah, *Beyond Belief: Essays on Religion in a Post-Traditional World* (1970). See also Wilfred Cantwell Smith's discussion of how the meaning of the word "belief" has changed over the centuries. *Faith and Belief* (1979), pp. 105–27.

29. *The Transfiguration of the Commonplace: A Philosophy of Art* (1981). I had entitled the present book, incidentally, long before Danto's appeared.

30. *Essays on English and American Literature*, ed. Anna Hatcher (1962), pp. 141–42, Spitzer's emphasis.

Chapter 2. Poetry and Reality

1. The two books that most fully summarize Wheelwright's work correlating the semantics of poetry with ontology are *The Burning Fountain: A Study in the Language of Symbolism*, 2d ed. rev. (1968), hereafter cited as *BF*, and *Metaphor and Reality* (1962), hereafter cited as *MR*. The original edition of *BF* was published in 1954 and will hereafter be cited as *BF*, 1st ed.

2. *MR*, pp. 21–31; *BF*, pp. 3–17.

3. *BF*, p. 5.

4. See *Language, Thought, and Reality: Selected Writings of Benjamin Lee Whorf*, ed. John B. Carroll (1956).

5. See *The Philosophy of Symbolic Forms*, trans. Ralph Manheim (1953).

6. See Heidegger's *Poetry, Language, Thought*, trans. Albert Hofstadter (1971), and Ricoeur's *The Symbolism of Evil*, trans. Emerson Buchanan (1st ed., 1967; 1969).

7. See *The Interpretation of Cultures: Selected Essays by Clifford Geertz* (1973).

8. See Earl Miner, "That Literature Is a Kind of Knowledge," *Critical Inquiry* (1976).

9. See *BF*, chap. 4, "The Limits of Plain Sense."

10. The most explicit—and also most extreme—of Wheelwright's critiques of the modern "idolatry" of steno-language is to be found in his essay "Poetry, Myth, and Reality," in *The Language of Poetry*, ed. Allen Tate (1942), pp. 3–33.

11. It should be noted that "conceptual discourse" as Wheelwright uses the term—and as I shall use it in subsequent chapters—denotes propositional discourse in which the message is in large part separable from the medium, and the reference (*Bedeutung*) from the sense (*Sinn*). The latter terminology, widely used in some circles, comes from Gottlob Frege. See Frege's "On Sense and Reference," in *Philosophical Writings of Gottlob Frege*, trans. Max Black and Peter Geach (1952). As I have already indicated, I do not mean my usage of the word "conceptual" to imply that metaphoric discourse is purely nonconceptual and prereflective. "Concepts" should thus be taken to mean "steno-concepts" as distinguished from metaphoric concepts.

12. See Bernard Meland, ed., *The Future of Empirical Theology* (1969), pp. 1–62.

13. To see this, one need only look at the scientific rationalism of Jean Piaget, whose influ-

ential epistemology is marked by a relatively temperate, but nevertheless unwavering, insistence that nothing be deemed cognitive that is not experimentally or logically demonstrable, and so capable of earning universal assent. (Yet Piaget does speak of a realm of "rational wisdom" that lies beyond the domain of strict cognition and where he locates such notions as freedom.) See *Insights and Illusions of Philosophy*, trans. Wolfe Mays (1971), esp. pp. 215–32.

14. Here Wheelwright is obviously echoing an observation made by countless others. For an excellent account of the theological consequences of the modern dominance of scientific language, and secularism in general, see Langdon Gilkey's *Naming the Whirlwind: The Renewal of God-Language* (1969).

15. I am not suggesting, of course, that Wheelwright's is the sole reaction against the modern tendency toward scientism and/or rationalism. One can hardly ignore the early Romantics or the existentialists like Kierkegaard and Nietzsche, Jaspers and Heidegger—all of whom opposed "objectivizing" discourse. One must also consider Bergson's vitalism, Cassirer's philosophy of symbolic forms, and American pragmatism. In literary criticism one naturally thinks of New Critics like Allen Tate, John Crowe Ransom, and Cleanth Brooks, for whom literature represents an autonomous form of language and a special kind of knowledge. At his best, however, Wheelwright provides noteworthy semantic grounding for an epistemology and ontology that would connect fact with value, intellect with feeling.

A different, but increasingly widespread, reaction to the impasse created by critical philosophy and empiricist epistemology has been to attempt to avoid the question of cognition altogether. Thus some followers of the later Wittgenstein seek to defend the meaningfulness of nonscientific language by describing the various "rules" of what they regard as the multiplicity of "language games," without assigning these "games" any truth-value. In a corresponding way practitioners of phenomenology consciously "bracket" questions of truth and reality so as to arrive, without presuppositions, at the fullest and subtlest possible account of phenomena as they appear in life experience, in the *Lebenswelt*. Although this often yields a sophisticated description of the contents of consciousness and experience, it does not itself provide an epistemology or ontology, nor is it ordinarily intended to. Likewise, certain American philosophers like Richard Rorty have returned to an earlier pragmatist orientation for insight into ways to abandon epistemology. Finally, it is to be noted that the vast array of approaches to language and culture that can roughly be categorized as kinds of structuralism or poststructuralism often are based either on the egalitarian assumption that semiotic systems exhibit no cognitive hierarchy or on the assumption that questions of truth are all moot. It should be apparent that Wheelwright's work addresses semantic, ontological, and epistemological issues consciously and systematically excluded from consideration by the above schools of thought.

16. Wittgenstein was an inspiration to the Circle but never officially joined it. It is now clear that the reason he did not was that he and the positivists were, at root, poles apart (though the positivists and a generation of Cambridge analytical philosophers never realized it). As Allan Janik and Stephen Toulmin show in their excellent study *Wittgenstein's Vienna* (1973), Wittgenstein was always greatly concerned with the literally unsayable, the mystical. The positivists, of course, were not.

17. For a good overview of logical positivism in its philosophical context see John Passmore, *A Hundred Years of Philosophy* (1st ed., 1957; 1968). See also the collection of essays and extensive bibliography found in *Logical Positivism*, ed. Alfred J. Ayer (1959).

18. Difficulties in applying the verifiability principle either to the principle itself or to statements of natural science led to many attempts to refine it, the "strong" version (found above) being progressively weakened over the years. Later, W. V. Quine challenged the whole analytic/synthetic distinction in his essay "Two Dogmas of Empiricism," *Philosophical Review* (1951).

19. See, for example, *BF*, pp. 58–66, and *BF*, 1st ed., pp. 296–97, where Wheelwright laments the influence of that "clever and perverse little book" by Richards called *Science and Poetry*.

20. *Poetries and Sciences: A Reissue of Science and Poetry (1926, 1935) with Commentary* (1970), p. 78.

21. Ibid., pp. 57–66.

22. The general tenor of Wheelwright's early counterattack can be gathered from his accusation, in "Poetry, Myth, and Reality," that positivism and other modern ideologies have made science and its language "the Great Dictator, to whom the spiritual republics of religion and poetry are yielding up their autonomy in bloodless defeat" (p. 9).

23. These terms are scattered throughout *BF*.

24. *MR*, p. 17.

25. *BF*, p. 74.

26. Ibid., pp. 73–74.

27. Cf. Wheelwright's contention that "steno-language represents a set of limiting cases, so to speak, in a universe of infinite possibilities" (*BF*, 1st ed., p. 54).

28. In fairness to Wheelwright it must be admitted that he himself criticizes this analogy. He does not withdraw it, however; and the sole defect he finds in it is that it does not allow for "differentiation" within the phenomenon of steno-language. We are still left to wonder why anyone would ever knowingly choose to use steno-language.

29. *BF*, p. 3.

30. See "On the Semantics of Poetry," *Kenyon Review* (1940); *MR*, pp. 37–38; *BF*, pp. 11–12.

31. See, for example, *BF*, pp. 16–17.

32. See "On the Semantics of Poetry." See also "Semantics and Poetry," in *Princeton Encyclopedia of Poetry and Poetics*, ed. Alex Preminger (1st ed., 1965; enl. ed., 1974), pp. 758–61.

33. "Semantics and Poetry," p. 759.

34. Robert T. Orr and Margaret C. Orr, *Wildflowers of Western America* (New York: Alfred A. Knopf, 1974), p. 100. My example.

35. *BF*, p. 17.

36. Ibid., pp. 11–12.

37. See, especially, chapter 4, "The Limits of Plain Sense."

38. *MR*, p. 39.

39. *BF*, pp. 36–39, 45–49. Cf. pp. 18–31, 56–72.

40. Murray Krieger explicitly identifies Wheelwright with the New Critics in *The New Apologists for Poetry* (1st ed., 1956; 1963), p. 9. See also R. S. Crane's essay "Criticism as Inquiry," in *The Idea of the Humanities and Other Essays Critical and Historical* (1967), 2:38–40.

41. See Richard Foster, *The New Romantics: A Reappraisal of the New Criticism* (1st ed., 1962; 1973), pp. 78, 148–49, and John Fraser, "Modern Poetics: 20th-Century American and British," in *Princeton Encyclopedia*, pp. 514–18.

42. *New Apologists*, p. 75.

43. An excellent critique of the New Critics' theories of poetic language is provided by Gerald Graff in his book *Poetic Statement and Critical Dogma* (1970).

44. *BF*, pp. 73–101. See also "Semantics and Poetry."

45. Wheelwright himself does not explicitly point out two different modes of "assertorial lightness," but he usually presumes that both are included in the first mode. When he does not presume this, he distinguishes between the declarative thrust of an assertion (which he calls its "seriousness") and its *steno*- declarative thrust (which he then calls its "weight"). But because, on other occasions, Wheelwright plainly assumes that "weight" refers to both of these components of assertions, I have thought it best to make them explicit.

46. *BF*, pp. 186–205.

47. Ibid., p. 188.

48. *MR*, pp. 172–73.

49. *BF*, p. 74.

50. Ibid., p. 73.

51. Ibid., p. 16.

52. "On the Semantics of Poetry," pp. 269, 282.

53. Ibid., p. 269.

54. See, especially, the latter portion of the essay.

55. *BF*, p. 102.

56. Ibid., p. 124.

57. *MR*, p. 130.

58. *BF*, p. 103.

59. "Semantics and Ontology," in *Metaphor and Symbol*, ed. L. C. Knights and Basil Cottle (1960), p. 5.

60. In a manner confusing to everyone, the terms of a metaphor have been variously labeled as subject and predicate, major subject and minor subject, subject and modifier, vehicle and tenor.

61. See *MR*, pp. 70–91. See also "Semantics and Ontology," pp. 5–7.

62. 1456 b, *Aristotle's Poetics: Translation and Analysis*, trans. Kenneth A. Telford (1961), p. 39.

63. *BF*, pp. 102–5.

64. *MR*, pp. 73–74.

65. Ibid., p. 80.

66. Ibid., p. 79.

67. *MR*, p. 81. Wheelwright's theory that metaphor combines diaphor and epiphor seems to address some of the issues Roman Jakobson raises when he calls into question the primacy of metaphor. And since considerable attention is currently being given to the work of Jakobson and of related structuralist linguists, a brief rejoinder from Wheelwright's perspective seems in order at this point. Jakobson has argued, on the basis of research on aphasia, that metonymy engages basically different thought processes from those engaged by metaphor and that these are no less fundamental than are those related to metaphor. It should be noted, therefore, that Wheelwright's concept of metaphor encompasses much of what Jakobson discusses under the two contrasting categories of metaphor and metonymy. Epiphor, like the trope Jakobson simply calls "metaphor," operates by virtue of similarity; diaphor, like metonymy, operates by virtue of contiguity. Does Wheelwright, then, merely have a looser, less discriminating notion of metaphor? I do not think so. Wheelwright's theory is that all "live" metaphors, even of the kind Jakobson considers to be purely metaphorical, involve some degree of diaphor as well as epiphor; thus they do not exclude metonymy. That the aphasic subjects referred to by Jakobson did not respond to metaphors in such a way as to identify in them the element of metonymy really proves nothing except that they were aphasics—and that Jakobson himself, under the influence of his substitution theory of metaphor, was not properly equipped to evaluate their responses. See Jakobson, "Two Aspects of Language and Two Types of Aphasic Disturbance," in *Fundamentals of Language*, with Morris Halle, 2d ed. rev. (1956).

68. *MR*, pp. 45–69; *BF*, pp. 102–23.

69. *MR*, p. 71.

70. Ibid.

71. Ibid., pp. 92–110.

72. Epiphoric symbols are found in abundance in eighteenth-century poetry, whereas diaphoric symbols are common in symbolist or imagist verse.

73. See *MR*, p. 128.

74. *Rule of Metaphor*, p. 352.

75. See *BF*, pp. 92–96, 186–205.

76. It is ironic, to say the least, that this assertion of the nonassertorial nature of poetry is found in a poem, "Ars Poetica" (1926).

77. *MR*, p. 50.

78. See, for example, *BF*, pp. 188–89.

79. *BF*, pp. 89–90.

80. See *MR*, p. 51, for a discussion of mimesis. Certain literary critics—notably the Chicago neo-Aristotelians—have been so struck by what they conceive to be the purely mimetic function of most literature that they have refused to consider any literary work a form of assertion unless it is *not* truly mimetic but overtly didactic. A mixture of mimesis and assertion is thus ruled out in principle. See Elder Olson, "William Empson, Contemporary Criticism, and Poetic Diction," in *Critics and Criticism: Ancient and Modern* (1952), esp. pp. 66–68.

81. See *BF*, pp. 32–55.

82. Beda Allemann has pointed out that there is a tendency in much contemporary literature to avoid what would classically have been thought to be "apt" metaphor (that is, epiphor). (See "Metaphor and Antimetaphor," in *Interpretation: The Poetry of Meaning*, ed. Stanley Romaine Hopper and David L. Miller, [1961]). But Allemann, like Wheelwright, argues that even this "antimetaphorical" approach to poetry is in a basic sense metaphoric. The difference between the contemporary and the classical literatures is that no longer is the element of rational resemblance emphasized. Thus, in Wheelwright's terms, we may say that the diaphoric has come to predominate over the epiphoric in much contemporary literature.

83. *BF*, pp. 3–6.

84. Ibid., p. 75.

85. Ibid.

86. Ibid., p. 205.

87. See ibid., pp. 186–205.

88. Colin Murray Turbayne's warnings against the dangers of metaphor in *The Myth of Metaphor*, rev. ed. (1st ed., 1962; 1970). See also Douglas Berggren, "The Use and Abuse of Metaphor," *Review of Metaphysics* (1962, 1963).

89. *BF*, p. 47.

90. Wheelwright (like most writers) makes no attempt to distinguish sharply between emotion and feeling. Two works that do make progress toward a more sophisticated terminology of affect are David Rapaport, *Emotions and Memory*, 5th ed. (1st ed., 1941; 1971) and Stephan Strasser, *Das Gemut* (1956), trans. Robert E. Wood as *Phenomenology of Feeling: An Essay on the Phenomena of the Heart* (1977). See also Amelie Oksenberg Rorty, ed., *Explaining Emotions* (1980).

91. *BF*, pp. 68–70.

92. Ibid., p. 70.

93. Ibid. Wheelwright's emphasis. In Frege's terms, we could say that here the reference is to some degree inseparable from the sense.

94. Ibid., pp. 67–72.

95. *MR*, pp. 164–67.

96. *BF*, pp. 46–48; *MR*, p. 153.

97. *BF*, p. 39.

98. See "On the Semantics of Poetry."

99. See *MR*, pp. 153–73; *BF*, pp. 18–31.

100. *New Apologists*, p. 75.

101. *BF*, p. 34.

102. *MR*, pp. 20, 153–73.

103. Ibid., pp. 154–64.

104. Ibid., pp. 167–68.

105. Ibid., p. 169.

106. Ibid., pp. 166–67 (my emphasis).

107. Ibid., pp. 172–73.

108. Ibid., p. 171.

109. Ibid., pp. 170–71.

110. See *BF*, p. 205. Like Ernst Cassirer, Wheelwright maintains that even the steno-assertions of science are limited in scope and applicability. But Wheelwright also holds, with Cassirer, that scientific assertions—unlike those of poetry—are sufficiently general to be able to contradict, corroborate, or build on other scientific statements. This is part of what it means for them to be steno-linguistic.

111. *MR*, p. 173.

112. *BF*, p. 205.

113. *MR*, pp. 171–72.

114. *BF*, p. 240.

115. Ibid., p. 28. See also "Poetry, Myth, and Reality."

116. Peckham is quoting from his own essay "A Little Plain Speaking on a Weary Subject," in "Foreword I" to Turbayne, *Myth of Metaphor*.

117. *Rule of Metaphor*, p. 295.

118. Ibid., p. 251.

119. "Presence and Reference in a Literary Text," *Critical Inquiry* (1979), pp. 489–510.

120. One thinks, for instance, of Roman Jakobson's thesis that the poetic function of language is "the set toward the message as such," the "focus on the message for its own sake." See "Linguistics and Poetics," in *Style and Language*, ed. Thomas A. Sebeok (1960). Obviously I am sympathetic with Gerald Graff's contention that "a continuity of assumptions connects the New Criticism with the more radical skepticisms of recent continentally influenced movements," including deconstruction (*Literature Against Itself*, p. 145). But Graff overstates his case. For a rather different view see Lentricchia, *After the New Criticism* (1980), and Geoffrey H. Hartman, *Criticism in the Wilderness: The Study of Literature Today* (1980).

121. *On the Margins of Discourse: The Relation of Literature to Language* (1978), p. 80.

122. Ibid., pp. 10, 41–75.

123. It is significant that, when Felix Martinez-Bonati wants to "correct" Professor Smith's position, he becomes even more extreme, saying that literary discourse is only and always "imaginary discourse represented by a conventionally designed pseudo-verbal icon." (*Fictive Discourse and the Structures of Literature*, trans. Philip Silver [1981], p. 157.) This sounds like the New Criticism carried to the nth degree.

124. "The Fictional Criticism of the Future," *TriQuarterly* (1975).

125. "Metaphor and the Central Problem of Hermeneutics," in *Hermeneutics and the Human Sciences*, ed. and trans. John B. Thompson (1981), p. 171.

126. *Metaphors We Live By* (1980).

127. Ibid., p. 5.

128. To use Frege's terms again, sense and reference are here quite separable, as in "morning star" and "evening star"—expressions that usually have an identical reference (Venus) but always have quite different senses.

129. For further complaints against stereotypical philosophical notions of ordinary language see Stanley Fish, "How Ordinary Is Ordinary Language?," *New Literary History* (1973),

and "Normal Circumstances, Literal Language, Direct Speech Acts, the Ordinary, the Everyday, the Obvious, What Goes Without Saying, and Other Special Cases," *Critical Inquiry* (1978).

130. See "White Mythology: Metaphor in the Text of Philosophy," *New Literary History* (1974).

131. "The Linguistic Moment in 'The Wreck of the Deutschland'," in *The New Criticism and After*, ed. Thomas Daniel Young (1976), p. 58.

132. "A Postscript on Metaphor," *Critical Inquiry* (1978), p. 162.

133. "Metaphor and Hermeneutics," p. 170.

134. *Rule of Metaphor*, p. 296.

135. Ibid.

136. Ibid., pp. 310, 303.

137. Ibid., p. 302.

138. Whitehead insists that the precise meaning of any word or statement cannot be determined apart from its context. Perfectly to conceive any one unit of meaning entails perfect conception of the whole and its internal relations, which is impossible. This applies even to logical terms and propositions and to mathematical statements like "one plus one equals two." See "Immortality," in *The Philosophy of Alfred North Whitehead*, ed. Paul Arthur Schilpp (1st ed., 1941; 1951), esp. pp. 698–700.

139. See n. 67 on Jakobson.

140. "Metaphor," in *Models and Metaphors* (1962), and "More about Metaphor," in *Metaphor and Thought*, ed. Ortony.

141. *MR*, pp. 45–69. Cf. Ricoeur, *Rule of Metaphor*, pp. 224, 313.

142. *Interpretation Theory: Discourse and the Surplus of Meaning* (1976), p. 68. Cf. Monroe Beardsley, "The Metaphorical Twist," *Philosophy and Phenomenological Research* (1962).

143. *Rule of Metaphor*, pp. 221, 173–215. See also "The Metaphorical Process as Cognition, Imagination, and Feeling," *Critical Inquiry* (1978), esp. pp. 153–55.

144. "Creativity in Language," *Philosophy Today* (1973).

145. *BF*, p. 107.

146. In recent years the view that literal falsity is essential to metaphor has been much criticized. See Black, "More about Metaphor"; Ted Cohen, "Notes on Metaphor," *Journal of Aesthetics and Art Criticism* (1976); and Monroe Beardsley's own second thoughts in "Metaphor and Falsity," *Journal of Aesthetics and Art Criticism* (1976).

147. This means, I think, that the reader or hearer typically realizes that a literally true statement (like "No man is an island") has a metaphoric dimension when the statement is encountered in a position of anticipated importance and yet is only minimally interesting at a literal level. Falsity is but one cue among many alerting the reader to metaphoric meanings.

148. In his later writings Wheelwright is careful to state that he does not consider religion and poetry to be "consubstantial." (See "Religion and Poetry" in the *Princeton Encyclopedia*, pp. 688–90). And in *BF* he admits that the ontological seriousness of even the more lightly asserted religious statements is decidedly greater than that of most poetry (p. 67). But Wheelwright nevertheless always stresses what he believes to be the close kinship between the poetic and the religious "sense of reality."

Chapter 3. Poetic Transfiguration

1. *The Art of T. S. Eliot* (1st ed., 1950; 1959), p. 44.

2. Throughout the remainder of this study I follow the common practice of abbreviating the title of each poem of the *Quartets*. "Burnt Norton" is abbreviated as "BN," "East Coker"

as "EC," "The Dry Salvages" as "DS," and "Little Gidding" as "LG." Unless otherwise noted, all references are to the text of *Collected Poems, 1909–1962* (1963). Textual variations are discussed in A. D. Moody, *Thomas Stearns Eliot: Poet* (1979), pp. 301–9.

3. *The Invisible Poet: T. S. Eliot* (1st ed., 1959; 1969), p. 296.

4. Leonard Unger, *T. S. Eliot: Moments and Patterns* (1956).

5. For a discussion of the thrush's "deception," see the next section of the present chapter.

6. *BF*, p. 243.

7. A negative judgment of this kind is in fact made by C. K. Stead in "The Imposed Structure of *Four Quartets*," in *T. S. Eliot: "Four Quartets," A Casebook*, ed. Bernard Bergonzi (1969), pp. 197–211.

8. Compare *BF*, pp. 244–45.

9. See Genesius Jones, *Approach to the Purpose: A Study of the Poetry of T. S. Eliot* (1964), p. 132.

10. Ibid.

11. See Staffan Bergsten, *Time and Eternity: A Study in the Structure and Symbolism of T. S. Eliot's "Four Quartets"* (1st ed., 1960; 1973), pp. 168–69.

12. Douglas Fox writes that "a supreme symbol of Buddhism is the lotus, for the image of this exquisite flower rising in its growth from the mud and murk of a pond to rest, at last, in sunlight is suggestive of the Buddhist's quest." *The Vagrant Lotus: An Introduction to Buddhist Philosophy* (1973), p. 37.

13. The idea of the deceptive nature even of one's deepest experiences is one central to the *Quartets*. It helps explain why the poem emphasizes that the single moment of bliss and/or insight must be complemented by a whole body of experience and a whole tradition of understanding (even if the latter is always in some measure questionable or inapplicable). The collective wisdom of the whole transcends the private and checks one's tendencies toward self-deception. For a reading of the *Quartets* and other Eliot poems that stresses their vision of the social rather than the private sphere, see Nathan A. Scott, Jr., "The *Polis* as 'Time's Covenant'," in *The Poetry of Civic Virtue* (1976), pp. 1–39.

14. See Bergsten, *Time and Eternity*, p. 40.

15. This thesis is supported by Kristian Smidt, *Poetry and Belief in the Work of T. S. Eliot* (1961), p. 221.

16. If the garden of unalloyed bliss is not where we humans belong as we participate in history, then the bird's declaration that "human kind cannot bear very much reality" is not so much an ironic condemnation of human limitations as it is a truthful description of them. When it banishes "us" from too long and immediate a contact with Reality, it is returning "us" to a more limited state of being where we rightly belong. As Eliot asserts in "Burnt Norton" II, "the enchainment of past and future / Woven in the weakness of the changing body, / Protects mankind from heaven and damnation / Which flesh cannot endure." The thrush's words, like these, reflect an orthodox religious belief that unmediated contact with the Divine or Ultimate Reality would be, for humans, so overwhelming in glory as well as in judgment that it would result in annihilation. To be protected from Reality as such is therefore a kind of blessing for us. (This point is made repeatedly by Rudolf Otto in *The Idea of the Holy*, trans. John W. Harvey, 2d ed. [London: Oxford University Press, 1950].)

But, more than this, the words of the thrush reflect a kind of theodicy—a theodicy the *Quartets* will increasingly require. The fact is that a disturbing question is raised by Eliot's stark depiction of human existence as being, at best, condemned to "partial ecstasy" and limited satisfaction even when it is obedient to divine requirements of prayer, humility, discipline, and patience. The question is this: How is the goodness or existence of God compatible with the suffering and anxiety caused by our having been created thus? We seem victims of malice or blind injustice. The bird's statement as to humanity's limited capacity for "bearing" reality excuses us of sole responsibility for our condition while also excusing God of injustice or malice. On the one hand, we are not solely responsible, because finitude occasionally graced with moments of vision is all we can hope for in our creaturely state. On the other hand, God is not unjust, because the special moments of illumination and beatitude come as signs of a reality ultimately supportive of human existence, although the moments themselves are rare events. Such moments are not our temporal home, nor are they required to be in order for life to be affirmed. Our anxiety—and consequently our misery—at being left in time is therefore an inappropriate response to our condition. How this could be so is the existential meaning of Incarnation and the explicitly Christian answer sought in the meditative quest represented by the *Quartets*.

17. Kenner, *Invisible Poet*, p. 312.

18. Ibid., p. 315.

19. Reprinted in Bergonzi, ed., *"Four Quartets": A Casebook*, pp. 254–59. It should be noted that, whereas Perkins uses his analysis to show what changes have taken place in the "protagonist" through the course of *Four Quartets*, I am more interested in what changes take place in the reader's perspective as that perspective is determined both by the "protagonist's" attitude and thought and by the relatively impersonal structure of the poetry. In any case, I believe the speaker in the *Quartets* is intended to be a representative human being and not—like Prufrock, for instance—a curiosity or an enigma. As such, he is usually self-effacing. It is his subject that matters and not his personality.

20. Ibid., pp. 257–58.

21. Eliot himself, in the role of critic, is partly to blame for promoting this sort of confusion. Although in some of his essays he extolled the virtues of poetry in which thought and feeling are fused, Eliot could be careless in formulating the relationship between these two components. And often "thought" was slighted in the process. Eliot at various times proclaimed, for instance, that poetry presents merely the *emotional equivalent* of thought; that it presents not belief itself, but only what it *feels like* to believe; that the poet, *qua* poet, does not think at all, and so forth. Indeed, he could state quite bluntly that poetry "is not intellectual but emotional." Plainly Eliot cannot be looked to for clear guidance concerning the problem at hand. See Fei-Pai Lu, *T. S. Eliot: The Dialectical Structure of His Theory of Poetry* (1966), pp. 40–70.

Chapter 4. The Dynamics of Poetic Structure

1. One of the most thorough, and most critical, analyses of this five-part structure is given by C. K. Stead in *The New Poetic: Yeats to Eliot* (1964). For a fascinating, if controversial, account of the relation of this structure to the structure of the whole work see Hugh Kenner, *The Invisible Poet: T. S. Eliot* (1959), pp. 289–323. Three of the best studies of structure that have played the analogy with musical form for all it is worth are Helen Gardner, *The Art of T. S. Eliot* (1st ed., 1950; 1959), Thomas R. Rees, *The Technique of T. S. Eliot: A Study of the Orchestration of Meaning in Eliot's Poetry* (1974); and Keith Alldritt, *Eliot's "Four Quartets": Poetry as Chamber Music* (1978). Some of the comparisons, especially with sonata-allegro form, are clearly useful but can also clearly be carried too far.

2. One notable exception to this widespread failing on the part of Eliot's critics is found in A. D. Moody's *Thomas Stearns Eliot: Poet* (1979), pp. 196–200, 238–41. But Moody's analysis, while in many ways illuminating, still does not reveal the various components of the structure that provide its special theological import; and Moody, like many other critics, is misled by Eliot's seeming "mysticism." Cf. my critique of William T. Moynihan's reading in the present chapter.

3. See *BF*, pp. 240–68.

4. Ibid., p. 241.

5. Ibid., pp. 241–42.

6. The best single volume of neo-Aristotelian theory and criticism has long been *Critics and Criticism: Ancient and Modern*, ed. R. S. Crane (1952), especially the essays by Crane, Elder Olson, and Richard McKeon. See also R. S. Crane, *The Languages of Criticism and the Structure of Poetry* (1953).

7. William T. Moynihan, "Character and Action in *Four Quartets*," in *T. S. Eliot: A Collection of Criticism*, ed. Linda W. Wagner (1974).

8. Ibid., pp. 80, 74.

9. Ibid., p. 83.

10. Ibid., pp. 83–84.

11. Ibid., pp. 73, 74.

12. Ibid., p. 73.

13. Gardner, *Art of Eliot*, p. 44.

14. I am convinced that Eliot's views of the relation of poetry and ideas to feeling have been misunderstood whenever it has been supposed that he does not see ideas and feelings as intimately related and to some extent co-inherent. Much of the inconsistency in Eliot's printed statements on this topic is due, I think, to Eliot's own varied use of the term "feeling." But what he is often driving at can be seen in even a cursory reading of the first chapter of his dissertation on F. H. Bradley. Indeed, that chapter should be required reading for anyone wanting to use Eliot's pronouncements as something more than slogans. I find especially pertinent Eliot's own observation, made in the course of elucidating Bradley's thought, that "we do not [in actual experience] find feeling without thought, or presentation without reflection." We might also keep in mind Eliot's statement that, for Bradley, feeling is the unity or confusion of perception and thought, will and desire; it is (quoting Bradley) "the general state of the total soul not yet at all differentiated into [its] special aspects." Thus Eliot and Bradley both consider "feeling" to be something similar to what I am here simply calling one's "whole being." I would argue, however, that even the "total soul" is to some extent "differentiated." *Knowledge and Experience in the Philosophy of F. H. Bradley* (1964), pp. 17, 19–20.

15. "Character and Action," p. 74.

16. Cf. Elder Olson's claim that the mimetic poet strives, in writing, simply to make a beautiful and pleasing whole, whereas Dante, in composing the *Comedy*, "is writing a scholastic treatise." "William Empson, Contemporary Criticism, and Poetic Diction," in *Critics and Criticism*, p. 68. See also ibid., pp. 63–67. R. S. Crane, it should be noted, treats the distinction between mimetic and didactic works chiefly as a matter of their form and "material nature" rather than purpose. But, as Olson's essay illustrates, the distinction necessarily implies differences in poetic purpose as well. See Crane, *Languages of Criticism*, pp. 156–58.

17. *Mysticism: A Study in the Nature and Development of Man's Spiritual Consciousness* (1st ed., 1911; 1961), p. 169.

18. Moynihan characterizes Underhill's third stage as that of "*purgation* bringing illumination," whereas it is clear (despite some grammatical complexity) that Underhill's description is of a stage of *illumination* that has been brought about by purgation. See *Mysticism*, p. 169, and "Character and Action," p. 83, my emphases.

19. See, for example, William Johnston, *The Still Point: Reflections on Zen and Christian Mysticism* (1971), and Sister Bernadette Counihan, "*Four Quartets*: An Ascent to Mount Carmel?," *Wisconsin Studies in Literature* (1969). Cf. Eloise Knapp Hay, *T. S. Eliot's Negative Way* (1982).

20. See Lyndall Gordon, *Eliot's Early Years* (1977), Appendix I, and Helen Gardner, *The Composition of "Four Quartets"* (1978), pp. 69–70.

21. For a short but lucid discussion of apophatic mysticism, see John F. Teahan, "Thomas Merton and the Apophatic Tradition," *Journal of Religion* 58 (July 1978): 263–87.

22. See Saint John of the Cross, *The Dark Night of the Soul*, book 2, chapts. 19 and 20. Here I am in agreement with Robert J. Andreach, who argues that Eliot—whose speaker in the *Quartets* never gets beyond the stage of active purgation—is "not really interested in spiritual growth that leads to illumination and on to union so much as he is interested in affirming the necessity of the spiritual life." *Studies in Structure: The Stages of the Spiritual Life in Four Modern Authors* (1964), p. 93.

23. T. S. Eliot, "The *Pensées* of Pascal," in *Selected Essays*, 3d ed. (1951), pp. 402–16. First published as the introduction to the Everyman Library edition of the *Pensées*, trans. W. F. Trotter (London: J. M. Dent, [1931]), pp. vii–xix.

24. See *Time and Eternity* (1st ed., 1960; 1973), p. 70.

25. Ibid.

26. Ibid., p. 69.

27. Bergsten seems not to have noticed the word "analogue."

28. Many editions of the *Pensées*, including that for which Eliot's essay serves as an introduction, alter Pascal's arrangement of topics in such a way as to suggest a more linear argument than Pascal had in mind. Even considering this, however, Eliot's account is definitely a simplification and a somewhat personal interpretation.

29. From A. J. Krailsheimer's introduction to his translation of the *Pensées* (London: Penguin Books, 1968), p. 26.

30. I follow Moynihan's practice of referring to the "I" of these poems as the "speaker" rather than as "Eliot." Although this may seem slightly artificial, it serves the purpose of reminding us that the "I" is a persona, however closely identified with Eliot himself.

31. With reference to Eliot's pilgrimage toward Anglo-Catholicism, Helen Gardner observes that "faith precedes faith in a regressive series." (*Art of Eliot*, p. 103.) Perhaps we should also say that faith is progressive as well.

32. See T. S. Eliot's preface to *Anabasis: A Poem*, by St. John Perse (1938).

Chapter 5. Poetic Metaphor and Poetic Purpose

1. My analysis presumes the reader has a basic familiarity with *Four Quartets* and with "East Coker" in particular.

2. *Four Quartets* begins with two epigrams from Heraclitus, of course, and "East Coker" itself contains many allusions to this pre-Socratic philosopher.

3. *The Well-Tempered Critic* (1963), p. 149. See also *Anatomy of Criticism: Four Essays* (1957), pp. 341–54. Cf. Frye's contention, in *The Great Code* (1981), that the Bible itself is largely "centripetal" in meaning, the two testaments forming a "double mirror, each reflecting the other but neither the world outside" (p. 78). This position seems to be modified when he admits that the Bible uses "proclaiming rhetoric." But Frye insists that this very concern for proclamation or assertion is what sets the Bible apart from literature as such, because, in his view, literature and the arts use language that is "purely imaginative and hence hypothetical" (p. 231).

4. "That Literature Is a Kind of Knowledge," *Critical Inquiry* (1976), p. 493.

5. It is rather surprising just how many of the descriptive details in these poems are based on actual observations. See Helen Gardner, *The Composition of "Four Quartets"* (1978).

6. Anyone who thought that dahlias can actually sleep would miss the metaphoric qualities of the poetic assertion that the dahlias sleep in the silence.

7. The "insistence" of the lane also informs us that lanes and roads in this poetic world are phenomena that guide one in times of transition. We are therefore not surprised when a later road "insists" on the direction toward Little Gidding.

8. In many poems, it should be observed, the most ontologically serious assertions are covert. They are implications that grow out of the whole, suggested more pointedly in some passages than in others, but never explicitly articulated. In other poems the explicit interpretations internal to the work are all false to the "facts" of the poem and to the realities of experience—but intentionally so. In such works (parodies, satires, absurdist art) the implicit ontological import is "argued" by demolishing inferior interpretations of the "truth." The implicit claim of such works may even be that there is no truth. But this one claim, at least, is asserted seriously, if only by implication.

9. By "thetical" I mean precisely what the *OED* means: "Of the nature of or involving direct or positive statement."

10. Because the poetic argument is metaphoric, the word "conclusion" is somewhat misleading even when applied to the third kind of assertion. Aside from the fact that such an assertion seems more like a "thesis" when one encounters it earlier in a poem, as one does in reading "In my beginning is my end," it is inconclusive simply because no poetic conclusion is ever absolutely conclusive, but only relatively so. The conclusion of a syllogism contains the import of the argument; it is that for the sake of which the argument exists. The heavier assertions in "East Coker," by contrast, never *contain* the essential meaning of the poem; they only serve to concentrate it and then release it.

11. For another argument to this effect see Walter A. Davis, *The Act of Interpretation: A Critique of Literary Reason* (1978), esp. pp. 122–27. I am delighted to discover that Professor Davis has independently arrived at similar conclusions as to the potential synthesis of argument and representation in literary art. It is not Davis's intention to examine in detail the dynamics of what he calls "dialectical mimesis," however—which is, in a sense, what I have tried to do here. And his notion of how such mimesis functions in relation to literary art in general is rather different from my own.

12. According to A. D. Moody, Eliot's literary models here are found "in the Tudor translations of Seneca, . . . in some of Marlowe's 'over-reaching' magniloquence; in Donne's *Anatomie of the World*; in the discourses upon cosmic disorder spoken by Titania in *A Midsummer Night's Dream* and Ulysses in *Troilus and Cressida*; and, of course, in Burton's *Anatomy*, and in Milton." (*Thomas Stearns Eliot: Poet* [1979] p. 212.) So precise a pinpointing of sources is best regarded as intelligent guesswork.

13. I cannot agree at this point with Keith Alldritt, who thinks that here "there is a tumbling succession of uneasy adjectival phrases and the sound of the lines, particularly the consonants, confirms a sense of thunderous violence." *Eliot's "Four Quartets": Poetry as Chamber Music* (1978), p. 79.

14. *The Art of T. S. Eliot*, (1st ed. 1950; 1959), p. 38.

15. *T. S. Eliot: The Longer Poems* (1976), p. 132.

16. T. S. Eliot, "East Coker," *"Four Quartets" Read by T. S. Eliot*, Caedmon, T C 1403, n.d.

17. We know that an earlier version of the poem contained, at some point, the line "The Archer's bow and Taurus' ire," which Eliot seems only reluctantly to have revised out of the later versions as a response to criticism from John Hayward. It is my judgment that this line could have followed quite naturally on the heels of "Hunt the heavens and the plains," where it would have rhymed perfectly with some slightly modified version of the next to last line. In that case the inner pair of lines in the closing quatrain would have rhymed exactly, thus mak-

ing the last quatrain as complete and symmetrical as the first. (See Gardner, *Composition*, pp. 16–17, 100–101.) Perhaps Eliot could not quite bring this off and still have the poem say what he needed it to say.

18. Literally, of course, the symmetry comes closer to being bilateral or even chiastic than it does to being radial. The radial aspect is suggested, however, in the context of a cycle of poems in which circular movement, still points, centers, and so forth are well established as being of major thematic and symbolic import.

19. I suspect, in fact, that a literal account of such moments would be a literal impossibility.

20. On the basis of evidence supplied by Helen Gardner, I have used a comma instead of a period after "lightning." See Gardner, *Composition*, pp. 104–5.

21. From a reference Eliot makes to "East Coker" in a letter written to Anne Ridler in 1941. See Gardner, *Composition*, p. 109.

22. In this connection it is worth noting that one of the early drafts of "The Dry Salvages" explicitly mentioned Atonement alongside Incarnation. See Gardner, *Composition*, pp. 146–47.

23. Ibid., p. 109.

24. Although Eliot acknowledges the dangers in Jansenism, he remarks in his essay on the *Pensées* that "a moment of Jansenism may naturally take place, and take place rightly, in the individual; particularly in the life of a man of great and intense intellectual powers." *Selected Essays*, 3d ed. (1951), p. 414.

25. It should be noted, however, that the poetic meter itself conveys not only a sense of the speaker's conviction but also a sense of the power of that into which he submits his life. For in each stanza the first three lines of iambic tetrameter broaden into a further line in pentameter, and finally into another in hexameter. However weak the one who speaks, it seems he has come into a power that will triumph in the end.

26. Helen Gardner points out, incidentally, that one of Karl Barth's favorite concepts is of the "point of intersection"—familiar enough to anyone who has read "The Dry Salvages." *Composition*, p. 145.

27. Eliot, in fact, says something like this in his Pascal essay, p. 408.

28. *The Longer Poems*, p. 96, Traversi's emphasis.

29. Ibid., p. 89.

30. Ibid., p. 111, Traversi's emphasis.

31. Ibid., p. 181.

32. "New Modes of Empirical Theology," in *The Future of Empirical Theology*, ed. Bernard Meland (1969), pp. 366, 368.

33. Ibid., p. 369.

34. Ibid., p. 370. Cf. Paul Tillich's well-known "method of correlation" in *Systematic Theology*, (1951–63), 1:62–64.

35. "Apologetics," in *Sacramentum Mundi*, ed. Karl Rahner (1968), 1:67, 69.

36. It is interesting that John Margolis makes a similar observation concerning the content of Eliot's essays: "So far as [Eliot] saw himself in the orthodox tradition of [the] Christian Fathers, perhaps he felt it unnecessary to describe more precisely the content of his faith. But so far as he hoped to convert to that faith a world increasingly separated from it, his lack of specificity seriously diminishes the impact of his argument." *T. S. Eliot's Intellectual Development* (1972), p. 214.

37. "Religion and Literature," in *Selected Essays*, p. 394.

Chapter 6. Poetry and Religious Reflection

1. "Apologetics," in *Sacramentum Mundi*, ed. Karl Rahner (1968), 1:67, 69.

2. See the bibliography for a listing of important works by "process" theologians indebted to Whitehead.

3. I am particularly in sympathy with the tenor of Meland's arguments in his most recent book, *Fallible Forms and Symbols: Discourses on Method in a Theology of Culture* (1976).

4. See *Risk and Rhetoric in Religion: Whitehead's Theory of Language and the Discourse of Faith* (1972).

5. Even Victor Lowe, who praises what he calls Whitehead's "philosophical theology," has to admit that Whitehead "does not in fact often speak of theology." See *Understanding Whitehead* (1962), p. 95.

6. *Process and Reality: An Essay in Cosmology* (1st ed., 1929; corrected ed., edited by David Ray Griffin and Donald W. Sherburne, 1978), hereafter cited as *PR*, p. 4 [6]. (Bracketed page numbers refer to the popular American Macmillan edition, 1929.)

7. Some idea of the complexity and liveliness of contemporary discussions within a broadly empirical tradition can be seen in the 500-page volume of essays collected and edited by Robert J. Swartz and published as *Perceiving, Sensing and Knowing* (1965). See also Jacob Joshua Ross, *The Appeal to the Given: A Study in Epistemology* (1970), and Ash Gobar, *Philosophic Foundations of Genetic Psychology and Gestalt Psychology* (1968).

8. *Adventures of Ideas* (1st ed., 1933; 1967), hereafter cited as *AI*, p. 175.

9. Ibid., pp. 177–78.

10. Ibid., p. 225.

11. *Modes of Thought* (1st ed., 1938; 1968), hereafter cited as *MT*, p. 114.

12. Ibid. See also p. 115.

13. For Whitehead's technical discussion of perception see, for example, *Symbolism: Its Meaning and Effect* (1st ed., 1927; 1959), hereafter cited as *Sym*.

14. See David Hume, *A Treatise of Human Nature*, especially book 1, pt. 3.

15. *PR*, pp. 170–73 [259–63].

16. Whitehead is no determinist, of course, and he speaks not only of an efficient cause, but also of a final one, and of creativity as well.

17. *MT*, p. 110.

18. Ibid.

19. Ibid.

20. *Religion in the Making* (1st ed., 1926; 1960), hereafter cited as *RM*, p. 97.

21. Ibid. Compare *MT*, p. 110.

22. *MT*, p. 166.

23. Ibid., p. 116.

24. Ibid.

25. Ibid., p. 102.

26. Ibid., p. 120.

27. *AI*, p. 217. See also *Sym*., pp. 13–16.

28. Whitehead's technical terms for these two modes of perception are "presentational immediacy" and "causal efficacy." See *Sym*., pp. 49–59.

29. *MT*, p. 72.

30. *AI*, p. 163.

31. *PR*, pp. 10–11 [15–16].

32. "Remarks," *Philosophical Review* (1937).

33. I am persuaded that the passage in question is misunderstood, for instance, when

Wilbur M. Urban writes that "it seems to confirm the suspicion which I have had all along, that the spirit of Whitehead's philosophy is after all fundamentally naturalistic." See "Whitehead's Philosophy of Language," in *The Philosophy of Alfred North Whitehead*, ed. Paul Arthur Schilpp (1st ed., 1941; 1951), p. 324.

34. *Whitehead's Categoreal Scheme and Other Papers* (1974), p. 1.

35. *PR*, p. 8 [11–12].

36. Ibid., p. ix [x].

37. *Meaning and Method: Prolegomena to a Scientific Philosophy of Religion and a Scientific Theology* (1972), pp. 51–57.

38. This would be what Nygren calls "inductive metaphysics." Nygren seems not to conceive of the possibility that induction could proceed on the basis of a fundamental reconception of the nature of experience. Ibid., pp. 48–50.

39. *PR*, p. 3 [4].

40. *MT*, p. 48.

41. *RM*, p. 82n.

42. *PR*, pp. 9–11 [14–16]. Cf. *MT*, pp. 48–49.

43. My terminology here is intentionally borrowed from Frederick Ferré. See *Language, Logic, and God* (1961), pp. 162–66, and *Basic Modern Philosophy of Religion* (1967), pp. 378–440.

44. This is my statement, not Whitehead's.

45. *PR*, p. 3–4 [4–6].

46. Ibid., p. 6 [9–10].

47. *AI*, p. 226.

48. *PR*, pp. 3–4 [4–6].

49. Despite some ambiguity in certain of Whitehead's statements, this conclusion seems to me inevitable if one is to take seriously Whitehead's repeated emphasis on the empirical character of his method. For corroboration of this interpretation see the unpublished dissertations of Stephen Franklin, "Speaking from the Depth: Alfred North Whitehead's Metaphysics of Propositions, Symbolism, Perceptions, Language, and Religion" (1976), pp. 216–28, and Bernard MacDougall Loomer, "The Theological Significance of the Method of Empirical Analysis in the Philosophy of A. N. Whitehead" (1942), pp. 80–97. That Whitehead and Charles Hartshorne differ both in practice and in theory at this point seems clear to me; but this is not so apparent to some other interpreters. For differing views on this subject, see the essays by David R. Griffin, Lewis S. Ford, and William M. O'Meara in *Two Process Philosophers: Hartshorne's Encounter with Whitehead*, ed. Lewis S. Ford (1973).

50. *PR*, pp. 3–4 [4–5].

51. Cf. Whitehead's statement that "a cosmology should above all things be adequate." *The Function of Reason* (1st ed., 1929; 1958), hereafter cited as *FR*, p. 86.

52. *PR*, p. 5 [7].

53. *MT*, p. 83.

54. Ibid., p. 168; *PR*, pp. 4–5 [6–8]. Cf. Aristotle's *Metaphysics* A, 982b.

55. *PR*, pp. 5–6 [8–9].

56. *MT*, p. 83.

57. *FR*, p. 78.

58. *PR*, p. 4 [6].

59. Ibid.

60. Ibid.

61. Ibid., p. 9 [14].

62. Ibid., pp. 4–5 [6–7].

63. *FR*, p. 78.

64. *MT*, pp. 48–49.
65. Ibid., pp. 1–2.
66. *FR*, p. 75.
67. *AI*, p. 166. See also *MT*, p. 82.
68. *AI*, p. 166.
69. *MT*, pp. 70–71. See also *PR*, pp. 5, 15–16 [7–8, 23–24].
70. *MT*, p. 70.
71. Ibid., p. 71.
72. See *RM*, pp. 26, 50.
73. *AI*, p. 167.
74. Ibid.
75. Ibid., pp. 167–69.
76. *RM*, p. 18.
77. Ibid.
78. *PR*, p. 16 [23]. See also *AI*, p. 71.
79. *PR*, p. 16 [23].
80. *MT*, pp. 102, 116, 120.
81. Ibid., p. 78.
82. *RM*, p. 120.
83. Ibid., pp. 137–39.
84. Ibid., pp. 31, 55, 138, 143. See also *FR*, p. 78.
85. Ibid., p. 31.
86. Ibid.
87. *AI*, p. 163.
88. *PR*, pp. 11–13 [16–20]. *RM*, p. 127.
89. See, for example, *AI*, p. 163.
90. *MT*, pp. 5, 39, 49.
91. Ibid., p. 49. See also *PR*, pp. 4–5, 12 [6–7, 17].
92. It should be pointed out that Whitehead sees language and thought as intimately inter-related but not completely identical, noting in this connection that "some of us" struggle to find words for ideas that are in some sense already present. See *MT*, pp. 34–35, 41.
93. *PR*, p. 9 [14].
94. *MT*, p. 9.
95. Ibid., pp. 5, 117.
96. *AI*, p. 226.
97. *Science and the Modern World* (1st ed., 1925; 1967), hereafter cited as *SMW*, pp. 92–94.
98. Ibid., pp. 84, 88.
99. *RM*, p. 130.
100. *MT*, pp. 5, 117.
101. *SMW*, pp. 75–80, my emphasis.
102. Ibid., p. 93.
103. *MT*, p. 5.
104. *SMW*, p. 89. By "naive experience" Whitehead means essentially what phenomenologists have meant by "lived experience."
105. *MT*, p. 174.
106. *PR*, p. 4 [6]. We will see, however, that Whitehead believes we can have knowledge of—and insight into—truths we cannot clearly articulate and that we can rationalize our deepest insights without ever completely exhausting their meaning.
107. Ibid., p. x [xiv]. See also ibid., p. 9 [14].
108. Ibid., p. 4 [6].

109. Ibid., p. 9 [14].
110. Ibid., p. 7 [13].
111. *FR*, p. 68. See also *PR*, pp. 11–12 [16–18], especially Whitehead's statement that "a precise language must await a completed metaphysical knowledge" and his very emphatic assertions to this effect in the essay "Immortality," in *Philosophy of Whitehead*, esp. pp. 698–700.
112. See, for example, *AI*, p. 128.
113. See *Philosophy of Whitehead*, pp. 698–700.
114. *PR*, p. 7 [11].
115. *AI*, p. 128.
116. *MT*, p. 174.
117. Ibid., p. 117.
118. *FR*, p. 80.
119. *FR*, p. 71; *PR*, p. 9 [14].
120. *MT*, pp. 12–13.
121. *RM*, pp. 141, 127.
122. Ibid., p. 31.
123. *MT*, p. 50.
124. *PR*, p. 208 [318].
125. Ibid., pp. 208–9, 338 [317–19, 513–14].
126. *MT*, p. 10.
127. *RM*, p. 149.
128. *MT*, p. 5.
129. *AI*, p. 159.
130. *MT*, p. 43.
131. *FR*, p. 81.
132. *SMW*, p. 89.
133. *AI*, p. 163.

Chapter 7. Transfiguration

1. Today there are few philosophers who would call assertions in the second class "meaningless." But the truth of such assertions is still very much in question.
2. See, for example, Anders Nygren, *Meaning and Method: Prolegomena to a Scientific Philosophy of Religion and a Scientific Theology* (1972), and D. Z. Phillips, *Faith and Philosophical Inquiry* (1971).
3. See Thomas Altizer et al., *Deconstruction and Theology* (1982); Mark C. Taylor, *Deconstructing Theology* (1982); John Dominic Crossan, *Cliffs of Fall: Paradox and Polyvalence in the Parables of Jesus* (1980); and Charles E. Winquist, ed., *The Archaeology of the Imagination* (1981).
4. *Philosophy and the Mirror of Nature* (1979), pp. 371–72.
5. *The Claim of Reason: Wittgenstein, Skepticism, Morality, and Tragedy* (1979), p. 241.
6. This, it seems to me, is the chief danger of the otherwise admirable pluralism of David Tracy in *The Analogical Imagination: Christian Theology and the Culture of Pluralism* (1981). Tracy's emphasis on the public character of various kinds of truth-claims is intended, of course, to counteract tendencies toward the privatization and atomization of truth. But his willingness here to embrace all kinds of "truths" seems at times to water down the whole idea—or different ideas—of what it means to make a truth-claim.
7. I do not mean here to reflect an essentialist concept of selfhood or to hypostasize

"being." I am using the term as a casual equivalent for "form of life" (Wittgenstein), "being-in-the-world" (Heidegger), or just "mode of existence."

8. Cf. a similar viewpoint in David Tracy, *Blessed Rage for Order: The New Pluralism in Theology* (1975), esp. pp. 91–118.

9. *AI*, p. 161.

10. *RM*, p. 120.

11. This has meant, of course, that I have consistently rejected Wheelwright's notion that only metaphoric language is expressive of "depth."

12. Tracy, *Blessed Rage*, esp. pp. 43–63.

13. See, for example, Schubert M. Ogden, "Present Prospects for Empirical Theology," and Bernard E. Meland, "Can Empirical Theology Learn Something from Phenomenology?," in *The Future of Empirical Theology*, ed. Bernard E. Meland (1969). See also John E. Smith, *Themes in American Philosophy: Purpose, Experience, and Community* (1970), and *Experience and God* (1968).

14. See *BF*, pp. 18–31.

15. For a recent discussion of this topic that emphasizes the possibility of, and need for, pragmatic tests of the validity and truth of both metaphysics and theology see Gordon P. Kaufman, "Metaphysics and Theology," in *The Theological Imagination: Constructing the Concept of God* (1981).

16. See Schubert M. Ogden, "What Is Theology?," *Journal of Religion* (1972).

17. Cf. Tillich, *Systematic Theology*, (1951–63), 1:59–66.

18. *Blessed Rage*, p. 43. For Tracy, "Christian fact" is roughly the equivalent of "Christian tradition."

19. Ibid., pp. 43–46.

20. See, for example, *RM*, pp. 115, 120; *MT*, pp. 102, 120.

21. See "The New Reformation," in *AI*, and also *RM* as a whole.

22. *Christ without Myth: A Study Based on the Theology of Rudolf Bultmann* (1961).

23. *The Reality of God* (1964).

24. See *Faith and Freedom: Toward a Theology of Liberation* (1979), and *The Point of Christology* (1982).

25. "The Task of Philosophical Theology," in *The Future of Philosophical Theology*, ed. Robert A. Evans (1971), pp. 55–84.

26. Ibid., p. 82.

27. Ibid., p. 81.

28. Ibid., p. 78.

29. Ibid.

30. See Ogden, "Myth and Truth," in *Reality of God*, pp. 99–119. Recently David Tracy has reminded us of a growing consensus in modern religious studies that all major religions are grounded not in pure concepts but in certain root metaphors forming "a cluster or network in which certain sustained metaphors both organize subsidiary metaphors and diffuse new ones." See Tracy, "Metaphor and Religion: The Test Case of Christian Texts," *Critical Inquiry* (1978), p. 91.

31. See, for example, Ogden's essay "Lonergan and the Subjectivist Principle," *Journal of Religion* (1971).

32. *Reality of God*, p. 118.

33. Ibid., pp. 118, 97.

34. *Reality of God*, esp. pp. 78–82. See also "Bultmann's Demythologizing and Hartshorne's Dipolar Theism," in *Process and Divinity: The Hartshorne Festschrift*, ed. William L. Reese and Eugene Freeman (1964), p. 507.

35. *Reality of God*, pp. 78 – 83.

36. "On Revelation," in *Our Common History as Christians: Essays in Honor of Albert C. Outler*, ed. John Deschner, Leroy T. Howe, and Klaus Penzel (1975), pp. 261 – 92.

37. *Reality of God*, p. 92.

38. Ibid., p. 97.

39. *RM*, p. 56.

40. Ibid., p. 31; pp. 76 – 77.

41. *Reality of God*, p. 97, my emphasis. See also ibid., pp. 92, 118.

42. Ibid., p. 92.

43. For an interesting restatement of what Ogden means by "metaphysics" and "metaphysical truth"—and it is somewhat different from what either Whitehead or Hartshorne means— see his article "The Criteria of Metaphysical Truth and the Sense of 'Metaphysics'," *Process Studies* (1975).

44. *MT*, p. 49.

45. See "Immortality," in *The Philosophy of Alfred North Whitehead*, ed. Paul Arthur Schilpp (1st ed., 1941; 1951), pp. 698 – 700. Cf. Nelson Goodman's contention that synonymy is a suspect notion. *Ways of Worldmaking* (1978), pp. 24 – 25.

46. *MT*, p. 50.

47. *RM*, p. 123.

48. Ibid., p. 65.

49. Ibid.

50. *MT*, p. 10.

51. *FR*, p. 75.

52. *RM*, p. 50.

53. *AI*, p. 159.

54. *MT*, p. 43.

55. *Reality of God*, p. 81.

56. Ibid., pp. 92, 97, 118.

57. Bernard Meland makes a similar argument in *Fallible Forms and Symbols: Discourses on Method in a Theology of Culture* (1976).

58. *Christology*, pp. 132 – 40. In this book Ogden also criticizes what he terms "revisionary" Christologies in general. Plainly, however, he sees his own thinking as "revisionary" in spirit. In any case, "revisionary" (Ogden's term) and "revisionist" (David Tracy's term) are not synonymous, and Ogden does fit Tracy's description of the "revisionist" theologian.

59. Ibid., pp. 135 – 47.

60. Ibid., pp. 140 – 46, Ogden's emphasis. Unfortunately, Ogden is not very informative about just what his particular kind of "transcendental" method would entail and about the way—if any—in which his approach to metaphysics would be empirical as well as a priori. See Ogden, "Metaphysical Truth," pp. 47 – 48, for further relevant discussion. I trust I have not misrepresented his ideas on this topic in any major respect. Ogden's position on language, at least, seems crystal clear.

61. Ibid., p. 145.

62. Ibid., pp. 142 – 46.

63. *AI*, pp. 117 – 18.

64. *Reality of God*, p. 95.

65. One possible retort to my argument is that, even though scientists expect their theories to be modified at a future date, they are with good reason insistent on both the necessity and possibility of precisely verbalized understanding. In fact, just because their discourse exhibits conceptual clarity and precision, they can tell in retrospect which ideas were precisely right and which were wrong, what was really understood and what was really misunderstood. But

even if true (a questionable assumption), this point would merely show that metaphysical theories and "total explanations" are in some respects very different from their scientific counterparts. Whatever one concludes with respect to scientific theories, it remains the case that every major metaphysical concept is closely interrelated with every other; consequently, any substantial "correction" of one concept alters the meaning of every other concept. Apart from a perfect metaphysical understanding, therefore, not one metaphysical concept can be completely precise or fully adequate.

66. Paul M. van Buren, *The Edges of Language: An Essay in the Logic of a Religion* (1972), esp. pp. 151–66.

67. See Max Black, "Metaphor," in *Models and Metaphors* (1962), p. 46. See also Black, "More about Metaphor," in *Metaphor and Thought*, ed. Andrew Ortony (1979), pp. 34–36.

68. *Knowing and Acting: An Invitation to Philosophy* (1976), p. 168.

69. Ibid., pp. 309–10, Toulmin's emphasis.

70. Ibid., p. 164.

71. Ibid.

72. Ibid. For further discussion of the whole idea of rational procedures and reason-giving see the first—and as yet only—volume of Stephen Toulmin's *Human Understanding: The Collective Use and Evolution of Concepts* (1972). Obviously Toulmin here more or less equates understanding with conceptualization, but he considerably broadens the scope of the term "concepts."

73. The above description of revisionist ideas differs slightly from that given by David Tracy, but mostly in emphasis. See *Blessed Rage*, esp. pp. 43–63, 91–118.

74. *AI*, p. 143.

75. *Knowing and Acting*, p. 164.

76. For an extensive discussion of the religious and theological role of "classics," see Tracy, *Analogical Imagination*, chapters 3–8.

77. Cf. Paul Ricoeur, "The Metaphorical Process as Cognition, Imagination, and Feeling," *Critical Inquiry* (1978).

78. "Creativity in Language," *Philosophy Today* (1973).

79. Ibid., p. 111.

80. "Metaphorical Process," p. 153.

81. *The Rule of Metaphor: Multidisciplinary Studies in the Creation of Meaning*, trans. Robert Czerny (1977), p. 214.

82. Of the large number of scholars who have called attention to a religious dimension within "secular" literature, at least a few should be noted here: Nathan A. Scott, Jr., *The Broken Center: Studies in the Theological Horizon of Modern Literature* (1966), and *Negative Capability: Studies in the New Literature and the Religious Situation* (1971); J. Hillis Miller, *The Disappearance of God: Five 19th-Century Writers* (1965), and *Poets of Reality: Six Twentieth-Century Writers* (1965); Amos N. Wilder, *Theology and Modern Literature* (1958), and *Theopoetic* (1976); Vincent Buckley, *Poetry and the Sacred* (1968); Wesley Kort, *Narrative Elements and Religious Meaning* (1975); and Giles B. Gunn, *The Interpretation of Otherness: Literature, Religion, and the American Imagination* (1979).

83. *Understanding Religious Life* (1976), pp. 1–9.

84. See David Tracy, "Metaphor and Religion: The Test Case of Religious Texts," *Critical Inquiry* (1978).

85. See Gerardus van der Leeuw, *Sacred and Profane Beauty: The Holy in Art*, trans. David E. Green (1963).

86. See *Rule of Metaphor*, chap. 8, esp. p. 302. See also the concluding section of chapter 2 of the present book.

87. I am inclined to use the word "meaning" in much the way Max Black does: as a sign for

"whatever a competent hearer may be said to have grasped when he [or she] succeeds in responding adequately to the actual or hypothetical verbal action consisting in the . . . utterance of the sentence(s) in question." "More about Metaphor," p. 24.

88. *Truth and Symbol* (from *Von der Wahrheit*), trans. Jean T. Wilde, William Kluback, and William Kimmel (orig. text, 1947; extract and translation, 1959), p. 51.

89. *The Symbolism of Evil*, trans. Emerson Buchanan (1st ed., 1967; 1969), p. 348.

90. *Understanding Whitehead* (1962), p. 24.

91. In this connection it is interesting to see what Charles Wesley says, writing of his own 1780 handbook of hymns: "It is large enough to contain all the important truths of our most holy religion, whether speculative or practical; yea to illustrate them all, and to prove them both by Scripture and reason." Frank Whaling, ed., *John and Charles Wesley: Selected Writings and Hymns*, Classics of Western Spirituality (New York: Paulist Press, 1981), pp. 175–76.

92. See Martin Heidegger, *Poetry, Language, Thought*, trans. Albert Hofstadter (1971).

93. See Charles Hartshorne's criticism of the classical theistic concept of love in *The Divine Relativity: A Social Conception of God* (1948).

94. *Philosophy*, trans. E. B. Ashton (orig. text, 1932; trans. 1969–71), 1:335, 334.

95. *PR*, p. 9 [14].

96. Dorothy Emmet, thinking along these lines, claims that now, in a time of searching for new metaphysical systems, *Four Quartets* itself can provide a sense of where, and in what dimensions of experience, the right "word" might be found. See *The Nature of Metaphysical Thinking* (1st ed., 1945; 1966), pp. 224–27.

97. *Rule of Metaphor*, pp. 257–313.

98. This point is made emphatically by Wolfgang Iser in *The Act of Reading: A Theory of Aesthetic Response* (1978).

99. See Michael Polanyi, *The Tacit Dimension* (1966).

100. For a rather different view see Gordon D. Kaufman, *An Essay on Theological Method* (1979), pp. 43–68.

101. *PR*, p. 4 [6].

102. On the nature of metaphysical "faith" assumptions see Frank B. Dilley, *Metaphysics and Religious Language* (1964), and John B. Cobb, Jr., *A Christian Natural Theology* (1965), p. 259. Cf. Stephen C. Pepper, *World Hypotheses: A Study in Evidence* (1st ed., 1941; 1970).

103. For a thoughtful and persuasive attempt to place ritual within the dialectic between theoretical knowledge and other kinds of knowledge see Theodore W. Jennings, "On Ritual Knowledge," *Journal of Religion* (1982).

104. Geoffrey Wainwright makes a similar point when he writes, "It is the Christian community that transmits the vision which the theologian, as an individual human being, has seen and believed." But Wainwright fails to do justice to the degree to which theology can also assume a public function. *Doxology: The Praise of God in Worship, Doctrine and Life* (1980), p. 3.

105. Much of what is said here concerning poetic metaphor could be applied to nonverbal arts through an analysis of artistic metaphor. But this is beyond the scope of the present book.

Selected Bibliography

Because of the selective nature of this bibliography the more specialized bibliographies cited below should be consulted for detailed and exhaustive treatment of the literature relevant to particular topics. Entries in the present bibliography are divided into the following categories: "Bibliographies," "Writings by Philip Wheelwright," "Writings Pertaining to T. S. Eliot and *Four Quartets*," "Writings Pertaining to Alfred North Whitehead and Process Theology," and "Other Basic Sources and Background Material."

Bibliographies

"Bibliography." In *Process Philosophy and Christian Thought*. Edited by Delwin Brown, Ralph E. James, Jr., and Gene Reeves. Indianapolis: Bobbs-Merrill, 1971.
"A Bibliography of the Writings of Philip Wheelwright." In *The Hidden Harmony*: *Essays in Honor of Philip Wheelwright*. Edited by Oliver Johnson, David Harrah, Peter Fuss, and Theodore Guleserian. New York: Odyssey Press, 1966.
Frank, Mechthild; Frank, Armin Paul; and Jochum, K. P. S. *T. S. Eliot Criticism in English, 1916–65*: *A Supplementary Bibliography*. Yeats Eliot Review Monograph, no. 1. Edmonton: Yeats Eliot Review, 1978.
Gallup, Donald C. *T. S. Eliot*: *A Bibliography*. 2d ed. London: Faber & Faber, 1969.
Martin, Mildred. *A Half-Century of Eliot Criticism*: *An Annotated Bibliography of Books and Articles in English, 1916–1965*. Lewisburg, Pa.: Bucknell University Press, 1972.
Ricks, Beatrice. *T. S. Eliot*: *A Bibliography of Secondary Works*. Metuchen, N.J.: Scarecrow Press, 1980.
Shibles, Warren A. *Metaphor*: *An Annotated Bibliography and History*. Whitewater, Wisc.: Language Press, 1971.
Woodbridge, Barry A., ed. *Alfred North Whitehead*: *A Primary-Secondary Bibliography*. Bowling Green, Ohio: Philosophy Documentation Center, Bowling Green State University, 1977.

Writings by Philip Wheelwright

"The Living Mind." *Symposium* 1 (April 1930):282–84.
"Notes on Meaning." *Symposium* 1 (July 1930):371–86.
"Poetry and Logic." *Symposium* 1 (October 1930):440–57.
"A Defence of Orthodoxy." *Symposium* 3 (January 1932):3–24.
"A Contemporary Classicist." *Virginia Quarterly Review* 9 (January 1933):155–60.
"*Moral Man and Immoral Society*." *Symposium* 4 (July 1933):373–82.
"Comment." *Symposium* 4 (October 1933):413–19.
A Critical Introduction to Ethics. Garden City, N.Y.: Doubleday, Doran, 1935, 3d ed. New York: Odyssey Press, 1959.
"On the Semantics of Poetry." *Kenyon Review* 2 (Summer 1940):263–83.
"The Failure of Naturalism." *Kenyon Review* 3 (Autumn 1941):460–72.
"Crisis Thinking." *Journal of Liberal Religion* 3 (Winter 1942):120–30.

"Poetry, Myth, and Reality." In *The Language of Poetry*. Edited by Allen Tate. Princeton, N.J.: Princeton University Press, 1942.

"Religion and Social Grammar." *Kenyon Review* 4 (Spring 1942):202–16.

"Semantics in a New Key." *Journal of Liberal Religion* 4 (Winter 1943):161–63.

"Eliot's Philosophical Themes." In *T. S. Eliot: A Study of His Writings by Several Hands*. Edited by B. Rajan. London: Dennis Dobson, 1947.

"Symbol, Metaphor and Myth." *Sewanee Review* 58 (Fall 1950):678–98.

"Notes on Mythopoeia." *Sewanee Review* 59 (Fall 1951):574–92.

"On Being, Knowing, Saying." *Sewanee Review* 60 (Spring 1952):347–62.

"Mimesis and Katharsis." In *English Institute Essays*. New York: Columbia University Press, 1952.

"Art as Language." *Sewanee Review* 62 (Spring 1954):292–304.

The Burning Fountain: A Study in the Language of Symbolism. 1954. Rev. ed. Bloomington, Ind.: Indiana University Press, 1968.

The Way of Philosophy. 1954. Rev. ed. New York: Odyssey Press, 1960.

"The Semantic Approach to Myth." *Journal of American Folklore* 68 (October 1955):473–81.

Philosophy as the Art of Living. Stockton, Calif.: College of the Pacific Publications, 1956.

"Rediscovering Ovid." *Sewanee Review* 64 (Spring 1956):283–96.

"Aesthetic Surface and Mythic Depth." *Sewanee Review* 65 (Spring 1957):278–92.

"*Reason and Life: The Introduction to Philosophy*." *Christian Scholar* 40 (March 1957):64–69.

"The Intellectual Light." *Sewanee Review* 65 (Summer 1958):397–412.

Heraclitus. Princeton, N.J.: Princeton University Press, 1959.

"Semantics and Ontology." In *Metaphor and Symbol*. Edited by L. C. Knights and Basil Cottle. London: Butterworths Scientific Publications, 1960.

Metaphor and Reality. Bloomington, Ind.: Indiana University Press, 1962.

Valid Thinking: An Introduction to Logic. New York: Odyssey Press, 1962.

"Bubers philosophische Anthropologie." In *Philosophen des zwanzigsten Jahrhunderts: Martin Buber*. Stuttgart: Kohlhammer Verlag, 1963.

"Catharsis," "Myth," "Philosophy and Poetry," "Religion and Poetry," "Semantics and Poetry." In *Princeton Encyclopedia of Poetry and Poetics*. Edited by Alex Preminger. 1965. Enl. and rev. ed. Princeton, N.J.: Princeton University Press, 1974.

Ed. *Berkeley, Principles, and Hume, Treatise: Part I*. Garden City, N.Y.: Doubleday, Doran, 1935.

Ed. *Bentham, James Mill, and J. S. Mill: Selections*. Garden City, N.Y.: Doubleday, Doran, 1936.

Ed. *The Presocratics*. New York: Odyssey Press, 1966.

Ed. and trans. *Aristotle: Selections*. Garden City, N.Y.: Doubleday, Doran, 1935. Enl. and rev. ed. New York: Odyssey Press, 1951.

Ed., with James Burnham. *The Symposium: A Quarterly Review of Criticism*. New York: Symposium Press, 1930–33.

With James Burnham. *Introduction to Philosophical Analysis*. New York: Holt, 1932.

With James Burnham. "Comment: Thirteen Propositions." *Symposium* 4 (April 1933):127–34.

With Peter Fuss. *Five Philosophers*. New York: Odyssey Press, 1963.

Writings Pertaining to T. S. Eliot and *Four Quartets*

Alldritt, Keith. *Eliot's "Four Quartets": Poetry as Chamber Music*. London: Woburn Press, 1978.

Andreach, Robert J. *Studies in Structure: The Stages of the Spiritual Life in Four Modern Authors*. New York: Fordham University Press, 1964.

Antrim, Harry. *T. S. Eliot's Concept of Language: A Study of Its Development*. Gainesville: University of Florida Press, 1971.

Bergonzi, Bernard. *T. S. Eliot*. New York: Macmillan, 1972.

———, ed. *"Four Quartets": A Casebook*. London: Macmillan, 1969.

Bergsten, Staffan. *Time and Eternity: A Study in the Structure and Symbolism of T. S. Eliot's "Four Quartets."* 1960. Reprint. New York: Humanities Press, 1973.

Blackmur, R. P. "Unappeasable and Peregrine: Behavior and the *Four Quartets*." *Thought* 26 (Spring 1951):50–76.

Blamires, Harry. *World Unheard: A Guide through Eliot's "Four Quartets."* London: Methuen, 1969.

Bodelson, Carl Adolf G. *T. S. Eliot's "Four Quartets": A Commentary*. Copenhagen: University Publications Fund, Rosenkilde & Bagger, 1966.

Bornstein, George. *Transformations of Romanticism in Yeats, Eliot, and Stevens*. Chicago: University of Chicago Press, 1976.

Brady, Ann. *Lyricism in the Poetry of T. S. Eliot*. Port Washington, N.Y.: Kennikat Press, National University Publications, 1978.

Braybrooke, Neville, ed. *T. S. Eliot: A Symposium for His Seventieth Birthday*. New York: Farrar, Straus and Cudahy, 1958.

Brett, R. L. *Reason and Imagination: A Study of Form and Meaning in Four Poems*. London: Published for University of Hall by Oxford University Press, 1960.

Buckley, Vincent. *Poetry and the Sacred*. London: Chatto & Windus, 1968.

Cattaui, Georges. *T. S. Eliot*. Translated by Claire Pace and Jean Stewart. London: Merlin Press, 1966.

Counihan, Sister Bernadette. "*Four Quartets*: An Ascent to Mount Carmel?" *Wisconsin Studies in Literature* 6 (1969):58–71.

Davie, Donald. "T. S. Eliot: The End of an Era." *Twentieth Century* 159 (April 1956):350–62. Reprinted in *"Four Quartets": A Casebook*. Edited by Bernard Bergonzi. London: Macmillan, 1969.

Donoghue, Denis. "T. S. Eliot's *Quartets*: A New Reading." *Studies* 54 (Spring 1965):41–62. Reprinted in *"Four Quartets": A Casebook*. Edited by Bernard Bergonzi. London: Macmillan, 1969.

Drew, Elizabeth. *T. S. Eliot: The Design of His Poetry*. New York: Charles Scribner's Sons, 1949.

Eliot, T. S. *The Sacred Wood*. London: Methuen, 1920.

———. *Homage to John Dryden*. London: Leonard and Virginia Woolf, 1924.

———. *Selected Essays, 1917–1932*. 1932. 3d enl. ed. London: Faber & Faber, 1951.

———. *The Use of Poetry and the Use of Criticism*. London: Faber & Faber, 1933.

———. *After Strange Gods*. London: Faber & Faber, 1934.

———. *Elizabethan Essays*. London: Faber & Faber, 1934.

———. *Essays Ancient and Modern*. London: Faber & Faber, 1936.

———. "Preface" to St. John Perse, *Anabasis: A Poem*. New York: Harcourt, Brace, 1938.

———. *The Idea of a Christian Society*. London: Faber & Faber, 1939. Reprint. New York: Harcourt, Brace, 1940.

———. *Notes towards the Definition of Culture*. London: Faber & Faber, 1948. Reprint. New York: Harcourt, Brace, 1949.

———. *On Poetry and Poets*. London: Faber & Faber, 1957.

———. *The Collected Plays*. London: Faber & Faber, 1962.

———. *The Collected Poems, 1909–1962*. New York: Harcourt, Brace and World, 1963.

————. *Knowledge and Experience in the Work of F. H. Bradley*. London: Faber & Faber, 1964.

————. *To Criticize the Critic and Other Writings*. New York: Farrar, Straus & Giroux, 1965.

Frank, Armin Paul. *Die Sehnsucht nach dem unteilbaren Sein: Motive und Motivation in der Literaturkritik T. S. Eliots*. Munich: Wilhelm Fink Verlag, 1973.

Frye, Northrop. *T. S. Eliot*. Edinburgh: Oliver and Boyd, 1963.

Gardner, Helen. *The Art of T. S. Eliot*. 1950. Reprint. New York: E. P. Dutton, 1959.

————. *T. S. Eliot and the English Poetic Tradition*. Nottingham: Nottingham University, 1966.

————. *The Composition of "Four Quartets."* London: Faber & Faber, 1978.

Gordon, Lyndall. *Eliot's Early Years*. Oxford: Oxford University Press, 1977.

Hahn, Paul D. *A Reformation of New Criticism: "Burnt Norton" Revisited*. Emporia State Research Studies, vol. 21, no. 1. Emporia, Kans.: Emporia State Press, 1972.

Harding, D. W. *Experience into Words*. London: Chatto & Windus, 1963.

Hay, Eloise Knapp. *T. S. Eliot's Negative Way*. Cambridge, Mass.: Harvard University Press, 1982.

Howarth, Herbert. *Notes on Some Figures behind T. S. Eliot*. Boston: Houghton Mifflin, 1964.

Islak, Fayek M. *The Mystical Philosophy of T. S. Eliot*. New Haven: College and University Press, 1970.

Johnston, William. *The Still Point: Reflections on Zen and Christian Mysticism*. New York: Harper & Row, 1971.

Jones, Genesius. *Approach to the Purpose: A Study of the Poetry of T. S. Eliot*. London: Hodder and Stoughton, 1964.

Kenner, Hugh. *The Invisible Poet: T. S. Eliot*. New York: McDowell, Obolensky, 1959. 2d ed. rev. New York: Harcourt, Brace & World, 1969.

————, ed. *T. S. Eliot: A Collection of Critical Essays*. Englewood Cliffs, N.J.: Prentice-Hall, 1962.

Leavis, F. R. "Eliot's Later Poetry." *Scrutiny* 11 (Summer 1942):60–71.

————. *The Living Principle: 'English' as a Discipline of Thought*. New York: Oxford University Press, 1975.

Lu, Fei-Pai. *T. S. Eliot: The Dialectical Structure of His Theory of Poetry*. Chicago: University of Chicago Press, 1966.

Lynch, William F. *Christ and Apollo: The Dimensions of the Literary Imagination*. New York: Sheed and Ward, 1960.

March, Richard, and March, Tambimuttu, eds. *T. S. Eliot: A Symposium*. Freeport, N.Y.: Books for Libraries Press, 1949.

Margolis, John D. *T. S. Eliot's Intellectual Development, 1922–1939*. Chicago: University of Chicago Press, 1972.

Martin, Graham, ed. *Eliot in Perspective: A Symposium*. New York: Humanities Press, 1970.

Martz, Louis. *The Poem of the Mind: Essays on Poetry—English and American*. London: Oxford University Press, 1966.

Matthiessen, F. O. *The Achievement of T. S. Eliot: An Essay on the Nature of Poetry*. 1935. 3d ed. rev. and enl. London: Oxford University Press, 1958.

Maxwell, D. E. S. *The Poetry of T. S. Eliot*. London: Routledge & Kegan Paul, 1952.

Miller, J. Hillis. *Poets of Reality: Six Twentieth-Century Writers*. Cambridge, Mass.: Harvard University Press, Belknap Press, 1965.

Milward, Peter C. *A Commentary on T. S. Eliot's "Four Quartets."* Tokyo: Hokuseido Press, 1968.

Moody, A. D. *Thomas Stearns Eliot: Poet*. Cambridge: Cambridge University Press, 1979.

Moore, Ronald. *Metaphysical Symbolism in T. S. Eliot's "Four Quartets."* Stanford Essays in Humanities, no. 9. Stanford, Calif.: Stanford University Press.

Moynihan, William T. "Character and Action in *Four Quartets." Mosaic* 6 (Fall 1972): 203–28. Reprinted in *T. S. Eliot: A Collection of Criticism.* Edited by Linda W. Wagner. New York: McGraw-Hill, 1974.

Nuttall, A. D. *A Common Sky: Philosophy and the Literary Imagination.* Berkeley, Calif.: University of California Press, 1974.

Olney, James. "Four Quartets." In *Metaphors of Self: The Meaning of Autobiography.* Princeton, N.J.: Princeton University Press, 1972.

Osterwald, Hans. *T. S. Eliot: Between Metaphor and Metonymy.* Swiss Studies in English, no. 96. Bern: Francke Verlag, 1978.

Partridge, Astley Cooper. *The Language of Modern Poetry: Yeats, Eliot, Auden.* London: Deutsch, 1976.

Perkins, David. "Rose Garden to Midwinter Spring: Achieved Faith in the *Four Quartets." Modern Language Quarterly* 23 (March 1962):41–45. Reprinted in *"Four Quartets": A Casebook.* Edited by Bernard Bergonzi. London: Macmillan, 1969.

Preston, Raymond. *"Four Quartets" Rehearsed.* New York: Sheed and Ward, 1946.

Rajan, Balachandra. *The Overwhelming Question: A Study of the Poetry of T. S. Eliot.* Toronto: University of Toronto Press, 1976.

———, ed. *T. S. Eliot: A Study of His Writings by Several Hands.* New York: Funk and Wagnalls, 1948.

Rees, Thomas R. *The Technique of T. S. Eliot: A Study in the Orchestration of Meaning in Eliot's Poetry.* The Hague: Mouton, 1974.

Rosenthal, M. L. *Sailing Into the Unknown: Yeats, Pound, and Eliot.* New York: Oxford University Press, 1978.

Schneider, Elisabeth Wintersteen. *T. S. Eliot: The Pattern in the Carpet.* Berkeley, Calif.: University of California Press, 1975.

Scott, Nathan A., Jr. *Rehearsals of Discomposure: Alienation and Reconciliation in Modern Literature.* New York: Columbia University Press, King's Crown Press, 1952.

———. *The Poetry of Civic Virtue: Eliot, Malraux, Auden.* Philadelphia: Fortress Press, 1976.

Smidt, Kristian. *Poetry and Belief in the Work of T. S. Eliot.* 1949. Rev. ed. London: Routledge & Kegan Paul, 1961.

Smith, Grover. *T. S. Eliot's Poetry and Plays.* 1950. Rev. ed. Chicago: University of Chicago Press, 1960.

Stead, C. K. *The New Poetic: Yeats to Eliot.* London: Penguin Books, 1964.

Tate, Allen, ed. *T. S. Eliot: A Collection of Critical Essays.* Englewood Cliffs, N.J.: Prentice-Hall, 1962.

———. *T. S. Eliot: The Man and His Work.* New York: Dell, Delta, 1966.

Thompson, Eric. *T. S. Eliot: The Metaphysical Perspective.* Carbondale, Ill.: Southern Illinois University Press, 1963.

Traversi, Derek. *T. S. Eliot: The Longer Poems.* New York: Harcourt Brace Jovanovich, 1976.

Unger, Leonard. *T. S. Eliot: Moments and Patterns.* Minneapolis: University of Minnesota Press, 1966.

———, ed. *T. S. Eliot: A Selected Critique.* New York: Rinehart, 1948.

Ward, David. *T. S. Eliot: Between Two Worlds.* London: Routledge & Kegan Paul, 1973.

Webb, Eugene. *The Dark Dove: The Sacred and Secular in Modern Literature.* Seattle: University of Washington Press, 1975.

Weiss, Klaus. *Das Bild des Weges: Ein Schlüssel zum Verständis des Zeitlichen und Überzeitlichen in T. S. Eliot's "Four Quartets."* Bonn: H. Bouvier, 1965.

Weitz, Morris. "T. S. Eliot: Time as a Mode of Salvation." *Sewanee Review* 60 (Winter

1952):48–64. Reprinted in *"Four Quartets"*: *A Casebook*. Edited by Bernard Bergonzi. London: Macmillan, 1969.

Wheelwright, Philip. "Eliot's Philosophical Themes." In *T. S. Eliot*: *A Study of His Writings by Several Hands*. Edited by B. Rajan. London: Dennis Dobson, 1947.

———. *The Burning Fountain*: *A Study in the Language of Symbolism*. 1954. Rev. ed. Bloomington, Ind.: Indiana University Press, 1968.

Williamson, George. *A Reader's Guide to T. S. Eliot*: *A Poem by Poem Analysis*. 1953. Rev. ed. New York: Noonday Press, 1955.

Writings Pertaining to Alfred North Whitehead and Process Theology

Biller, Alan David. "Whitehead's Conception of Speculative Philosophy." Ph.D. dissertation, Columbia University, 1970.

Brown, Delwin; James, Ralph E., Jr.; Reeves, Gene, eds. *Process Philosophy and Christian Thought*. Indianapolis: Bobbs-Merrill, 1971.

Burgers, J. M. *Experience and Conceptual Activity*. Cambridge, Mass.: M.I.T. Press, 1965.

Christian, William A. *An Interpretation of Whitehead's Metaphysics*. New Haven: Yale University Press, 1959.

Cobb, John B., Jr. *A Christian Natural Theology*. Philadelphia: Westminster Press, 1965.

———. *The Structure of Christian Existence*. Philadelphia: Westminster Press, 1967.

———. *God and the World*. Philadelphia: Westminster Press, 1969.

Cousins, Ewert H., ed. *Process Theology*: *Basic Writings*. New York: Newman Press, 1971.

Crosby, Donald A. "Language and Religious Language in Whitehead's Philosophy." *Christian Scholar* 50 (Fall 1967):210–21.

———. "Whitehead on the Metaphysical Employment of Language." *Process Studies* 1 (Spring 1971):38–54.

Dean, William. "Radical Empiricism and Religious Art." *Journal of Religion* 61 (April 1981):168–87.

Eisendrath, Craig R. *The Unifying Moment*: *The Psychological Philosophy of William James and Alfred North Whitehead*. Cambridge, Mass.: Harvard University Press, 1971.

Emmet, Dorothy M. *Whitehead's Philosophy of Organism*. London: Macmillan, 1932.

Ford, Lewis S., ed. *Two Process Philosophers*: *Hartshorne's Encounter with Whitehead*. AAR Studies in Religion, no. 5. Tallahassee, Fla.: American Academy of Religion, 1973.

———. *The Lure of God*: *A Biblical Background for Process Theism*. Philadelphia: Fortress Press, 1978.

Franklin, Stephen Theodore. "Speaking from the Depth: Alfred North Whitehead's Metaphysics of Propositions, Symbolism, Perceptions, Language, and Religion." 2 vols. Ph.D. dissertation, University of Chicago, 1976.

Green, Juliana. "Alfred North Whitehead on the Ontological Principle: A Critique of Early Modern Epistemology in *Process and Reality*." Ph.D. dissertation, University of Chicago, 1974.

Hall, David L. *The Civilization of Experience*: *A Whiteheadian Theory of Culture*. New York: Fordham University Press, 1973.

Hartshorne, Charles. *Man's Vision of God and the Logic of Theism*. Chicago: Willett, Clark, 1941.

———. *The Divine Relativity*: *A Social Conception of God*. New Haven: Yale University Press, 1948.

————. *Reality as Social Process: Studies in Metaphysics and Religion*. Glencoe, Ill.: Free Press, 1953.

————. *The Logic of Perfection and Other Essays in Neo-classical Metaphysics*. La Salle, Ill.: Open Court, 1962.

————. *Anselm's Discovery*. La Salle, Ill.: Open Court, 1965.

————. *A Natural Theology for Our Time*. La Salle, Ill.: Open Court, 1967.

————. *Whitehead's Philosophy: Selected Essays, 1935–70*. Lincoln, Neb.: University of Nebraska Press, 1972.

Kline, George L., ed. *Alfred North Whitehead: Essays on His Philosophy*. Englewood Cliffs, N.J.: Prentice-Hall, 1963.

Lazlo, Ervin. *Beyond Scepticism and Realism: A Constructive Exploration of Husserlian and Whiteheadian Methods of Inquiry*. The Hague: Nijhoff, 1966.

Leclerc, Ivor. *Whitehead's Metaphysics: An Introductory Exposition*. New York: Macmillan, 1958.

————, ed. *The Relevance of Whitehead*. New York: Macmillan, 1961.

Loomer, Bernard M. "The Theological Significance of the Method of Empirical Analysis in the Philosophy of A. N. Whitehead." Ph.D. dissertation, University of Chicago, 1942.

————. "Empirical Theology within Process Thought." In *The Future of Empirical Theology*. Edited by Bernard E. Meland. Chicago: University of Chicago Press, 1969.

Lowe, Victor. *Understanding Whitehead*. Baltimore: Johns Hopkins University Press, 1962.

Lundeen, Lyman T. *Risk and Rhetoric in Religion: Whitehead's Theory of Language and the Discourse of Faith*. Philadelphia: Fortress Press, 1972.

Mack, Robert Donald. *The Appeal to Immediate Experience: Philosophical Method in Bradley, Whitehead, and Dewey*. New York: King's Crown Press, 1945.

Martin, R. M. *Whitehead's Categoreal Scheme and Other Papers*. The Hague: Martinus Nijhoff, 1974.

Meland, Bernard E. *Faith and Culture*. New York: Oxford University Press, 1953.

————. *The Realities of Faith: The Revolution in Cultural Forms*. New York: Oxford University Press, 1962.

————. "The Empirical Tradition in Theology at Chicago." In *The Future of Empirical Theology*. Edited by Bernard E. Meland. Chicago: University of Chicago Press, 1969.

————. "Can Empirical Theology Learn Something from Phenomenology?" In *The Future of Empirical Theology*. Edited by Bernard E. Meland. Chicago: University of Chicago Press, 1969.

————. *Fallible Forms and Symbols: Discourses on Method in a Theology of Culture*. Philadelphia: Fortress Press, 1976.

Neville, Robert C. *Reconstruction of Thinking*. Albany, N.Y.: State University of New York Press, 1981.

Ogden, Schubert M. *Christ without Myth*. New York: Harper & Row, 1961.

————. *The Reality of God*. New York: Harper & Row, 1963.

————. "Bultmann's Demythologizing and Hartshorne's Dipolar Theism." In *Process and Divinity: The Hartshorne Festschrift*. Edited by William L. Reese and Eugene Freeman. La Salle, Ill.: Open Court, 1964.

————. "Present Prospects for Empirical Theology." In *The Future of Philosophical Theology*. Edited by Bernard E. Meland. Chicago: University of Chicago Press, 1969.

————. "Lonergan and the Subjectivist Principle." *Journal of Religion* 51 (July 1971):155–72.

————. "The Task of Philosophical Theology." In *The Future of Philosophical Theology*. Edited by Robert A. Evans. Philadelphia: Westminster Press, 1971.

————. "What Is Theology?" *Journal of Religion* 52 (January 1972):22–40.

————. "The Criteria of Metaphysical Truth and the Sense of 'Metaphysics'." *Process Studies* 5 (Spring 1975):47–48.

————. "On Revelation." In *Our Common History as Christians: Essays in Honor of Albert C. Outler*. Edited by John Deschner, Leroy T. Howe, and Klaus Penzel. New York: Oxford University Press, 1975.

————. *Faith and Freedom: Toward a Theology of Liberation*. Nashville: Abingdon, 1979.

————. *The Point of Christology*. San Francisco: Harper & Row, 1982.

Peters, Eugene. *The Creative Advance: An Introduction to Process Philosophy as a Context for Christian Faith*. St. Louis: Bethany Press, 1966.

Pittenger, Norman. *God in Process*. London: S. C. M. Press, 1967.

Pols, Edward. *Whitehead's Metaphysics*. Carbondale, Ill.: Southern Illinois University Press, 1967.

Redding, Earl W. "Aesthetic, Religious, and Moral Intuition in the Philosophy of Alfred North Whitehead." Ph.D. dissertation, University of Miami, 1969.

Reese, William L., and Freeman, Eugene, eds. *Process and Divinity: Philosophical Essays Presented to Charles Hartshorne*. La Salle, Ill.: Open Court, 1964.

Schilpp, Paul Arthur, ed. *The Philosophy of Alfred North Whitehead*. Library of Living Philosophers, vol. 3. New York: Tudor Press, 1941. Rev. ed. La Salle, Ill.: Open Court, 1951.

Schmidt, Paul F. *Perception and Cosmology in Whitehead's Philosophy*. New Brunswick, N.J.: Rutgers University Press, 1967.

Sherburne, Donald W. *A Key to Whitehead's Process and Reality*. New York: Macmillan, 1966.

————. *A Whiteheadian Aesthetic*. New Haven: Yale University Press, 1961.

Thompson, Kenneth F., Jr. *Whitehead's Philosophy of Religion*. The Hague: Mouton, 1971.

Whitehead, Alfred North. *The Organization of Thought, Educational and Scientific*. London: Williams and Norgate, 1917.

————. *An Enquiry Concerning the Principles of Natural Knowledge*. Cambridge: Cambridge University Press, 1919.

————. *The Concept of Nature*. Cambridge: Cambridge University Press, 1920.

————. *Science and the Modern World*. 1925. Reprint. New York: Macmillan, 1967.

————. *Religion in the Making*. 1926. Reprint. New York: Macmillan, 1960.

————. *Symbolism: Its Meaning and Effect*. 1927. Reprint. New York: Macmillan, 1959.

————. *The Aims of Education and Other Essays*. 1929. Reprint. New York: Macmillan, 1967.

————. *The Function of Reason*. 1929. Reprint. Princeton, N.J.: Princeton University Press, 1958.

————. *Process and Reality: An Essay in Cosmology*. New York: Macmillan, 1929. Corrected ed., edited by David Ray Griffin and Donald W. Sherburne. New York: Free Press, 1978.

————. *Adventures of Ideas*. 1933. Reprint. New York: Macmillan, 1967.

————. "Remarks." *Philosophical Review* 46 (March 1937):178–86.

————. *Modes of Thought*. 1938. Reprint. New York: Macmillan, 1968.

————. "Immortality." In *The Philosophy of Alfred North Whitehead*. Edited by Paul Arthur Schilpp. Library of Living Philosophers, vol. 3. New York: Tudor Press, 1941. Rev. ed. La Salle, Ill.: Open Court, 1951.

————. *Essays in Science and Philosophy*. New York: Philosophical Library, 1947.

————. *Dialogues of Alfred North Whitehead*. As recorded by Lucian Price. Boston: Little, Brown, 1954.

Wieman, Henry Nelson. *Religious Experience and Scientific Method*. New York: Macmillan, 1926.

————. *The Source of Human Good*. Chicago: University of Chicago Press, 1946.

Williams, Daniel Day. *God's Grace and Man's Hope*. New York: Harper & Brothers, 1949.

———. "How Does God Act?: An Essay in Whitehead's Metaphysics." In *Process and Divinity*. Edited by William L. Reese and Eugene Freeman. La Salle, Ill.: Open Court, 1964.

———. *The Spirit and the Forms of Love*. New York: Harper & Row, 1968.

Other Basic Sources and Background Material

Abrams, M. H. "The Newer Criticism: Prisoner of Logical Positivism?" *Kenyon Review* 17 (Winter 1955):139–43.

———. "The Deconstructive Angel." *Critical Inquiry* 3 (Spring 1977): 425–38.

Allemann, Beda. "Metaphor and Antimetaphor." In *Interpretation: The Poetry of Meaning*. Edited by Stanley R. Hopper and David Miller. New York: Harcourt, Brace & World, 1967.

Altieri, Charles. "Presence and Reference in a Literary Text: The Example of Williams' 'This Is Just to Say.'" *Critical Inquiry* 5 (Spring 1979):489–510.

———. *Act and Quality: A Theory of Literary Meaning and Humanistic Understanding*. Amherst: University of Massachusetts Press, 1981.

Altizer, Thomas. *The Self-Embodiment of God*. New York: Harper & Row, 1977.

———, et al. *Deconstruction and Theology*. New York: Crossroad, 1982.

Aristotle. *The Basic Works of Aristotle*. Edited by Richard McKeon. New York: Random House, 1941.

———. *Poetics*. Translated by Kenneth A. Telford. Chicago: Henry Regnery, 1965.

Arnheim, Rudolf. *Toward a Psychology of Art: Collected Essays*. Berkeley, Calif.: University of California Press, 1966.

Austin, J. L. *How to Do Things with Words*. Edited by J. O. Urmson. Oxford: Clarendon Press, 1962.

Ayer, A. J. *Language, Truth, and Logic*. 2d ed. New York: Dover, 1952.

———, ed. *Logical Positivism*. Glencoe, Ill. Free Press, 1959.

Ballard, Edward G. "Metaphysics and Metaphor." *Journal of Philosophy* 45 (April 1948): 208–14.

Barfield, Owen. *Poetic Diction: A Study in Meaning*. New York: McGraw Hill, 1928. 3d ed. Middletown, Conn.: Wesleyan University Press, 1973.

Beardsley, Monroe C. *Aesthetics: Problems in the Philosophy of Criticism*. New York: Harcourt, Brace & World, 1958.

———. "The Metaphorical Twist." *Philosophy and Phenomenological Research* 22 (March 1962):293–307.

———. "Metaphor." In *Encyclopedia of Philosophy*. Edited by Paul Edwards. New York: Macmillan, 1967.

———. "Metaphor and Falsity." *Journal of Aesthetics and Art Criticism* 35 (Winter 1976): 218–22.

Bellah, Robert N. *Beyond Belief: Essays on Religion in a Post-Traditional World*. New York: Harper & Row, 1970.

Berggren, Douglas. "An Analysis of Metaphorical Meaning and Truth." Ph.D. dissertation, Yale University, 1959.

———. "The Use and Abuse of Metaphor." *Review of Metaphysics* 16 (December 1962):237–58; (March 1963):450–72.

Binkley, Timothy. "The Truth and Probity of Metaphor." *Journal of Aesthetics and Art Criticism* 33 (Fall 1974):171–80.

Black, Max. *Models and Metaphors*. Ithaca, N.Y.: Cornell University Press, 1962.

————. *The Labyrinth of Language*. New York: Praeger, 1968.

————. "More about Metaphor." In *Metaphor and Thought*. Edited by Andrew Ortony. Cambridge: Cambridge University Press, 1979.

————. "How Metaphors Work: A Reply to Donald Davidson." *Critical Inquiry* 6 (Autumn 1979):131–43.

Blackmur, R. P. *Language as Gesture*. New York: Harcourt, Brace, 1952.

————. *The Lion and the Honeycomb*. New York: Harcourt, Brace, 1954.

Booth, Wayne C. *The Rhetoric of Fiction*. Chicago: University of Chicago Press, 1961.

————. *Modern Dogma and the Rhetoric of Assent*. Notre Dame, Ind.: University of Notre Dame Press, 1974.

————. *Critical Understanding: The Powers and Limits of Pluralism*. Chicago: University of Chicago Press, 1979.

Brooks, Cleanth. *Modern Poetry and the Tradition*. Chapel Hill, N.C.: University of North Carolina Press, 1939.

————. *The Well Wrought Urn: Studies in the Structure of Poetry*. New York: Reynal and Hitchcock, 1947.

————. "Metaphor and the Function of Criticism." In *Spiritual Problems in Contemporary Literature*. Edited by Stanley R. Hopper. New York: Harper & Brothers, 1952.

————. "Metaphor, Paradox, and Stereotype." *British Journal of Aesthetics* 5 (October 1965):315–38.

Bruner, Jerome S. *On Knowing: Essays for the Left Hand*. Cambridge, Mass.: Harvard University Press, 1962.

Bruns, Gerald L. *Modern Poetry and the Idea of Language: A Critical and Historical Study*. New Haven: Yale University Press, 1974.

Bultmann, Rudolf. *Existence and Faith: Shorter Writings*. Edited and translated by Schubert M. Ogden. Cleveland: World, Meridian Books, 1960.

————. "New Testament and Mythology." Revised translation by Reginald H. Fuller. In *Kerygma and Myth: A Theological Debate*. Edited by Hans Werner Bartsch. New York: Harper & Row, Torchbook, 1961.

Burke, Kenneth. *The Philosophy of Literary Form*. Baton Rouge, La.: Louisiana State University Press, 1941.

————. *Language as Symbolic Action: Essays on Life, Literature, and Method*. Berkeley, Calif.: University of California Press, 1966.

Cassirer, Ernst. *The Philosophy of Symbolic Forms*. Translated by Ralph Manheim. 3 vols. New Haven: Yale University Press, 1953.

Cavell, Stanley. *The Claim of Reason: Wittgenstein, Skepticism, Morality, and Tragedy*. Oxford: Oxford University Press, 1979.

Chafe, Wallace L. *Meaning and the Structure of Language*. Chicago: University of Chicago Press, 1970.

Chomsky, Noam. *Aspects of the Theory of Syntax*. Cambridge, Mass.: M.I.T. Press, 1965.

Cohen, Ted. "Figurative Speech and Figurative Acts." *Journal of Philosophy* 72 (November 1975):669–84.

————. "Notes on Metaphor." *Journal of Aesthetics and Art Criticism* 34 (Spring 1976): 249–59.

Crane, R. S. *The Languages of Criticism and the Structure of Poetry*. Toronto: University of Toronto Press, 1953.

————. "Criticism as Inquiry." In *The Idea of the Humanities and Other Essays Critical and Historical*. 2 vols. Chicago: University of Chicago Press, 1967.

————, ed. *Critics and Criticism: Ancient and Modern*. Chicago: University of Chicago Press, 1952.

Crossan, John Dominic. *In Parables: The Challenge of the Historical Jesus*. New York: Harper & Row, 1973.

————. *Cliffs of Fall: Paradox and Polyvalence in the Parables of Jesus*. New York: Seabury, Crossroad Books, 1980.

Culler, Jonathan. *Structuralist Poetics: Structuralism, Linguistics, and the Study of Literature*. Ithaca, N.Y.: Cornell University Press, 1975.

————. *The Pursuit of Signs: Semiotics, Literature, Deconstruction*. Ithaca, N.Y.: Cornell University Press, 1981.

————. *On Deconstruction: Theory and Criticism after Structuralism*. Ithaca: Cornell University Press, 1982.

Danto, Arthur. *The Transfiguration of the Commonplace: A Philosophy of Art*. Cambridge, Mass.: Harvard University Press, 1981.

Davidson, Donald. "What Metaphors Mean." *Critical Inquiry* 5 (Autumn 1978):31–47.

Davis, Walter. *The Act of Interpretation: A Critique of Literary Reason*. Chicago: University of Chicago Press, 1978.

Derrida, Jacques. "White Mythology: Metaphor in the Text of Philosophy." Translated by F. C. T. Moore. *New Literary History* 6 (1974):5–74.

————. *Writing and Difference*. Chicago: University of Chicago Press, 1978.

Detweiler, Robert. *Story, Sign, and Self: Phenomenology and Structuralism as Literary-Critical Methods*. Philadelphia: Fortress Press, 1978.

Dewey, John. *Art as Experience*. 1934. Reprint. New York: G. P. Putnam's Sons, Capricorn Books, 1958.

Dilley, Frank B. *Metaphysics and Religious Language*. New York: Columbia University Press, 1964.

————. "The Irrefutability of Belief Systems." *Journal of the American Academy of Religion* 43 (June 1975):214–23.

Dufrenne, Mikel. *The Phenomenology of Aesthetic Experience*. Translated by Edward S. Casey, Albert A. Anderson, Willis Domingo, and Leon Jacobson. Evanston, Ill.: Northwestern University Press, 1973.

Eco, Umberto. *A Theory of Semiotics*. Bloomington, Ind.: Indiana University Press, 1976.

Edie, James M. *Speaking and Meaning: The Phenomenology of Language*. Bloomington, Ind.: Indiana University Press, 1976.

Emmet, Dorothy. *The Nature of Metaphysical Thinking*. 1945. Rev. ed. Philadelphia: Westminster Press, 1971.

Farley, Edward. *Ecclesial Reflection: An Anatomy of Theological Method*. Philadelphia: Fortress Press, 1982.

Ferré, Frederick. *Language, Logic, and God*. New York: Harper & Row, 1961.

————. "Mapping the Logic of Models in Science and Theology." *Christian Scholar* 46 (Spring 1963):9–39.

————. *Basic Modern Philosophy of Religion*. New York: Charles Scribner's Sons, 1967.

————. "Metaphors, Models, and Religion." *Soundings* 51 (Fall 1968):327–45.

Fish, Stanley. "How Ordinary Is Ordinary Language?" *New Literary History* 5 (Autumn 1973):41–54.

————. "Normal Circumstances, Literal Language, Direct Speech Acts, the Ordinary, the Everyday, the Obvious, What Goes without Saying, and Other Special Cases." *Critical Inquiry* 4 (Summer 1978):625–44.

Flew, Antony, and MacIntyre, A. C., eds. *New Essays in Philosophical Theology*. London: S. C. M. Press, 1955.

Foster, Richard. *The New Romantics: A Reappraisal of the New Criticism.* Bloomington, Ind.: Indiana University Press, 1962.

Foucault, Michel. *The Order of Things: An Archaeology of the Human Sciences.* New York: Random House, Vintage Books, 1973.

Fox, Douglas. *The Vagrant Lotus: An Introduction to Buddhist Philosophy.* Philadelphia: Westminster Press, 1973.

Fraser, John. "Modern Poetics: 20th-Century American and British." In *Princeton Encyclopedia of Poetry and Poetics.* Edited by Alex Preminger. 1965. Enl. and rev. ed. Princeton, N.J.: Princeton University Press, 1974.

Frege, Gottlob. "On Sense and Reference." In *Philosophical Writings of Gottlob Frege.* Translated by Max Black and Peter Geach. Oxford: Blackwell, 1952.

Frye, Northrop. *Anatomy of Criticism.* Princeton, N.J.: Princeton University Press, 1957.

―――. *The Well-Tempered Critic.* Bloomington, Ind.: Indiana University Press, 1967.

―――. *The Great Code: The Bible and Literature.* New York: Harcourt Brace Jovanovich, 1981.

Funk, Robert W. *Language, Hermeneutic, and Word of God: The Problem of Language in the New Testament and Contemporary Theology.* New York: Harper & Row, 1966.

Gadamer, Hans-Georg. *Truth and Method.* Translated by Garrett Barden and John Cumming. New York: Seabury Press, 1975.

Geertz, Clifford. *The Interpretation of Cultures: Selected Essays.* New York: Basic Books, 1973.

Gendlin, Eugene T. *Experiencing and the Creation of Meaning: A Philosophical and Psychological Approach to the Subjective.* Glencoe, Ill.: Free Press, 1962.

Gerhart, Mary. *The Question of Belief in Literary Criticism: An Introduction to the Hermeneutical Theory of Paul Ricoeur.* Stuttgarter Arbeiten zur Germanistik, no. 54. Stuttgart: Akademischer Verlag Hans-Dieter Heinz, 1979.

Gilkey, Langdon. *Naming the Whirlwind: The Renewal of God-Language.* Indianapolis: Bobbs-Merrill, 1969.

―――. "New Modes of Empirical Theology." In *The Future of Empirical Theology.* Edited by Bernard E. Meland. Chicago: University of Chicago Press, 1969.

Gobar, Ash. *Philosophic Foundations of Genetic Psychology and Gestalt Psychology: A Comparative Study of the Empirical Basis, Theoretical Structure, and Epistemological Groundwork of European Biological Psychology.* The Hague: Nijhoff, 1968.

Gombrich, E. H. *Art and Illusion: A Study in the Psychology of Pictorial Representation.* 1960. Rev. ed. Princeton, N.J.: Princeton University Press, 1961.

Goodman, Nelson. *The Languages of Art: An Approach to a Theory of Symbols.* Indianapolis: Bobbs-Merrill, 1968.

―――. *Ways of Worldmaking.* Indianapolis: Hackett Publishing Company, 1978.

Graff, Gerald. *Poetic Statement and Critical Dogma.* Evanston, Ill.: Northwestern University Press, 1970.

―――. *Literature Against Itself: Literary Ideas in Modern Society.* Chicago: University of Chicago Press, 1979.

Gunn, Giles. *The Interpretation of Otherness: Literature, Religion, and the American Imagination.* New York: Oxford University Press, 1979.

Habermas, Jürgen. *Knowledge and Human Interests.* Translated by Jeremy J. Shapiro. Boston: Beacon Press, 1971.

Hamburger, Michael. *The Truth of Poetry: Tensions in Modern Poetry from Baudelaire to the Nineteen-sixties.* New York: Harcourt Brace Jovanovich, 1969.

Hart, Ray L. *Unfinished Man and the Imagination.* New York: Herder and Herder, 1968.

Hartman, Geoffrey H. *Criticism in the Wilderness: The Study of Literature Today.* New Haven: Yale University Press, 1980.

Hartt, Julian N. *Theological Method and Imagination*. New York: Seabury Press, Crossroad Books, 1977.

Heidegger, Martin. *On the Way to Language*. Translated by Peter D. Hertz. New York: Harper & Row, 1968.

———. *Poetry, Language, Thought*. Translated by Albert Hofstadter. New York: Harper & Row, 1971.

Heimbeck, Raeburne S. *Theology and Meaning: A Critique of Metatheological Scepticism*. London: George Allen and Unwin, 1969.

Heller, Erich. "The Hazard of Modern Poetry." In *The Disinherited Mind*. Cleveland: World Publishing Co., Meridian Books, 1959.

Henle, Paul, ed. *Language, Thought, and Culture*. Ann Arbor, Mich.: University of Michigan Press, 1958.

Herschberger, Ruth. "The Structure of Metaphor." *Kenyon Review* 5 (Summer 1943):433–43.

Hesse, Mary. *Models and Analogies in Science*. Notre Dame, Ind.: University of Notre Dame Press, 1966.

Hester, Marcus B. *The Meaning of Poetic Metaphor*. The Hague: Mouton, 1967.

High, Dallas M., ed. *New Essays on Religious Language*. New York: Oxford University Press, 1969.

Hirsch, E. D., Jr. *Validity in Interpretation*. New Haven: Yale University Press, 1967.

Hofstadter, Albert. *Truth and Art*. New York: Columbia University Press, 1965.

Holland, Norman N. *The Dynamics of Literary Response*. New York: Oxford University Press, 1968.

Hopper, Stanley Romaine, and Miller, David L., eds. *Interpretation: The Poetry of Meaning*. New York: Harcourt, Brace & World, 1967.

Ingarden, Roman. *The Cognition of the Literary Work of Art*. Translated by Ruth Ann Crowley and Kenneth R. Olson. Evanston, Ill.: Northwestern University Press, 1973.

Iser, Wolfgang. *The Act of Reading: A Theory of Aesthetic Response*. Baltimore: Johns Hopkins University Press, 1978.

Jakobson, Roman. "Two Aspects of Language and Two Types of Aphasic Disturbance." In *Fundamentals of Language*. With Morris Halle. 2d ed. rev. The Hague: Mouton, 1956.

———. "Linguistics and Poetics." In *Style in Language*. Edited by Thomas A. Sebeok. Cambridge, Mass.: M.I.T. Press, 1960.

Jameson, Fredric. *The Prison-House of Language: A Critical Account of Structuralism and Russian Formalism*. Princeton, N.J.: Princeton University Press, 1972.

———. *The Political Unconscious: Narrative as a Socially Symbolic Act*. Ithaca, N.Y.: Cornell University Press, 1981.

Jaspers, Karl. *Truth and Symbol* (from *Von der Wahrheit* [1947]). Translated by Jean T. Wilde, William Kluback, and William Kimmell. New Haven: College and University Press, 1959.

———. *Philosophy*. Translated by E. B. Ashton. 3 vols. Chicago: University of Chicago Press, 1969–71.

Jennings, Theodore W. "On Ritual Knowledge." *Journal of Religion* 62 (April 1982):111–27.

Katz, Jerrold J. *Semantic Theory*. New York: Harper & Row, 1972.

Kauffmann, S. Bruce. "Charting a Sea Change: On the Relationships of Religion and Literature to Theology." *Journal of Religion* 58 (October 1978):405–27.

Kaufman, Gordon D. *An Essay on Theological Method*. Rev. ed. AAR Studies in Religion, no. 11. Missoula, Mont.: Scholars Press, 1979.

———. *The Theological Imagination: Constructing the Concept of God*. Philadelphia: Westminster Press, 1981.

Knights, L. C., and Cottle, Basil, eds. *Metaphor and Symbol*. London: Butterworths Scientific Publications, 1960.

Kort, Wesley. *Narrative Elements and Religious Meaning*. Philadelphia: Fortress Press, 1975.

Kovacs, Brian W. "Philosophical Foundations for Structuralism." *Semeia* 10 (1978):85–105.

Krieger, Murray. *The New Apologists for Poetry*. Minneapolis: University of Minnesota Press, 1956.

———. *The Play and Place of Criticism*. Baltimore: Johns Hopkins University Press, 1967.

———. *Poetic Presence and Illusion: Essays in Critical History and Theory*. Baltimore: Johns Hopkins University Press, 1979.

Kuhns, Richard. *Structures of Experience: Essays on the Affinity between Philosophy and Literature*. New York: Basic Books, 1970.

Lakoff, George, and Johnson, Mark. *Metaphors We Live By*. Chicago: University of Chicago Press, 1980.

Lang, Berel. *Art and Inquiry*. Detroit: Wayne State University Press, 1975.

Langer, Susanne. *Philosophy in a New Key*. 1942. Rev. ed. Cambridge, Mass.: Harvard University Press, 1951.

———. *Feeling and Form*. New York: Charles Scribner's Sons, 1953.

Lawler, Justus George. *Celestial Pantomime: Poetic Structures of Transcendence*. New Haven: Yale University Press, 1979.

Leeuw, Gerardus van der. *Sacred and Profane Beauty: The Holy in Art*. Translated by David E. Green. New York: Holt, Rinehart and Winston, 1963.

Lentricchia, Frank. *After the New Criticism*. Chicago: University of Chicago Press, 1980.

Levin, Samuel R. *The Semantics of Metaphor*. Baltimore: Johns Hopkins University Press, 1977.

———. "Standard Approaches to Metaphor and a Proposal for Literary Metaphor." In *Metaphor and Thought*. Edited by Andrew Ortony. Cambridge: Cambridge University Press, 1979.

Lévi-Strauss, Claude. *Structural Anthropology*. Translated by Claire Jacobson and Brooke Schoepf. New York: Basic Books, 1963.

———. *The Savage Mind*. Chicago: University of Chicago Press, 1966.

Lonergan, Bernard J. F. *A Study of Human Understanding*. New York: Longman's, 1958.

———. *Method in Theology*. New York: Seabury Press, 1972.

McCanles, Michael. "The Literal and the Metaphorical: Dialectic of Interchange." *Publications of the Modern Language Association of America* 91 (March 1976):279–90.

McFague, Sallie. *Speaking in Parables: A Study in Metaphor and Theology*. Philadelphia: Fortress Press, 1975.

———. *Metaphorical Theology: Models of God*. Philadelphia: Fortress Press, 1982.

Macquarrie, John. *Twentieth-Century Religious Thought*. London: S. C. M. Press, 1963.

———. *God-talk: An Examination of the Language and Logic of Theology*. London: S. C. M. Press, 1967.

Malbon, Elizabeth Struthers. "Structuralism, Hermeneutics, and Contextual Meaning." *Journal of the American Academy of Religion* 51 (June 1983).

Martin, F. David. *Art and the Religious Experience: The "Language" of the Sacred*. Lewisburg, Pa.: Bucknell University Press, 1972.

Martinez-Bonati, Felix. *Fictive Discourse and the Structures of Literature: A Phenomenological Approach*. Translated by Philip W. Silver. Ithaca, N.Y.: Cornell University Press, 1981.

Martland, Thomas R. *Religion as Art: An Interpretation*. Albany: State University of New York Press, 1981.

Metz, Johannes-Baptist. "Apologetics." In *Sacramentum Mundi*. Edited by Karl Rahner. 6 vols. New York: Herder and Herder, 1968.

Miller, J. Hillis. *The Disappearance of God: Five 19th-Century Writers.* 1963. Reprint. New York: Schocken Books, 1965.

———. "The Linguistic Moment in 'The Wreck of the Deutschland.'" In *The New Criticism and After.* Edited by Thomas Daniel Young. Charlottesville: University Press of Virginia, 1976.

Miner, Earl. "That Literature Is a Kind of Knowledge." *Critical Inquiry* 2 (Spring 1976): 487–518.

Mulder, John R., ed. *Literature and Religion: The Convergence of Approaches. Journal of the American Academy of Religion,* Supplement 47 (June 1979).

Nygren, Anders. *Meaning and Method: Prolegomena to a Scientific Philosophy of Religion and a Scientific Theology.* Translated by Philip S. Watson. Philadelphia: Fortress Press, 1972.

Ong, Walter. "Metaphor and the Twinned Vision." *Sewanee Review* 62 (Spring 1955):193–201.

Ortony, Andrew, ed. *Metaphor and Thought.* Cambridge: Cambridge University Press, 1979.

Paivo, Allan. *Imagery and Verbal Processes.* New York: Holt, Rinehart and Winston, 1971.

Passmore, John. *A Hundred Years of Philosophy.* 1957. Reprint. Harmondsworth, Eng.: Penguin Books, 1966.

Pepper, Stephen C. *World Hypotheses: A Study in Evidence.* Berkeley, Calif.: University of California Press, 1942.

Perkins, David. *A History of Modern Poetry from the 1890s to the High Modernist Mode.* Cambridge, Mass.: Harvard University Press, Belknap Press, 1976.

Perrin, Norman. *Jesus and the Language of the Kingdom: Symbol and Metaphor in New Testament Interpretation.* Philadelphia: Fortress Press, 1976.

Phelan, James. *Worlds from Words: A Theory of Language in Fiction.* Chicago: University of Chicago Press, 1981.

Phillips, D. Z. *Faith and Philosophical Inquiry.* New York: Schocken, 1971.

———. *Religion without Explanation.* Oxford: Basil Blackwell, 1977.

Piaget, Jean. *Insights and Illusions of Philosophy.* Translated by Wolfe Mays. New York: World Publishing Co., Meridian Books, 1971.

Polanyi, Michael. *Personal Knowledge: Towards a Post-Critical Philosophy.* Chicago: University of Chicago Press, 1958.

———. *The Tacit Dimension.* Garden City, N.Y.: Doubleday, Anchor, 1966.

Polanyi, Michael, with Prosch, Harry. *Meaning.* Chicago: University of Chicago Press, 1975.

Pratt, Mary Louise. *Toward a Speech Act Theory of Literary Discourse.* Bloomington, Ind.: Indiana University Press, 1976.

Quine, W. V. "Two Dogmas of Empiricism," *Philosophical Review* 60 (January 1951):20–43.

———. *Word and Object.* Cambridge, Mass.: M.I.T. Press, 1964.

———. "A Postscript on Metaphor." *Critical Inquiry* 5 (Autumn 1978):161–62.

Ramsey, Ian T. *Religious Language.* New York: Macmillan, 1963.

———. *Models and Mystery.* Oxford: Oxford University Press, 1964.

Ransom, John Crowe. *The World's Body.* New York: Charles Scribner's Sons, 1938.

Rapaport, David. *Emotions and Memory.* 1941. 5th ed. New York: International Universities Press, 1971.

Richards, I. A. *Principles of Literary Criticism.* New York: Harcourt, Brace, 1925.

———. *The Philosophy of Rhetoric.* London: Oxford University Press, 1936.

———. *Poetries and Sciences: A Reissue of Science and Poetry (1926, 1935) with Commentary.* New York: W. W. Norton, 1970.

Ricoeur, Paul. *The Symbolism of Evil.* Translated by Emerson Buchanan. New York: Harper & Row, 1967.

———. "Creativity in Language: Word, Polysemy, Metaphor." *Philosophy Today* 17 (Summer

1973):97–111. Reprinted in *The Philosophy of Paul Ricoeur*. Edited by Charles E. Reagan and David Stewart. Boston: Beacon Press, 1978.

———. "Philosophy and Religious Language." *Journal of Religion* 54 (January 1974):71–85.

———. *Interpretation Theory: Discourse and the Surplus of Meaning*. Fort Worth: Texas Christian University Press, 1976.

———. *The Rule of Metaphor: Multi-Disciplinary Studies of the Creation of Meaning in Language*. Translated by Robert Czerny, with Kathleen McLaughlin and John Costello. Toronto: University of Toronto Press, 1977.

———. "Toward a Hermeneutic of the Idea of Revelation." Translated by David Pellauer. *Harvard Theological Review* 70 (Jan.-April 1977):1–37. Reprinted in *Essays on Biblical Interpretation*. Edited by Lewis S. Mudge. Philadelphia: Fortress Press, 1980.

———. "The Metaphorical Process as Cognition, Imagination, and Feeling." *Critical Inquiry* 5 (Autumn 1978):143–59.

———. "Naming God." Translated by David Pellauer. *Union Seminary Quarterly Review* 34 (Summer 1979):215–27.

———. "Metaphor and the Central Problem of Hermeneutics." In *Hermeneutics and the Human Sciences*. Edited and translated by John B. Thompson. Cambridge: Cambridge University Press, 1981.

Riffaterre, Michael. *Semiotics of Poetry*. Bloomington, Ind.: Indiana University Press, 1978.

Rogers, Robert. *Metaphor: A Psychoanalytic View*. Berkeley: University of California Press, 1978.

Rorty, Amelie Oksenberg, ed. *Explaining Emotions*. Berkeley: University of California Press, 1980.

Rorty, Richard. *Philosophy and the Mirror of Nature*. Princeton, N.J.: Princeton University Press, 1979.

Ross, Jacob Joshua. *The Appeal to the Given: A Study in Epistemology*. London: George Allen and Unwin, 1970.

Sacks, Sheldon, ed. "Special Issue on Metaphor." *Critical Inquiry* 5 (Autumn 1978).

Scholes, Robert. *Structuralism in Literature: An Introduction*. New Haven: Yale University Press, 1974.

———. "The Fictional Criticism of the Future." *TriQuarterly* 34 (Fall 1975):233–47.

Schrag, Calvin O. *Experience and Being: Prolegomena to a Future Ontology*. Evanston, Ill.: Northwestern University Press, 1969.

Scott, Nathan A., Jr. *The Broken Center: Studies in the Theological Horizon of Modern Literature*. New Haven: Yale University Press, 1966.

———. *Negative Capability: Studies in the New Literature and the Religious Situation*. New Haven: Yale University Press, 1969.

———. *The Wild Prayer of Longing: Poetry and the Sacred*. New Haven: Yale University Press, 1971.

———, ed. *The New Orpheus: Essays toward a Christian Poetic*. New York: Sheed and Ward, 1964.

Searle, John. *Speech Acts*. Cambridge: Cambridge University Press, 1969.

Segal, Sydney Joelson, ed. *Imagery: Current Cognitive Approaches*. New York: Academic Press, 1971.

Sewell, Elizabeth. *The Orphic Voice: Poetry and Natural History*. New Haven: Yale University Press, 1960.

Shibles, Warren. *An Analysis of Metaphor*. The Hague: Mouton, 1971.

Smith, Barbara Herrnstein. *On the Margins of Discourse: The Relation of Literature to Language*. Chicago: University of Chicago Press, 1978.

Smith, John E. *Experience and God*. New York: Oxford University Press, 1968.

————. *The Analogy of Experience*: *An Approach to Understanding Religious Truth*. New York: Harper & Row, 1973.

Smith, Wilfred Cantwell. *Faith and Belief*. Princeton, N.J.: Princeton University Press, 1979.

Spitzer, Leo. *Essays on English and American Literature*. Edited by Anna Hatcher. Princeton, N.J.: Princeton University Press, 1962.

Strasser, Stephan. *Phenomenology of Feeling*: *An Essay on the Phenomena of the Heart*. Translated by Robert E. Wood. Pittsburgh: Duquesne University Press, 1977.

Streng, Frederick. *Understanding Religious Life*. 2d ed. rev. Encino, Calif.: Dickenson Publishing Co., 1976.

Swartz, Robert J., ed. *Perceiving, Sensing, and Knowing*. Garden City, N.Y.: Doubleday, Anchor Books, 1965.

Taylor, Mark C. *Deconstructing Theology*. Chico, Calif.: Scholars Press / New York: Crossroad, 1982.

Tillich, Paul. *The Religious Situation*. Translated by H. Richard Niebuhr. New York: Henry Holt, 1932.

————. *The Protestant Era*. Translated by James Luther Adams. Chicago: University of Chicago Press, 1948.

————. *Systematic Theology*. 3 vols. Chicago: University of Chicago Press, 1951–63.

————. *Dynamics of Faith*. New York: Harper & Row, 1957.

————. *Theology of Culture*. Edited by Robert C. Kimball. London: Oxford University Press, 1959.

Tolbert, Mary Ann. *Perspectives on the Parables*: *An Approach to Multiple Interpretations*. Philadelphia: Fortress Press, 1979.

Toulmin, Stephen. *Reason in Ethics*. Cambridge: Cambridge University Press, 1964.

————. *Human Understanding*. Vol. 1, *The Collective Use and Evolution of Concepts*. Princeton, N.J.: Princeton University Press, 1972.

————. *Knowing and Acting*: *An Invitation to Philosophy*. New York: Macmillan, 1976.

Toulmin, Stephen; Hepburn, Ronald W.; and MacIntyre, Alasdair. *Metaphysical Beliefs*. 1957. Rev. ed. London: S. C. M. Press, 1978.

Toulmin, Stephen, and Janik, Allen. *Wittgenstein's Vienna*. New York: Simon and Schuster, 1973.

Tracy, David. *Blessed Rage for Order*: *The New Pluralism in Theology*. New York: Seabury, Crossroad Books, 1975.

————. "Metaphor and Religion: The Test Case of Christian Texts." *Critical Inquiry* 5 (Autumn 1978):91–106.

————. *The Analogical Imagination*: *Christian Theology and the Culture of Pluralism*. New York: Crossroad, 1981.

Turbayne, Colin Murray. *The Myth of Metaphor*. New Haven: Yale University Press, 1962. Rev. ed. with appendix by R. Eberle. Columbia, S.C.: University of South Carolina Press, 1970.

Turner, Victor. *The Ritual Process*: *Structure and Anti-Structure*. Chicago: Aldine Publishing Co., 1969.

————. *Dramas, Fields and Metaphors*: *Symbolic Action in Human Society*. Ithaca, N.Y.: Cornell University Press, 1974.

Tyler, Stephen. *The Said and the Unsaid*: *Mind, Meaning, and Culture*. New York: Harcourt Brace Jovanovich, Academic Press, 1978.

Ullmann, Stephen. *Semantics*: *An Introduction to the Science of Meaning*. Oxford: Basil Blackwell, 1962.

Underhill, Evelyn. *Mysticism*: *A Study in the Nature and Development of Man's Spiritual Consciousness*. 1911. Reprint. New York: E. P. Dutton, 1961.

Urban, Wilbur Marshall. *Language and Reality*. London: Allen and Unwin, 1931.

Urmson, J. O. *Philosophical Analysis: Its Development between the Two World Wars*. London: Clarendon Press, 1956.

Van Buren, Paul M. *The Edges of Language: An Essay in the Logic of a Religion*. New York: Macmillan, 1972.

Vaught, Carl. *The Quest for Wholeness*. Albany, N.Y.: State University of New York Press, 1982.

Vivas, Eliseo. *Creation and Discovery*. Chicago: Henry Regnery, 1955.

Wainwright, Geoffrey. *Doxology: The Praise of God in Worship, Doctrine, and Life*. New York: Oxford University Press, 1980.

Walsh, Dorothy. *Literature and Knowledge*. Middletown, Conn.: Wesleyan University Press, 1969.

Wellek, René. *The Attack on Literature and Other Essays*. Chapel Hill, N.C.: University of North Carolina Press, 1982.

Werner, Heinz, and Kaplan, Bernard. *Symbol Formation: An Organismic-Developmental Approach to Language and the Expression of Thought*. New York: John Wiley & Sons, 1963.

Whalley, George. *Poetic Process: An Essay in Poetics*. London: Routledge & Kegan Paul, 1953.

Whorf, Benjamin Lee. *Language, Thought, and Reality: Selected Writings*. Edited by John B. Carroll. Cambridge, Mass.: M.I.T. Press, 1956.

Wicker, Brian. *The Story-Shaped World: Fiction and Metaphysics*. Notre Dame, Ind.: Notre Dame University Press, 1975.

Wilder, Amos N. *Theology and Modern Literature*. Cambridge, Mass.: Harvard University Press, 1958.

―――. *The New Voice: Religion, Literature, Hermeneutics*. New York: Herder and Herder, 1969.

―――. *Theopoetic*. Philadelphia: Fortress Press, 1976.

Wimsatt, W. K., Jr. *The Verbal Icon: Studies in the Meaning of Poetry*. Lexington, Ky.: University of Kentucky Press, 1954.

Winquist, Charles E., ed. *The Archaeology of the Imagination*. JAAR Thematic Studies, vol. 48, no. 2. Chico, Calif.: Scholars Press, 1981.

Wittgenstein, Ludwig. *Tractatus Logico-Philosophicus*. Translated by D. F. Pears and B. F. McGuinness. London: Routledge and Kegan Paul, 1961.

―――. *Philosophical Investigations*. Translated by G. E. M. Anscombe. 3d ed. London: Basil Blackwell, 1968.

Wolterstorff, Nicholas. *Art in Action: Toward a Christian Aesthetic*. Grand Rapids: William B. Eerdmans, 1980.

―――. *Works and Worlds of Art*. Oxford: Oxford University Press, 1980.

Wood, Robert E. *The Future of Metaphysics*. Chicago: Quadrangle Books, 1970.

Index